Come, Lord Jesus

Other books by John Piper

Battling Unbelief
Bloodlines: Race, Cross, and the Christian
Brothers, We Are Not Professionals
Coronavirus and Christ
The Dangerous Duty of Delight
Desiring God
Does God Desire All to Be Saved?
Don't Waste Your Life
Expository Exultation
Fifty Reasons Why Jesus Came to Die
Finally Alive
Five Points
Future Grace
God Is the Gospel
God's Passion for His Glory
A Godward Heart
A Godward Life
Good News of Great Joy
A Hunger for God
Lessons from a Hospital Bed
Let the Nations Be Glad!
A Peculiar Glory
The Pleasures of God
Providence
Reading the Bible Supernaturally
Seeing and Savoring Jesus Christ
Sex, Race, and the Sovereignty of God (formerly *A Sweet and Bitter Providence*)
Spectacular Sins
Taste and See
Think
This Momentary Marriage
What Is Saving Faith?
What Jesus Demands from the World
When I Don't Desire God
Why I Love the Apostle Paul

Come, Lord Jesus

Meditations on the Second Coming of Christ

John Piper

WHEATON, ILLINOIS

Come, Lord Jesus: Meditations on the Second Coming of Christ
Copyright © 2023 by Desiring God Foundation
Published by Crossway
    1300 Crescent Street
    Wheaton, Illinois 60187

Cover design: Jeff Miller, Faceout Studios
First printing 2023
Printed in the United States of America

Unless otherwise indicated, Scripture quotations are from the ESV® Bible (The Holy Bible, English Standard Version®), copyright © 2001 by Crossway, a publishing ministry of Good News Publishers. Used by permission. All rights reserved. The ESV text may not be quoted in any publication made available to the public by a Creative Commons license. The ESV may not be translated into any other language.

Scripture quotations marked KJV are from the King James Version of the Bible. Public domain.

Scripture quotations marked NASB are taken from the New American Standard Bible®, copyright © 1960, 1971, 1977, 1995, 2020 by The Lockman Foundation. Used by permission. All rights reserved. www.lockman.org.

All emphases in Scripture quotations have been added by the author.

Hardcover ISBN: 978-1-4335-8495-4
ePub ISBN: 978-1-4335-8498-5
PDF ISBN: 978-1-4335-8496-1
Mobipocket ISBN: 978-1-4335-8497-8

Library of Congress Cataloging-in-Publication Data
Names: Piper, John, 1946– author.
Title: Come, Lord Jesus : meditations on the second coming of Christ / John Piper.
Description: Wheaton, Illinois : Crossway, 2023. | Includes bibliographical references and index.
Identifiers: LCCN 2022011807 (print) | LCCN 2022011808 (ebook) | ISBN 9781433584954 (hardcover) | ISBN 9781433584961 (pdf) | ISBN 9781433584978 (mobi) | ISBN 9781433584985 (epub)
Subjects: LCSH: Second Advent—Meditations.
Classification: LCC BT886.3 .P57 2023 (print) | LCC BT886.3 (ebook) | DDC 236/.9—dc23/eng/20220815
LC record available at https://lccn.loc.gov/2022011807
LC ebook record available at https://lccn.loc.gov/2022011808

Crossway is a publishing ministry of Good News Publishers.

LSC			32	31	30	29	28	27	26	25	24	23
13	12	11	10	9	8	7	6	5	4	3	2	1

To
George Eldon Ladd

the first to show me that
the whole New Testament
is eschatological

Contents

PART 1

REASONS TO LOVE
CHRIST'S APPEARING

THE MIRACLE
WE SEEK: LOVE

THE AIM OF THIS BOOK IS TO HELP YOU love the second coming of Jesus Christ. The contents and title were inspired partly by the biblical prayers "Come, Lord Jesus!" (Rev. 22:20), and "Our Lord, come!" (1 Cor. 16:22). But mainly the book was inspired by the heart affection beneath these prayers, which Paul expressed in 2 Timothy 4:8:

> There is laid up for me the crown of righteousness, which the Lord, the righteous judge, will award to me on that day, and not only to me but also to all who have *loved his appearing*.

A crown of righteousness is promised to those who *love* the second coming of Christ. We pray for his appearing, because we love his appearing. The prayer "Come, Lord Jesus" is rooted in something deeper: "I love your appearing!"

This book is about the reality that awakens such love and how that awakening happens. This love involves desiring, longing, and hoping. It is not an action of the body. It is a spiritual affection of the heart. By *spiritual*, I mean brought into being and formed by the Holy Spirit. It is not surprising that the Holy Spirit would bring into being the heart's love for the coming of Christ, for the Spirit's most essential work in the human heart is to glorify Jesus. Jesus says of the Spirit, "He will glorify me" (John 16:14).

Therefore, our Spirit-awakened love for the second coming is not a Christ-neglecting fascination with an event. It is a Christ-enthralled longing for his presence and glory. It is an extension of our love for Christ—the kind of love Jesus was seeking in Matthew 10:37: "Whoever loves father or mother more than me is not worthy of me, and whoever loves son or daughter more than me is not worthy of me." Any love for the second coming that is not an extension of this supreme affection for Jesus himself is not the Christ-exalting work of the Holy Spirit. It is not the love to which Paul promised a crown. It is not what I am aiming at.

Therefore, this book aims at a miracle that the book alone cannot achieve—namely, Spirit-created affections. But that aim is no different from all Christian teaching and preaching and counseling and serving, which seek to build faith in Jesus, and rescue people from divine judgment, and stir up Christ-exalting righteousness. All such faith and rescue and righteousness are works of the Spirit of God (Rom. 5:9; Eph. 2:8; Phil. 1:29; 2 Thess. 1:11). Human means—like books—are not decisive. God is.

But human means *are* divinely appointed. When God intends to open the eyes of the spiritually blind to see the glory of Christ and his coming, he sends a human messenger and says, "I am sending *you* to open their eyes, so that they may turn from darkness to light" (Acts 26:17–18). That's how God awakens love for the second coming. He opens the eyes of the blind to see the greatness, the glory, and the worth of Christ's coming. He does it through the biblical truth about Christ's coming and through human teachers who point to that truth. That's what I aim to do in this book.

1

All Who Have Loved His Appearing

LET'S MAKE SURE THAT the biblical text where this book takes its stand can bear the weight:

> I am already being poured out as a drink offering, and the time of my departure has come. I have fought the good fight, I have finished the race, I have kept the faith. Henceforth there is laid up for me the crown of righteousness, which the Lord, the righteous judge, will award to me on that day, and not only to me but also to *all who have loved his appearing*. (2 Tim. 4:6–8)

Does the *appearing* referred to in verse 8 actually refer to the second coming of Christ, or does it refer to his first coming, his incarnation? Considered by itself, the word *appearing* (ἐπιφάνεια) can refer to his first coming. Of the five other uses of this word by the apostle Paul, four refer to the second coming (2 Thess. 2:8; 1 Tim. 6:14; 2 Tim. 4:1; Titus 2:13). But one refers to the first coming:

> [God] saved us and called us to a holy calling, not because of our works but because of his own purpose and grace, which he gave us in Christ Jesus before the ages began, and which now has been

manifested through the *appearing* [ἐπιφανείας] of our Savior Christ Jesus, who abolished death and brought life and immortality to light through the gospel. (2 Tim. 1:9–10)

So there is nothing in the word *appearing* itself that demands a reference to the second coming. But four observations incline me to think that in 2 Timothy 4:8 Paul means "all who have loved his [*second*] appearing."

First, the nearest use of the word, seven verses earlier, refers to the second coming: "I charge you in the presence of God and of Christ Jesus, who is to judge the living and the dead, and by his *appearing* and his kingdom: preach the word" (2 Tim. 4:1–2).

Second, in verse 10 Paul contrasts those who "have loved his appearing" (2 Tim. 4:8) with Demas, who "deserted me, *having loved the present age*" (my translation). Calling attention to Demas's love for "the *present* age" contrasts him with those who love the second coming of Christ, because the second coming brings the "*end* of the age" (Matt. 13:40; 24:3; 28:20). The second coming brings to an end the very thing Demas has come to love most. Those who love the second coming, however, prefer the arrival of Christ over all that this present fallen age can give.

Third, Paul's reference to his being rewarded on "that day" (2 Tim. 4:8) creates the expectation that what follows will relate to "that day"— namely, the day of Christ's second coming. (For Paul's use of "that day" as a reference to Christ's second coming, see 1 Thess. 5:4; 2 Thess. 1:10; 2:3; 2 Tim. 1:12, 18.) In this flow of thought, it would be strange for Paul to revert to the first appearing of Christ.

The fourth observation that inclines me to take 2 Timothy 4:8 as a reference to the *second* appearing of Christ, rather than the first, is that Paul sees the first appearing as precisely designed to fit us for the second. Notice how he argues in Titus 2:11–13:

The grace of God has *appeared* [ἐπεφάνη, the verb form of the Greek noun behind the word *appearing*], bringing salvation for all people, training us to renounce ungodliness and worldly passions, and to live self-controlled, upright, and godly lives in the present age, [eagerly[1]] waiting [προσδεχόμενοι] for our blessed hope, the *appearing* [ἐπιφάνειαν] of the glory of our great God and Savior Jesus Christ.

Boiling it down, Paul says that the grace of God *appeared* the first time to bring into being a people who would eagerly wait for Christ's second *appearing* with uprightness and godliness. In other words, the first appearing prepares us for the second. We have much to love about the first appearing of Christ. But as great as it was, climaxing in the cross and the resurrection of Jesus, it was all designed to bring into being a people and a new reality that would find climactic expression at the second coming.

So I think Paul would say that the test of our proper affection for the first coming of Christ is the measure of our affection for the second. Or to say it another way, the test of our love for the Christ who *has* appeared is our longing for the Christ who *will* appear. Therefore, I believe I am building on a good foundation when I say that the aim of this book is to help people love the second coming of Christ. To such people, Christ, the righteous judge, will award the crown of righteousness.

Why a Crown for Loving His Appearing?

Why does Paul connect the crown of righteousness with love for Christ's appearing? Why does he say, "The righteous judge, will award [the crown of righteousness] . . . to all who have loved his appearing" (2 Tim. 4:8)? Why not say that the Lord will give a crown "to all who have finished their race," or "to all who have fought the good fight," or "to all who have kept the faith"? That is what Paul seems to be leading up to when he says in 2 Timothy 4:7–8:

1   This Greek verb, προσδέχομαι, in most of its uses carries the connotation of waiting with eagerness, or gladly welcoming, Mark 15:43; Luke 2:25, 38; 23:51; Rom. 16:2; Phil. 2:29; Heb. 10:34; Jude 21.

I have fought the good fight, I have finished the race, I have kept the faith. Henceforth there is laid up for me the crown of righteousness, which the Lord, the righteous judge, will award to me on that day, and not only to me but also to all who . . .

It certainly sounds as if Paul is going to say, "Not only do I get a wreath for fighting the good fight, but so does everyone else who . . . *fights the good fight*." "Not only am I awarded a wreath for finishing the race, but so is everyone else who . . . *finishes the race*." "Not only will the judge give *me* a crown for keeping the faith, but he will give that crown also to all who . . . *keep the faith*." That's what we expect. But that is not what Paul says.

He says in effect, "Just as I will receive a crown for the *fight fought*, and the *race finished*, and the *faith kept*, so also will everyone else who . . . *has loved the Lord's appearing*." Why? Why does Paul replace "fighting the fight" and "finishing the race" and "keeping the faith" with "loving the Lord's appearing"?

My suggestion is that welling up in Paul's mind, as he thinks about his fight and race and faith, is his own decades-long desire for the Lord's appearing that exerted such a keeping power in his life. In other words, as he thought back over the battles he had fought, and the endurance demanded by the marathon of his life, and the temptations to forsake his faith for the pleasures of the world, what rose in his consciousness was the sustaining power of the preciousness of what he saw coming at the Lord's appearing. He loved it. And that love kept him.

Why Demas Did Not Finish

Two contextual clues show us that Paul was thinking this way. One is the link we have already seen between 2 Timothy 4:8 and what follows about Demas in verse 10:

Henceforth there is laid up for me the crown of righteousness, which the Lord, the righteous judge, will award to me on that day,

and not only to me but also to all who have loved his appearing.
Do your best to come to me soon. For Demas deserted me, *having
loved the present age*, and went to Thessalonica. (2 Tim. 4:8–10,
my translation)

Demas did not fight on. He did not finish his race. He did not keep
the faith. He is the opposite of what Paul is urging Timothy, and us,
to be. He says to Timothy, "Endure suffering [*fight!*] . . . fulfill your
ministry [*finish!*]" (2 Tim. 4:5). Don't stop fighting and running. Paul
gives *himself* as a model for Timothy to follow and *Demas* as a model
not to follow. But the language he chooses to describe Demas's faith
is *love* language, not the language of fighting or running or keeping.
Demas quit fighting and quit running and quit keeping, because he
"*loved* the present age." He did *not* love the Lord's appearing.

So in the example of Demas, Paul makes explicit what is in his mind
in verses 6–8, namely, the connection between what we *love* and whether
we *endure*. He makes plain that promising the crown of righteousness
to those who have *loved* the Lord's appearing (2 Tim. 4:8) is in perfect
harmony with the promise that he would receive that same crown for
his good fight and finished race and kept faith. They are in harmony
because loving the Lord's appearing was essential for his lifelong endurance. It was the root of that fruit.

Why the Itchers Did Not Finish the Race

Another contextual clue shows that Paul sees loving the Lord's appearing as essential to fighting the good fight and finishing the race and
keeping the faith. It is found in the preceding verses:

The time is coming when people will not endure sound teaching,
but having itching ears they will accumulate for themselves teachers
to suit their own passions, and will turn away from listening to the
truth and wander off into myths. (2 Tim. 4:3–4)

Here Paul prepares us for what he will say about Demas. The issue is that professing Christians will "turn away" from the truth. (Demas had seemed to be Paul's faithful partner, Col. 4:14.) They will "wander off." But why? The reason Paul mentions is not intellectual struggles or relational conflicts or sincere doubts. What he mentions is "itching ears" for teaching that will "suit their own passions."

The word *passions* is simply the common word for *desires* (ἐπι-θυμίας). It is the language of *love*. It is similar to 2 Timothy 4:8 ("have *loved* the Lord's appearing") and verse 10 ("having *loved* the present age"). The reason they "turn away" and "wander off" is that they *love* (crave, long for, desire) the wrong things. They quit fighting the fight. They stop running the race. They cease keeping the faith. Because, like Demas, they love this age. They do not *love* the Lord's appearing.

It is not surprising, therefore, that Paul says *his* crown will be awarded because of a well-fought fight and a well-run race and persevering faith, while *their* crown will be awarded because they have loved the Lord's appearing. These are not separate standards for awarding crowns. They are the same standard. In one, Paul focuses on the inner spiritual affection of love for the Lord and his coming. And in the other, Paul focuses on the resulting fight for perseverance.

How Important Is It to Love the Second Coming?

This relationship between *loving* and *fighting* is so important for us to see because it shows how crucial it is that we love the Lord's second coming. This love is not marginal. It is not optional. It is a means by which Christians are kept from falling away. It is a condition of the Christian heart that protects us from the destructive Demas-like love for this age. It is a thrilling glimpse of the prize at the end of life's marathon that keeps us running (Phil. 3:14). Loving the Lord's coming is an extension into the future of loving the Lord now. And loving the Lord now is essential to being a Christian.

The closest New Testament parallel to 2 Timothy 4:8 is James 1:12:

Blessed is the man who remains steadfast under trial, for when he has stood the test he will receive the crown of life, which God has promised to those who love him.

James 1:12	2 Timothy 4:7–8
steadfast under trial	fought the good fight, finished the race
the crown of life	the crown of righteousness
those who love him	those who loved his appearing

Two key differences in wording confirm how much is at stake in loving the Lord's appearing. James speaks of *loving the Lord himself* where Paul speaks of *loving the Lord's appearing*. And James promises a *crown of life* where Paul promises a *crown of righteousness*. These are not contrary pictures. Both teach that what is at stake in loving the Lord and his appearing is final salvation. The "crown of life" signifies the final inheritance of eternal life (cf. Titus 3:7); and the "crown of righteousness" signifies that this eternal life is the inheritance of those whose saving faith was confirmed by the fruit of righteousness.[2]

2 The term "crown of righteousness" could possibly represent the final act by which God declares us to be justified. But I have taken it to mean an award for a life whose justifying faith was confirmed with the fruit of righteousness. I do this for two reasons. One is that Paul's use of the term "righteous judge" in 2 Tim. 4:8 is not based on a courtroom scene (suggesting justification) but on an athletic scene where the judge is rightly deciding if the athletes fought and ran by the rules. "An athlete is not crowned unless he competes according to the rules" (2 Tim. 2:5). The other reason is that awarding Christians a crown for a life marked by the fruit of righteousness is what Paul, and the rest of the New Testament authors, taught. Such teaching simply acknowledges that "faith apart from works is dead" (James 2:26), and we are saved "through sanctification" (2 Thess. 2:13), and there is a "holiness without which no one will see the Lord" (Heb. 12:14), and "whoever does not practice righteousness is not of God" (1 John 3:10). This is not perfectionism. We will not be perfect until we see the Lord Jesus face-to-face (Phil. 3:12; 1 John 3:2). And it is not justification by works. It is the uniform teaching of the New Testament that to enter heaven one must have a wedding garment (Matt. 22:11–14) and that garment is "the righteous deeds of the saints" (Rev. 19:8). These "righteous deeds" do not earn heaven or replace faith as the sole

Therefore, loving the Lord Jesus, and its extension in loving his coming, is an essential mark of a true Christian. Paul says at the end of 1 Corinthians, "If anyone does not love the Lord, let him be accursed. Our Lord, come!" (16:22, my translation). In other words, no one is a Christian—no one is saved—who does not love the Lord Jesus. And it is striking that just as Paul links *loving* the Lord with the Lord's coming in 2 Timothy 4:8, so here he links *not loving* the Lord with the Lord's coming: "Let him be accursed. Our Lord, come!" In other words, just as the crown of righteousness is awarded to the lovers of Christ at the day of his coming, so will the curse be pronounced on the nonlovers of Christ at the day of his coming.

Place of Grace

Someone might stumble over the fact that the very next verse in 1 Corinthians 16 says, "The *grace* of the Lord Jesus be with you" (16:23). One might ask, "How can Paul make love for Christ essential for escaping God's curse, and then declare that *grace* is the way Christ relates to his people?"

The answer has two parts. First, grace is the divine power that gave us spiritual life in the first place so that our hearts were able to love Christ (Eph. 2:5). "The *grace* of our Lord overflowed for me with the faith and *love* that are in Christ Jesus" (1 Tim. 1:14). Second, the ongoing blessings of grace flow to us in the channels of love for Christ that grace itself has created. This is why Paul says in Ephesians 6:24, "Grace be with all who love our Lord Jesus Christ with love incorruptible." Loving Christ (and thus his coming) is the channel through which more grace flows to us. This is also why both James and Peter say, "God opposes the proud but *gives grace to the humble*" (James 4:6; 1 Pet. 5:5).

---

instrument of God's being 100 percent for us. They are the "obedience that comes from faith" (Rom. 1:5, my translation; Heb. 11:8), the "[works] of faith" (2 Thess. 1:11). They are the fruit of the Spirit (Gal. 5:22–23). Or, as Paul said in Phil. 1:10–11, Christians will be found on "the day of Christ, filled with the fruit of righteousness."

The point is that even though grace is what created the humility in the first place, it is to the humble that God gives "more grace" (James 4:6). When the apostles speak of God's grace flowing to those who love Christ (Eph. 6:24), and grace flowing to the humble (1 Pet. 5:5), they are not describing different hearts—one humble and one loving. There is one Christian heart. It has been brought low in humility, and it loves Christ and his coming.

Therefore, when Paul says that the person who does *not love* the Lord will be cursed at his coming, and the person who *loves* the Lord will receive a crown of righteousness at his coming, he is not undermining or contradicting the decisive role of sovereign grace. God's grace is the mighty plan and power that, before the creation of the universe, had guaranteed the salvation of God's people. "[God] saved us and called us to a holy calling, not because of our works but because of his own purpose and *grace*, which he gave us in Christ Jesus before the ages began" (2 Tim. 1:9). The grace that gave us life and revealed to us the infinitely precious glory of Christ—in his person and in his coming— was given to us before the universe was created.

Love for the Second Coming Is Essential

The point we are stressing is that love for Jesus and, by extension, love for his coming, are essential to being a Christian. Jesus himself taught this truth more than once. He said to the Jewish leaders, who claimed to know God but rejected Jesus, "If God were your Father, you would love me" (John 8:42). In other words, if you don't love me, you don't have God as your Father. And as we have seen before, Jesus said, "Whoever loves father or mother more than me is not worthy of me, and whoever loves son or daughter more than me is not worthy of me" (Matt. 10:37). What that verse makes clear is that loving Jesus cannot be reduced to doing external things that he commands. That is not what love for father and mother and son and daughter means. This love is what we have called an *affection* of the heart, not a set of deeds done by the body. And in the case of love for Jesus and his coming, it is a *spiritual* affection—a work of the Holy Spirit in our lives. Without this love, God is not our Father, and Jesus is not our Savior.

Means to a Miracle

Perhaps it is obvious, therefore, why I am pursuing a deeper, more authentic, more unshakable love for Christ's coming, and would like to bring you with me. The aim is that we experience a Christ-enthralled longing for his presence and glorification. Only a divine act in our hearts can bring that about. So the question we turn to now is, How can a natural act, like writing or reading a book, be a means to that miraculous end?

2

How Can a Book Awaken Love
for Christ's Appearing?

SINCE THE AIM OF THIS BOOK is to help you love the second coming of Christ, how can that actually happen? How can the *natural* acts
of writing and reading a book result in the *supernatural* experience of
love for Christ and his coming?

Loving the Appearing of Christ Is a Work of the Holy Spirit

In chapter 1, I argued that what the Bible means by love for Christ's
second coming is not a merely natural fascination with an astounding
event. Rather, it is a Christ-enthralled longing for his presence and
glorification. That Christ-enthralled longing is a supernatural experience. It is a spiritual affection of the heart that the fallen, sinful human
heart cannot produce. It is a work of the Holy Spirit.

Paul explains that "the natural person does not accept the things
of the Spirit of God, for they are folly to him, and he is not able
to understand them because they are spiritually discerned" (1 Cor.
2:14). The "natural person" is simply the normal person who does not
have the Spirit of God inhabiting and transforming his heart by faith.
Jude described the natural person like this: "These are natural people,

not having the Spirit [ψυχικοί, πνεῦμα μὴ ἔχοντες]" (Jude 19, my translation).

Another way of describing the "natural person" is to speak of him as having "the mind of the flesh" or being "in the flesh." *Flesh*, in Paul's ordinary use of the word, refers to fallen human nature considered as independent from God and uninfluenced by the indwelling Spirit. In this condition, people are at odds with God. And in that condition of alienation and resistance, they do not and cannot submit to God's instruction. So Paul says:

> The mind of the flesh is hostile to God, for it does not submit to God's law; indeed, it cannot. Those who are in the flesh cannot please God. You, however, are not in the flesh but in the Spirit, if in fact the Spirit of God dwells in you. Anyone who does not have the Spirit of Christ does not belong to him. (Rom. 8:7–9, my translation)

The point I am drawing out of Paul's teaching about the "natural person" and the "mind of the flesh" is that none of us will ever discern or embrace the greatness and beauty and value of the coming of Christ without the supernatural work of the Holy Spirit in our hearts. We may be fascinated with prophetic thoughts, or captivated by end-time predictions, or agitated by a fearful future. But none of that requires a supernatural transformation of the fallen human heart. So without the work of the Spirit, we will not love the second coming as Paul intends in 2 Timothy 4:8. We will not experience this love as a Christ-enthralled longing for his presence and glorification.

Seeing the Glory of His Appearing Creates the Savoring

So we turn back to the question raised above: How can the *natural* acts of writing and reading a book result in the *supernatural* experience of love for Christ and his coming? I answered in chapter 1 that God opens the spiritually blind eyes of *natural* people to see the greatness, the glory, and the worth of Christ's coming. He does it through biblical truth about Christ's appearing and through human teachers who point to that truth. He does it, for example, through books.

So I am saying that authentic *love* for Christ's coming is awakened and intensified by the spiritual *sight* of Christ's greatness and glory and worth in his coming. There is a *seeing* that creates the *savoring*. There is a spiritual *light* that creates the sweetness of the *longing*. Paul spoke of "having the eyes of your hearts enlightened, that you may *know* what is the hope to which he has called you" (Eph. 1:18). This knowing is *not* the kind of knowing that the devil has. The devil knows about the second coming and the day of judgment. We know this because when Jesus intruded on the devil's domain, the demons complained that he had "come here to torment us *before the time*" (Matt. 8:29)—that is, before the day appointed for their final judgment. They know very well what the second coming of Christ will mean for them.

That kind of knowing is not our goal. We do not need to have the eyes of our hearts enlightened by God in order to know the way demons know. That is natural knowledge. It does not require the work of the Holy Spirit. Paul was not praying in Ephesians 1:18 that God would enlighten the eyes of our hearts so that we could share the knowledge of demons. He was praying for a kind of "knowing" that only the Holy Spirit can give. He was praying for a knowledge of the *reality* of our hope that would actually produce *rejoicing* in our hope! He was praying for the supernatural experience of *desiring* and *loving* our hope. He was praying that we would *love* the appearing of Christ.

And that *loving* is the effect of a spiritually illumined *knowing*. If our love for the second coming were conjured up by methods that short-circuited a knowledge of truth, the love would not honor Christ. The affections that magnify Christ are affections awakened by a true sight of Christ—a true knowledge of Christ. So it is with the second coming. The only love for Christ's appearing that honors Christ is love that is awakened by a true knowledge of his appearing.

So the natural act of providing knowledge (like writing this book) goes hand in hand with the supernatural experience of seeing the greatness and glory and worth of Christ *through* that knowledge.

News, Glory, and Light

Paul illustrates this connection between supernatural sight of glory and the natural knowledge of the truth. He says:

> The god of this world has blinded the minds of the unbelievers, to keep them from seeing the light of the gospel of the glory of Christ, who is the image of God. For what we proclaim is not ourselves, but Jesus Christ as Lord, with ourselves as your servants for Jesus' sake. For God, who said, "Let light shine out of darkness," has shone in our hearts to give the light of the knowledge of the glory of God in the face of Jesus Christ. (2 Cor. 4:4–6)

Verse 4 describes what people are blinded from seeing. Verse 6 describes the overcoming of that blindness by God's supernatural intervention. Verse 4 has three elements.

First, there is *gospel*, that is, "good news." There is real, factual news. There are objective facts about who Christ is and what he has done. As Paul says in 1 Corinthians 15:1–4, "I would remind you, brothers, of the gospel . . . that Christ died for our sins in accordance with the Scriptures, that he was buried, that he was raised on the third day in accordance with the Scriptures." This is real, objective, factual news.

Second, there is "glory." Paul refers to "the gospel of the *glory* of Christ" (2 Cor. 4:4). The news is objective fact, but it communicates more than mere happenings. It carries in it a glory—a beauty, a radiance, a worth, a greatness of Christ. Rightly told, the *news* of Christ is a window onto the *glory* of Christ. But a person can hear the news and not see the glory for what it is.

Third, there is "light" that may or may not be seen by those who hear the news of this glory. Paul speaks of "the *light* of the gospel of the glory of Christ" (2 Cor. 4:4). This light is what Satan, "the god of this world" (see also John 12:31; 14:30; 16:11; Eph. 2:2), conceals if he can. He is not as concerned whether people hear the *news*, or even whether they hear the news told so as to point to Christ's *glory*. To be sure, he hates the news and the glory. But a person can hear the "gospel of the glory of Christ" and still be firmly in the bondage of Satan. But if a person sees the *light* of that gospel of glory, Satan has lost him. He is born again. He belongs to God. Seeing that "light" is a supernatural experience.

This miracle of sight is described in verse 6. Again, there are the same three elements.

First, there is the news, only this time it is called "knowledge." This is the objective content of the truth about Christ and what he has done.

Second, there is "glory." Just as verse 4 spoke of "the *gospel* of the glory," so verse 6 speaks of "the *knowledge* of the glory." In verse 4, it is the "glory of Christ, who is the image of God." In verse 6, it is the "glory of God in the face of Jesus Christ." It is one divine glory—Christ's glory as he images God the Father, and God's glory as he shines in the face of Christ. One divine glory.

Third, there is "light." Only here in verse 6, God enables the heart to see it. Satan's blinding is overcome. "God, who said, 'Let light shine out of darkness,' has shone in our hearts to give the light of the knowledge of the glory of God in the face of Jesus Christ." "The knowledge [or news] of the glory" is now, by God's intervention, communicated as a kind of "light" that reveals the glory as *glorious* to the heart of the one who sees it. The heart's experience of this light goes beyond anything the "natural person" or Satan can experience. This is a seeing that compels savoring. This is a seeing that becomes treasuring.

And when this seeing is a seeing of the glory of the second coming of Christ, it is a *seeing* that becomes a *loving*. This is how it happens that any of us "have loved his appearing" (2 Tim. 4:8). God shines in our hearts to give the light of the knowledge of the glory of God in the coming of Christ. That experience of God's heart illumination is called, by Paul, *loving* the appearing of the Lord. It is a spiritual affection rooted in real, glorious, objective facts revealed in Scripture. It is mediated through true knowledge of those facts. This is how a book may become the means of your loving the second coming. Thus, the natural act of providing knowledge (like writing this book) goes hand in hand with the supernatural experience of seeing the greatness and glory and worth of Christ in his coming.

Example of Peter and John the Baptist

What we have seen from 2 Corinthians 4:4–6 is also visible in a remarkably different way in the teaching of Jesus. Here again, we see that when our aim is a supernatural experience of objective reality, there are always two steps to get there. One is natural; the other is supernatural—the *natural* presentation of the reality to our minds, and then God's *supernatural* illumination to cause us to see divine glory in that reality. Consider an illustration of these two steps in the ministry of Jesus.

There came a point for John the Baptist when the ministry of Jesus fell short of his expectations of how the coming Messiah would act. John was in prison, which itself was troubling, if the messianic kingdom was about to dawn. From prison, therefore, he sent word to Jesus and said, "Are you the one who is to come, or shall we look for another?" (Matt. 11:3). What was at stake here was John the Baptist's faith in Jesus as the Messiah.

At this point, Jesus might have prayed for John that God would supernaturally illumine his heart to see the self-authenticating glory of Jesus in the facts that John already knew. In fact, Jesus may have done just that. We don't know. But we do know what Jesus definitely did. Jesus said to John's messengers:

Go and tell John what you hear and see: the blind receive their sight and the lame walk, lepers are cleansed and the deaf hear, and the dead are raised up, and the poor have good news preached to them. And blessed is the one who is not offended by me. (Matt. 11:4–6)

In other words, Jesus made sure that John had the facts. The news. The knowledge.

Now compare this transaction between Jesus and John the Baptist to a transaction between Jesus and Peter. Instead of waiting for Peter to ask Jesus about whether he was the Messiah or not, the way John did, Jesus takes the initiative and asks the disciples, "Who do you say that I am?" To which Peter replies, "You are the Christ [*Christos* is Greek for *Messiah*], the Son of the living God." To this Jesus responds, "Blessed are you, Simon Bar-Jonah! For flesh and blood has not revealed this to you, but my Father who is in heaven" (Matt. 16:15–17).

Jesus recognized in Peter's answer that a miracle had happened. God had "revealed" something to Peter beyond what "flesh and blood" could see. It was more than factual knowledge that men and devils can attain by their own resources. It is more than the mere fact that Jesus is the Son of God. The devil knows that Jesus is the Son of God. Hence the unclean spirit says to Jesus, "I know who you are—the Holy One of God" (Mark 1:24). But the devil's knowledge is a hating knowledge, not a loving knowledge. The devil "knows," but "he does not . . . know as he ought to know" (1 Cor. 8:2).

The devil had not seen Jesus as gloriously precious. He had seen him only as an offensive threat. He had not seen the magnificence of Jesus as the magnificence of a treasure. But Peter's recognition of Jesus went beyond what natural men and devils can see. His sight was "blessed." The devil's wasn't. "*Blessed* are you, Simon." He was blessed because his sight was a God-given transforming sight of Christ. He had experienced the miracle of 2 Corinthians 4:6. God had "shone in [his heart] to give the light of the knowledge of the glory of God in the face of Jesus Christ."

Now consider what these two encounters—with John the Baptist and with Peter—teach us about natural knowledge and supernatural love. They show that when our aim is a supernatural experience of objective reality, there are always two steps to get there: one natural, the other supernatural. Both John and Peter needed factual knowledge about Jesus. They needed a natural presentation of reality to their minds. Peter had this knowledge from living with Jesus as a close disciple. John was reminded of it by Jesus: "Go and tell John what you hear and see." And both needed the supernatural intervention of God to illumine natural knowledge with the kind of "light" that would turn a Jewish wonder worker into a treasure of infinite worth (Matt. 13:44).

What then is the answer to the question we posed at the beginning of this chapter? Since the aim of this book is to help you love the second coming of Christ, how can that actually happen? How can the *natural* act of writing and reading a book result in the *supernatural* experience of love for Christ and his coming? Now we have seen the answer. It can happen if I communicate accurately "good news" and "knowledge" about the glory of Christ in his coming, and if God shines in your heart with the divine light of that glory (2 Cor. 4:6). It can happen if I tell you accurately the glories of the second coming that are really there in the Bible, and if God reveals their heart-satisfying worth, which flesh and blood cannot (Matt. 11:1–6; 16:17). In other words, it can happen if I impart objective truth through my writing, and if God imparts spiritual light through your reading.

Foundations of Truth about the Second Coming

You can see an implicit assumption in what I just said, which I want to make explicit with some explanation. I am assuming the truth of biblical teaching about the second coming. I am not assuming it without reason. But that reasoning is in another book, *A Peculiar Glory: How the Christian Scriptures Reveal Their Complete Truthfulness.*[1] Here I am assuming that what the Bible teaches about the second coming is true. If you have questions about that, one way forward is to read this book in order to "test everything; hold fast what is good" (1 Thess. 5:21). Test to see if I handle the Scriptures accurately, and read with the prayer that God would confirm to your mind and heart what is really true. In other words, the book itself might be a means God uses to increase your confidence in the Scriptures.

One of the reasons I linger here to emphasize the truth of Scripture is that this is what the apostle Peter does in his second letter when he begins to deal with the question of the second coming of Christ. Peter is about to address skeptics who asked, "Where is the promise of his coming?" (2 Pet. 3:4). But before he gives his answers to their skepticism, he lays the foundation of his truthfulness.

He lays two foundations: first, his own eyewitness experience of Christ on the Mount of Transfiguration and, second, the confirmation of Old Testament Scriptures, which were inspired by God. I will deal with Peter's teaching about the second coming in chapter 20. Here I am only pointing out that he is eager to lay foundations for the truthfulness of his teachings, which is what I want to do as well.

He says, first, "We did not follow cleverly devised myths when we made known to you the power and coming of our Lord Jesus Christ, but we were eyewitnesses of his majesty" (2 Pet. 1:16). Peter is aware that people are led astray by end-time myths. He wants no part of it. He is not a myth maker or a myth follower. His claims to truth are based on his own eyewitness experience of Jesus's teachings and actions.

His reference to seeing Christ's "majesty" refers to his being with Christ on the Mount of Transfiguration (Matt. 17:1–8). "When . . . the voice was borne to him by the Majestic Glory, 'This is my beloved Son, with whom I am well pleased' [Matt. 17:5], we ourselves heard this very

---

1 John Piper, *A Peculiar Glory: How the Christian Scriptures Reveal Their Complete Truthfulness* (Wheaton, IL: Crossway, 2016).

voice borne from heaven, for we were with him on the holy mountain" (2 Pet. 1:17–18). We will deal in chapter 13 with why Peter connects the transfiguration with the second coming ("the power and coming of our Lord Jesus Christ," 2 Pet. 1:16), but for now the point is simply this: Peter wants to distance himself as far as possible from speculative myths. He wants only to teach truth for which there is good reason. He wants a reasonable foundation under all that he says. I share that goal.

Second, he moves from the foundation of his own eyewitness experience of Jesus to the foundation of the inspired Scriptures, which for him meant the Old Testament (although he refers in 3:16 to the letters of Paul as part of the Scriptures). He says:

> And we have the prophetic word [the Scriptures] more fully con-
> firmed, to which you will do well to pay attention. . . . For no
> prophecy was ever produced by the will of man, but men spoke from
> God as they were carried along by the Holy Spirit. (2 Pet. 1:19, 21)

This is one of the clearest teachings in the Bible concerning the divine inspiration of the Old Testament Scriptures. Peter believed, with good reason (Jesus believed the same, Matt. 5:17–18; John 10:35), that the authors of the Old Testament were not acting on their own. They were carried along by the Spirit. What they wrote was not only *their* word. It was *God's*. Therefore, Peter was eager to lay a double foundation under his teaching about the second coming—namely, the eyewitness accounts of Jesus and the God-inspired Scriptures. I share Peter's eagerness. And I share his confidence in the eyewitness stories of Jesus and in the inspired Scriptures.

Words That Will Never Be Shaken

I cannot move on without drawing attention to the very same concern of Jesus to make sure we see his own teaching as a rock-solid, unwavering ground for our understanding of the second coming. In the longest and most detailed treatment of the end times in the New Testament Gospels, namely Matthew 24, Jesus says this: "Heaven and earth will pass away, but my words will not pass away" (24:35). Jesus was aware that all kinds of false prophets and false christs and false teaching would challenge a right understanding of the second coming (Matt. 24:10–11, 24). Therefore, he wanted to emphasize that in all the shaking of the world that will come, his words will never be shaken from their truthfulness. There is a good foundation for knowing what we need to know about the second coming.

Savoring the Truth We See

When I say that this book could be a means of your loving the appearing of Christ, if I impart objective truth through my writing, and if God imparts spiritual light through your reading, the objective truth I have in mind is nothing other than what the Bible teaches. I claim no authority of my own. If I am faithful to what the Bible teaches, I have good hope that God will be pleased to do his miraculous light-giving work so that many will not only see the facts of Christ in his coming, but see them as glorious and precious—more precious than all this world. That is my aim—that you would savor the truth you see, and that all of us would find ourselves among the number of those "who have loved [the Lord's] appearing" (2 Tim. 4:8).

3

The Glory of Christ as the Primary Reality of His Coming

The Heart of the Matter, Part 1

I HAVE ARGUED THAT LOVE for the appearing of the Lord Jesus is a *spiritual affection*—an affection, or heart feeling, created (in its origin) and formed (in its nature) by the Holy Spirit. One implication of this is that there are different kinds of affections—kinds of love—for his appearing. Some of these are *not* spiritual and are *not* the love to which Paul promises a crown of righteousness (2 Tim. 4:8). So my goal in this book includes the effort to prevent a kind of love for the second coming that has catastrophic results.

Helping Us Avoid Catastrophic Results at His Coming

What I mean by "catastrophic results" is what Jesus warns about in Matthew 7:21–23. He says that on "that day"—the day of his coming in judgment—some of those who seemed to love his appearing will be shocked that they are turned away from Christ's presence:

> Not everyone who says to me, "Lord, Lord," will enter the kingdom of heaven, but the one who does the will of my Father who is in

heaven. On that day many will say to me, "Lord, Lord, did we not prophesy in your name, and cast out demons in your name, and do many mighty works in your name?" And then will I declare to them, "I never knew you; depart from me, you workers of lawlessness."

The reason I say that these false disciples seemed to *love* the Lord's appearing is that they wanted to be included on "that day." They *wanted* in. They called Jesus "Lord." They may have sung a worship song like I did in the 1980s: "I love you, *Lord*, and I lift my voice to worship you. O my soul, rejoice." But Jesus turns them away. In spite of all their religious affirmations (about his lordship) and all their achievements (in doing "many mighty works"), he says that their works came from a lawless spirit. They were not humbly submissive to God and his laws. There was a controlling streak of independence. Concerning their worship songs, in effect, Jesus said, "This people honors me with their lips, but their heart is far from me; in vain do they worship me" (Matt. 15:8–9). How shall we love the appearing of the Lord Jesus in a way that avoids this catastrophic result on the day of his coming?

Heart of the Matter at His Coming

One answer is to ask honestly what we really love about the appearing of the Lord and then to compare that to what he will really bring at his coming. Or to say it another way, does our *love* for his coming fit with his *purposes* in coming? In a sense, the entirety of this book is an effort to help us answer this question. But in this chapter, I want to penetrate to the heart of the matter, that is, the heart of Christ's ultimate purpose in coming again. This purpose will be the test of whether our love for his coming fits with his purposes in coming.

The heart of the matter has to do, first, with the primary, objective reality of the Lord's coming, which is his *glory*—by which I always mean *himself* manifest as glorious. We are going to see that there is an astonishing focus on the Lord's glory at his coming. That's why I call it the *primary* objective reality. But the heart of the matter that I am talking about consists not only in the objective glory of Christ but also, secondly, in our *experience* of that glory on the day of his coming.

It's the relationship between these two—Christ's glory and our experience of it—that is the heart of the matter that I am talking about. The heart of the matter is how we experience the glory of Christ in his coming. Christ is coming not only to display his glory, but also to have his glory experienced in a certain way. Grasping this relationship between Christ's purpose to reveal his glory and his purpose that it be experienced a certain way will help us know whether our love for his appearing is authentic or not. Does it fit with his purposes in his coming?

How Did Jesus Reveal Defective Love for His First Coming?

Before I show this from the biblical texts about Christ's *second* coming, consider how it was also the heart of the matter at his *first* coming. Virtually all Israel hoped for the first coming of the Messiah. Many, one could say, *loved* his appearing. But many of those same people stumbled over his appearing. Their way of hoping or loving did not accord with Christ's purpose in coming. Something was wrong in the hearts of many who considered themselves faithful Jews. Something was wrong with their love for God and for the coming of his Messiah.

Here is one way Jesus drew out the defect. Read the following text from John's Gospel with this question in mind: Does this passage have anything to say about whether we will be glad at Christ's second coming?

You do not have his word abiding in you, for you do not believe the one whom he has sent. You search the Scriptures because you think that in them you have eternal life; and it is they that bear witness about me, yet you refuse to come to me that you may have life. I do not receive glory from people. But I know that you do not have the love of God within you. I have come in my Father's name, and you do not receive me. If another comes in his own name, you will receive him. How can you believe, when you receive glory from one another and do not seek the glory that comes from the only God? (John 5:38–44)

They would have said they loved God. But Jesus says, "You do not have the love of God within you." They would have said they loved the coming of God's Messiah. But he is there in front of them, and Jesus says, "You do not receive me." What was the problem?

Jesus puts his finger on the heart of the matter in verse 44: "How can you believe, when you receive glory from one another and do not seek the glory that comes from the only God?" This is a rhetorical question that is intended to make a statement. When he says, "How can you?" he means, "You can't." Can't what? They can't believe in Jesus. They can't receive Jesus for who he really is. Why not? It has to do with the way they experience glory.

Jesus describes their heart disposition like this: "You receive glory from one another and do not seek the glory that comes from the only God." What does that mean? It means at least this: you love to be commended by other people more than you want the commendation of God. Why would that be? Because you love to be associated with human greatness more than God's greatness. Why would that be? Because behind this disinterest in God's commendation and God's association is a devaluing of God himself as the greatest treasure in the universe. Which is why Jesus says, "You do not have the love of God within you" (John 5:42). You don't treasure the glory of God above all things.

That, Jesus says, *is why you cannot receive me. As long as that is your heart disposition, you cannot receive me for who I really am.* Why would that be? Jesus points to the answer with the words, "If another comes in his *own* name, you will receive him" (John 5:43). Why? Because he would be self-exalting like you, and his existence would not be a standing indictment of your self-exaltation. When Jesus comes humbly, obediently, sacrificially in his *Father's* name (John 5:43), his very existence indicts the self-exalting lovers of human glory. That is why they cannot receive him. They are not ready to join Jesus in treasuring the glory of the Father above all human glory.

The point of dealing with John 5:38–44 has been to illustrate how even at the first coming of the Messiah there was a catastrophic result for many who "loved his appearing." It happened because the Messiah they wanted was not the Messiah they saw. Jesus's purposes in coming did not fit with their desires. They "loved his appearing" in a way that proved false. It did not accord with who he really was. They would have been happy with the appearing of a Messiah who confirmed their love affair with human glory, and their devaluing of God's glory. But that was not the purpose of Jesus's coming.

This experience of some Jews with the first coming of Jesus points to the heart of the matter at his second coming, namely, the way his glory is going to be experienced when he comes. So let's turn to those texts that highlight the glory of Christ in his coming and then notice what kind of human response to that glory actually accords with Christ's purpose.

Paul: The Glory of Christ Is What Appears!

The apostle Paul, more directly than any other biblical writer, makes the glory of Christ central to the second coming. He says, for example, that Christians are "waiting for our blessed hope, *the appearing of the glory of our great God and Savior Jesus Christ*" (Titus 2:13). There are dozens of things Paul might have said about what makes our hope a "*blessed* hope" (μακαρίαν ἐλπίδα)—a happy hope. But what he says here is that what will make it happy is the appearing of *glory*—the glory of our great God and Savior Jesus Christ. Jesus is our Savior. He is our God. And he is great. And therefore, when he appears, this greatness will be manifest to the world as glory. So of all Paul might have said about what makes Christ's coming a happy hope, what he focuses on is glory.

The primacy of this glory appears not only in how it will make Christians happy (μακάριος), but also in how losing that glory will be destructive for unbelievers.

> The Lord Jesus [will be] revealed from heaven with his mighty angels in flaming fire, inflicting vengeance on those who do not know God and on those who do not obey the gospel of our Lord Jesus. They will suffer the punishment of eternal destruction, away from the presence of the Lord and *from the glory of his might*, when he comes on that day. (2 Thess. 1:8–10)

Human beings are made in the image of God (Gen. 1:27). This means, at least, that we are made to image forth the glory of God—to see it, love it, and be transformed by it so as to reflect it. This will be the deepest, highest, longest joy of God's human creation. Therefore, to be cut off from the glory of God is to lose the entire wonder and joy for which we were designed in creation. It will be the underlying sorrow of all "eternal destruction." Thus, Paul makes glory central to the second coming both for believers as our "happy hope" and for unbelievers as their greatest loss.

Peter: First Sufferings, Then Glories

The apostle Peter pointed to the supreme importance of glory by focusing our attention on the ages-long plan of God to bring Christ through suffering (in his first coming) to glory (at his second coming). He does this three times.

> Concerning this salvation, the prophets who prophesied about the grace that was to be yours searched and inquired carefully, inquiring what person or time the Spirit of Christ in them was indicating when he predicted *the sufferings of Christ and the subsequent glories*. (1 Pet. 1:10–11)

The prophets saw dimly how the sufferings and the glory of the Messiah would be related to each other. "They searched and inquired." They certainly would have said that his glory would follow his suffering. He *will* be triumphant at the last. His kingdom will be without end (Isa. 9:7). But they could not see clearly how the sufferings and the glories were connected, or how long it would be until the glories would be revealed after the sufferings. What they could see, and what Peter saw just as clearly, is that the central reality of our future expectation is the glory of Christ.

> Beloved, do not be surprised at the fiery trial when it comes upon you to test you, as though something strange were happening to you. But rejoice insofar as you share Christ's sufferings, that you may also rejoice and be glad *in the revelation of his glory*.[1] (1 Pet. 4:12–13, my translation)

Just as Paul makes "the appearing of the glory" central to the second coming (Titus 2:13), so Peter makes it central to the hope of Christ's suffering people. Just as Christ himself walked first through suffering on the way to the "subsequent glories," so also his people do the same. "Rejoice insofar as you share Christ's *sufferings*, that you may also rejoice and be glad in the revelation of his *glory*." In fact, Peter says that how we respond to our sufferings now decides how we will experience the glory later. Rejoice in your sufferings "so that" you might rejoice in the glory.

Then, third, Peter speaks from his own experience of the sufferings of Christ and again underlines the centrality of the coming glory:

---

1   "The revelation of his glory" is clearly a reference to the second coming, as we can see from the way Peter uses this term *revelation*, for example, in 1 Pet. 1:7: ". . . so that the tested genuineness of your faith—more precious than gold that perishes though it is tested by fire—may be found to result in praise and glory and honor *at the revelation of Jesus Christ*." See also 1 Pet. 1:13: "Therefore, preparing your minds for action, and being sober-minded, set your hope fully on the grace that will be brought to you *at the revelation of Jesus Christ*."

> I exhort the elders among you, as a fellow elder and a witness of the
> sufferings of Christ, as well as a partaker in *the glory that is going to
> be revealed* . . . (1 Pet. 5:1)

So Peter provides a threefold reinforcement of Paul's focus on the
centrality of the glory of Christ at his second coming. (1) Peter sum-
marizes the prophets' message with these words: "sufferings" for the
Messiah's first coming and "glories" for his second (1 Pet. 1:11). (2) He
describes the second coming of Christ with the summary phrase "the
revelation of his glory" (1 Pet. 4:13, my translation). (3) When he describes his own expectation of the second coming, he sums it up with
the hope-filled reality that he will be "a partaker in the glory" (1 Pet.
5:1). Prophets anticipate the glory. Suffering Christians anticipate the
glory. Peter anticipates the glory. Glory—that is, Christ in his revealed
glory—is the central reality of the second coming.

Jesus's Prediction of a Triple Glory at His Coming

This united focus on the primacy of divine glory at the second coming
is not surprising given the way Jesus himself describes his own return.
He speaks repeatedly of the future glory of his coming. At the end of
his life, in his prayer for the disciples (present and future, John 17:20),
Jesus prays, "Father, I desire that they also, whom you have given me,
may be with me where I am, *to see my glory*" (John 17:24).

That glory is not exhausted by, but surely includes, the glory to be
revealed at the Lord's second coming. For example, in Luke 9:23–27,
Jesus refers to a triple glory at his coming:

> If anyone would come after me, let him deny himself and take up
> his cross daily and follow me. For whoever would save his life will
> lose it, but whoever loses his life for my sake will save it. For what
> does it profit a man if he gains the whole world and loses or forfeits
> himself? For whoever is ashamed of me and of my words, of him

will the Son of Man be ashamed when he comes in *his glory* and *the glory of the Father* and *of the holy angels*. But I tell you truly, there are some standing here who will not taste death until they see the kingdom of God.[2]

By "triple glory," I mean these three glories referred to in verse 26: "of him will the Son of Man be ashamed when he comes in [1] his glory and [2] the glory of the Father and [3] of the holy angels." Why this triple-barreled shot from the gun of glory? The reason lies in the logical function of the sentence, signaled by the initial word *for*.

Verse 26 is given as a ground (*for*, γὰρ) for why it is utterly futile to try to save your life by refusing to deny yourself for Christ's sake (Luke 9:23). If you try to save your life (Luke 9:24) and gain the whole world (9:25)—by being ashamed of Jesus in this world, and by loving the glory of man—you are making a horrible mistake. Why? Answering that question is the point of Luke 9:26: because (γὰρ) the glory you thought to gain by avoiding shame for Christ, and by gaining the whole world, is ludicrously small compared to the triple glory you would see and enjoy and be part of at Christ's second coming.

In other words, the glory of Christ and the Father and the angels—all intended to magnify the majesty of Christ in his coming—is emphasized by Jesus as the primary reality of his return. And he does emphasize his glory in a way that has a present effect on what we value in this life. Do we value avoiding shame and getting the world's glory, or do we value the glory of Christ and the prospect of being part of that great revelation at his coming?

Christ's Predictions of His Coming with Great Glory

Another example of how Jesus focuses on the glory of his coming is found in the picture he paints of the final judgment in Matthew 25:31–46. It opens like this:

2 In chapter 13, I try to show how verse 27 relates to the following transfiguration and the second coming.

> When the Son of Man comes *in his glory*, and all the angels with him, then he will sit on *the throne of his glory*. Before him will be gathered all the nations, and he will separate people one from another as a shepherd separates the sheep from the goats. (Matt. 25:31–32, my translation)

When Jesus comes in the last day and makes a division between sheep and goats in judgment, his coming will be "in his *glory*," and the throne he sits on will be a throne of *glory*. Glory is the primary reality in Jesus's description of his second coming.

I will mention only two more passages from Jesus's words that show the primacy of glory at the Lord's coming:

> There will be signs in sun and moon and stars, and on the earth distress of nations in perplexity because of the roaring of the sea and the waves, people fainting with fear and with foreboding of what is coming on the world. For the powers of the heavens will be shaken. And then they will see the Son of Man coming in a cloud with power and *great glory*. (Luke 21:25–27)

> Then will appear in heaven the sign of the Son of Man, and then all the tribes of the earth will mourn, and they will see the Son of Man coming on the clouds of heaven with power and *great glory*. (Matt. 24:30)[3]

Both these texts emphasize that Christ is coming with "great glory." All suffering and shame are behind him. The great reversal—glory for suffering—will be made public to the whole world at his second coming. It will not be a temporary glory marred by some later reversal. It will be an "eternal glory" (2 Tim. 2:10; 1 Pet. 5:10).

---

3   In chapter 16, I deal with the view that seeks to limit such passages to a historical fulfillment in the destruction of Jerusalem in AD 70, with no reference to a final, global coming of Christ at the end of the age. I try to show why I think that effort is mistaken.

This emphasis from Jesus on the *glory* of his second coming is a clear warrant for Paul and Peter to treat Christ's glory as the primary reality of his coming. That is, in fact, what they do. Our "happy hope" (μακαρίαν ἐλπίδα) is summed up by Paul in the words "the appearing of the *glory* of our great God and Savior Jesus Christ" (Titus 2:13). For Peter, the summary of Christ's coming is the revelation of his *glory* (1 Pet. 4:13, my translation).

Turning to the End-Time Experience of His Glory

We have seen from Paul and Peter and Jesus an astonishing focus on the Lord's *glory* at his coming. The primary objective reality of the second coming is the glory of Christ—or Christ revealed in great glory. We are now in a position to focus on the *experience* of that glory in the lives of believers when the Lord comes. This prepares us for what I have called the heart of the matter—the relationship between Christ's glory and our experience of it. Grasping this relationship will help us avoid an inauthentic love of Christ's coming. It will help us love Christ's appearing as we ought. We turn now to the biblical focus on our experience of Christ's glory at his coming.

4

Experiencing the Glory of Christ
with Joyful Amazement

The Heart of the Matter, Part 2

THIS CHAPTER COMPLETES THE EFFORT to show the heart of the matter in Christ's coming. I am arguing that it is found in the relationship between *Christ's glory* as the primary reality of the second coming and the *experience* of that glory in the hearts of God's people. In chapter 3, we saw that Paul and Peter and Jesus all spoke of the glory of Christ as the primary reality of his coming. His coming is the revelation of his *glory* (1 Pet. 4:13). It is "the appearing of the *glory* of our great God and Savior Jesus Christ" (Titus 2:13). It is his coming "in his *glory* . . . [when] he will sit on the throne of his *glory*" (Matt. 25:31, my translation).

In this chapter, we shift from focusing on the glory itself and focus on the experience of God's people at his coming as they encounter this glory. How do God's people respond to the revelation of his glory? And how does this relationship between revelation and response show itself to be the heart of the matter?

"Worship Me and I Will Give You All the Kingdoms"

Surprisingly, Satan's temptation of Jesus in Matthew 4:8–10 sheds penetrating light on the relationship between the glory of Christ in his coming and the experience of that glory by those who see him:

> Again, the devil took him to a very high mountain and showed him all the kingdoms of the world and their glory. And he said to him, "All these I will give you, if you will fall down and worship me." Then Jesus said to him, "Be gone, Satan! For it is written, 'You shall worship the Lord your God and him only shall you serve.'"

To see how this relates to Christ's glory at his coming and our experience of it, I need to make explicit something implicit in the texts we looked at in chapter 3. For example, when Jesus says that at his coming the Son of Man "will sit on the *throne* of his glory" (Matt. 25:31), he implies that his *reign* as King and Judge is part of his glory. That is what *throne* signifies. Implicit in this, and all other references to Christ's glory, is his reign over all the kingdoms of the world. Christ is not coming to share his reign with competing rulers. His glory is the glory of one who sits on the throne of the universe— the "throne of his glory."

Now consider the way Satan offers Jesus just this—universal rule. "The devil . . . showed him all the kingdoms of the world and their glory. And he said to him, 'All these I will give you, if you will fall down and worship me'" (Matt. 4:9–10). The devil is trying to distract Jesus from the path of obedience and suffering that will culminate in this very reality—his rule over "all the kingdoms of the world and their glory." They will be rightly his as the perfectly obedient Son of God. Precisely because of his suffering, he will rule. He was obedient unto death; "*therefore* God has highly exalted him . . . so that at the name of Jesus every knee should bow" (Phil. 2:8–10). Jesus knew this. What

Satan offers him will be his if he is obedient unto death. That is obvious to him. So he is not swayed.

But less obvious is something implicit in the way Satan reasons. He says, in effect, "I will give you the rulership over all the world's kingdoms and their glory if you will worship me." Jesus does not deny that Satan could do this. It is not a laughable proposition, as if Satan had no claim on the kingdoms. Three times, Jesus calls Satan "the ruler of this world" (John 12:31; 14:30; 16:11). Paul calls him "the god of this world" (2 Cor. 4:4) and "the prince of the power of the air" (Eph. 2:2). And John writes that "the whole world lies in the power of the evil one" (1 John 5:19). None of these statements contradicts God's all-pervasive, all-governing providence. God has his reasons for giving Satan so much leash in this age.[1] Jesus's way of responding to Satan was not to question his power over the kingdoms of the world.

Why Satan Preferred Being Worshiped over Ruling All

We are left with the perplexing question, Why was Satan willing to part with his power over the kingdoms of the world? Why was he willing to give this power and authority to Jesus? The first part of the answer is this: because, in exchange for this power and authority, he would have the worship of Jesus. In other words, instead of having power and authority over the kingdoms of the world, Satan would have the worship of the one who had power and authority over the kingdoms.

Granted, Satan was a fool to think he could get the Son of God to waver in his path of obedience and suffering. But was he a fool to propose this exchange of universal power for worship? Authority for worship? Ownership for worship? No, he was not. And seeing why this is so sheds penetrating light on the relationship between the glory of Christ at his coming and the experience of that glory by those who see him.

1   See chapters 18 and 19 ("Satan and Demons" and "The Ongoing Existence of Satan") in John Piper, *Providence* (Wheaton, IL: Crossway, 2021), 255–86.

What Satan sees rightly is that the one who is worshiped over all is the one for whom all exists, regardless of who has the immediate rulership of all. If I worship you for giving me the nations, then I acknowledge that the nations exist for your sake. Letting Jesus have world rulership would not have been a loss for Satan, if Jesus ruled the world for Satan's sake. And that is what worship means. It means that Jesus would acknowledge Satan as his greatest allegiance and greatest treasure. And not just *acknowledge* but revere and admire and respect and value. This is what *worship* means. Without this it is hypocrisy, not worship.

Here's the crucial implication: raw power or authority over nations is not the ultimate tribute to Christ. Satan was willing to let Jesus have that, because he knew the ultimate tribute is not to rule all things but to be admired and treasured for ruling. The ultimate tribute is not to own all things but to be admired and treasured for ownership. Why is that? Because while, in one sense, rule and ownership are glorious, to be worshiped—to be revered and admired and treasured—is an even greater glory. One might be a powerful, all-owning potentate but hated by all his subjects. This would not be glorious.

Satan saw this, probably from the moment he was created. The Son of God would prove to be glorious not only because of the absoluteness of his ownership and rule, but also because the day would come when millions of creatures would treasure him above all things. His glory would shine not only because he would be acknowledged as owning and ruling all treasures, but also because he would be worshiped as the greatest treasure.

What Satan saw and never forgot was that the ultimate aim of God, in creating the universe and setting in motion a great world history, was not the *partial* glorification of his Son in the absoluteness of his ownership and power and wisdom and grace, but rather the *full* glorification of his Son in being surrounded by millions of worshiping people who don't just acknowledge his preeminence in all things (Col. 1:18), but admire him, revere him, love him, treasure him as their greatest portion in life (Ps. 73:26; Lam. 3:24). This is what Satan wanted for himself. Ownership and rule of kingdoms would come to nothing without this.

Revelation of Glory Completed in Worship

The point of focusing on Satan's temptation of Jesus has been to penetrate to the heart of the matter concerning the relationship between the glory of Christ in his coming and the experience of that glory by those who see him. The inference is this: it is true to say that the glory of Christ is the primary *objective* reality revealed at the second coming (as we saw from numerous texts in chapter 3), but without the *subjective* reality of how people *experience* that glory, we miss the heart of the matter. If there is no heartfelt worship, no delighting in, no treasuring of the glory, the ultimate aim of God fails. Satan knew this. We need to know it. Absolutely crucial to God's ultimate purpose in the second coming is not only that the glory of Christ be revealed, but that it be loved. Rightly loved.

Coming to Be Glorified and Marveled At

We turn now to a passage that brings these two realities together—the glory of Christ at his coming, and the experience of that glory in the hearts of his people. Paul wrote 2 Thessalonians largely to deal with issues surrounding the second coming of Christ. He wanted to help the church see God's purpose "in all your persecutions and in the afflictions that you are enduring" (2 Thess. 1:4), and to relate that purpose to the second coming. And he wanted to help the church deal with people who were quitting their jobs and becoming idlers, evidently because they thought "the day of the Lord has come" (2 Thess. 2:2; 3:6).

The part of this letter that concerns us now is 2 Thessalonians 1:10. Here's the context of verses 5–10:

This [persecution and affliction you are enduring] is evidence of the righteous judgment of God, that you may be considered worthy of the kingdom of God, for which you are also suffering—since indeed God considers it just to repay with affliction those who afflict you, and to grant relief to you who are afflicted as well as to us, when the Lord Jesus is revealed from heaven with his mighty angels in flaming fire, inflicting vengeance on those who do not know God and on those who do not obey the gospel of our Lord Jesus. They will suffer the punishment of eternal destruction, away from the presence of the Lord and from the glory of his might, when he comes on that day to be glorified in his saints, and to be marveled at among all who have believed, because our testimony to you was believed.

We will return to this text in chapters 8 and 9 for a closer look at its numerous important parts, but now the focus is on verse 10: ". . . when [Christ] comes on that day *to be glorified* [ἐνδοξασθῆναι²] in his saints, and *to be marveled at* [θαυμασθῆναι] among all who have believed."

This is one of the clearest statements of purpose for the second coming in all the Bible. It is *Christ's* purpose. He is coming, Paul says, for this twofold purpose: to be glorified and to be marveled at. Among other God-designed purposes for the second coming, this statement brings us to the ultimate purpose—the purpose that is not a means to any other purpose, but is an end in itself.

How Do Being Glorified and Marveled at Relate?

The reason this text is so relevant for our consideration at this point is that the words "be glorified" and "be marveled at" reveal what I have called the heart of the matter, namely, the relationship between the

2   Only here and in verse 12 does Paul use the compound word ἐνδοξασθῆναι (*en-doxasthēnai*) instead of the more common δοξάζω. In both cases, the verb is followed by a prepositional phrase with *en* (v. 10, ἐν τοῖς ἁγίοις αὐτοῦ, "in his saints"; and v. 12, ἐν ὑμῖν, "in you"). Thus the intent seems to be to draw attention to the fact that this act of glorifying is rooted *within* the saints. It is not exclusively internal. But it is rooted there. It is not simply an act of glorifying detached from the human heart, as if one might say, "even the rocks and mountains and stars glorify God." They certainly do, by simply reflecting his glory as their Maker, but he is not glorified "in them" as he is "in his saints."

glory of Christ in his coming and the experience of that glory in the hearts of his people. What is the relationship between Christ's being glorified at his coming and Christ's being marveled at in his coming?

To glorify is to make the glory of the Lord manifest. To display it. To cause it to be seen for the greatness that it is. To magnify it—as a telescope, not a microscope (not making something small look bigger than it is, but making something unimaginably big look more like what it really is). This may be done with *words* of praise, or with *actions* that draw attention to the greatness and worth and beauty of the Lord.

To marvel at, on the other hand, is an act of the human heart and mind. It is the awakening of what we have called an affection—a heart feeling of astonishment or amazement or awe. The word itself need not imply a positive emotion. It may be simply astonishment with no sense of joyful admiration, as when Jesus "marveled [ἐθαύμαζεν] because of their unbelief" (Mark 6:6). But in 2 Thessalonians 1:10, it is positive. Very positive. Jesus is returning to earth for this! The hope of the second coming is a "*happy* hope" (μακαρίαν ἐλπίδα, Titus 2:13). We will "*rejoice and be glad* when his glory is revealed" (1 Pet. 4:13). The marveling that Jesus is coming to receive is *joyful* marveling.

When we put the two together—being glorified and being marveled at—what we see is that *glorifying* is the outward fruit of displaying the Lord's glory, and *marveling* is the inward root of amazed admiration and of being in awe of that glory. When marveling is added to glorifying, it is more clear that the glorifying involves not just external reflection, but also internal affection. The glory of Christ is reflected in his people not as the sunlight is reflected in the unfeeling moon, but as the lover's presence is reflected in the beloved's radiant face.

I have called this the heart of the matter. Christ will return not only to be seen and shown as glorious, but to be marveled at as glorious. He is coming for an objective *presentation* of his glorious person, and he is coming to be *experienced* for the glorious person that he is. He is coming to be *acknowledged* for his glory and to be *admired* for his glory. His aim is that his appearing be *known* universally and that it be *loved* intensely.

But it is not as though these two aims are separate, standing side by side like two trophies on Jesus's mantel. The heart of the matter is that the inward marveling-admiring-loving response to Jesus's coming is essential to the authenticity of our outward glorification of his greatness. Without the marveling, the glorifying would be hollow. This is what Satan saw. Even if he had all the glory of all the kingdoms of the world as owner or ruler, it would be hollow without being worshiped. It is the worship, the admiration, the marveling, the love that causes the glorification to be full instead of hollow.

Christian Hedonism—Again!

I have devoted the last fifty years of my life to putting the truth on display that *God is most glorified in us when we are most satisfied in him.* I have called it Christian Hedonism. Here we meet this truth again. And it is the heart of the matter. From beginning to end, God does all things for his glory. This truth runs through the whole Bible.[3]

> *For my name's sake* I defer my anger
>   *for the sake of my praise* I restrain it for you,
>   that I may not cut you off.
> Behold, I have refined you, but not as silver;
>   I have tried you in the furnace of affliction.
> *For my own sake, for my own sake*, I do it,
>   for *how should my name be profaned?*
>   *My glory I will not give to another.* (Isa. 48:9–11)

God created us for his glory at the beginning (Isa. 43:6–7); he sent his Son into the world the first time for his glory (Luke 2:14; John

---

3 For a collection of texts to show this, see John Piper, "Biblical Texts to Show God's Zeal for His Own Glory," Desiring God, November 24, 2007, https://www.desiringgod.org/.

12:27–28); and at the second coming of Christ, history as we know it will reach its crescendo for his glory (2 Thess. 1:10). God's creation is a God-centered, Christ-exalting universe. World history is a God-centered, Christ-exalting history. "All things were created through [Christ] and for [Christ]" (Col. 1:16). Everything that happens, and everything that exists, is designed ultimately by God to communicate the full array of his excellencies.[4] He "works all things according to the counsel of his will" (Eph. 1:11).

But that is not the heart of the matter. The heart of the matter is that this ultimate purpose of God's glorification in Jesus Christ happens most fully and climactically when God's people *experience* his glory as profoundly marvelous. I say *profoundly* because moderate affections reflect poorly on the beloved. God did not command us to love him with half our heart or two-thirds of our heart, but "with *all* [our] heart" (Matt. 22:37). "Serve him with all your heart" (Josh. 22:5). "Trust in the LORD with all your heart" (Prov. 3:5). "Seek [him] with all your heart" (Jer. 29:13). "Return to [him] with all your heart" (Joel 2:12). "Rejoice and exult with all your heart" (Zeph. 3:14). Even though we fall short of this destiny in this life, we will not fall short on that day. Christ is not returning to receive moderate marveling.

On that day, when we see him, we will be changed so as to feel what we ought (1 John 3:2). And that feeling of the heart—that glory-inspired marveling—will be the ultimate purpose of all things. God in Christ will be most glorified in our being most satisfied in him. The divine aim is not only the revelation of glory. Nor is the aim only the joyful marveling of the saints. Rather, the aim is both—the glory calling forth the joyful marveling, the joyful marveling confirming the worth and beauty and greatness of the glory. This is the heart of the matter. This is the divine purpose of all things.

4 The support and explanation for this claim is laid out in Piper, *Providence*.

Avoiding the Catastrophic Results of Defective Love

We are now in a position to circle back to the practical, personal aim of chapters 3 and 4: to prevent a kind of love for the second coming that has catastrophic results. We saw such catastrophic results at the second coming in Matthew 7:21–23, and we saw catastrophic results at the first coming in John 5:38–44. Both involved defective love for Christ's appearing. Their love for the Messiah's coming did not fit with the Messiah's purposes in coming.

The issue was glory. "How can you believe, when you receive glory from one another and do not seek the glory that comes from the only God?" (John 5:44). They loved the glory that comes from man, not the glory that comes from God. But Christ did not come to confirm fallen human beings in their love affair with human praise. He came to create a people who would experience the Copernican revolution of putting God at the center of the solar system of their lives, not themselves. Christ came the first time to die for sinners so that the suicidal love of self-glorification would be replaced with the all-satisfying experience of God-glorification. "He died for all, that those who live might no longer live for themselves but for him who for their sake died and was raised" (2 Cor. 5:15).

But many in Christ's day loved the appearing of the Messiah in a way that made Jesus's goal in coming seem abhorrent. It contradicted their love for human praise. It contradicted their view of God as one who approved of their self-exaltation in righteousness (Luke 18:11–14). It made belief in the true Jesus impossible (John 5:44). Their love for the appearing of Christ put them at odds with Christ and proved catastrophic.

Self-Humbling, Christ-Exalting Love for His Appearing

Having laid bare the heart of the matter in Christ's second coming, we may now test ourselves. Does our love for Christ's appearing fit with his purposes in coming? The heart of the matter is that he is coming to be glorified and marveled at. Christ's purpose in coming is radically Christ-exalting. He means for his own glory to be front and center. He means for it to flash from horizon to horizon unmistakably (Luke 17:24). And he means for that glory to shine most brightly in the joyful marveling of his people. We will not be the center of attention. He will. And the glory of his centrality will be our joy. Our marveling at his supreme glory will complete his glorification and will be the height of our jubilation.

The utterly urgent questions for us are, Does this offend us? Does it grate against some remaining craving in our heart to be the center of attention? Does it seem egocentric to us that Christ's purpose is that Christ be exalted? Or have we experienced what Christ died for: the radical transformation that causes us to love Christ's coming to be glorified? When Paul said that the Lord would give the crown of righteousness to "all who have loved his appearing" (2 Tim. 4:8), this is the love he had in mind. A love that joyfully marvels at the coming of the all-glorious Christ to receive the joy-filled marveling of his people.

5

The Grace Being Brought to You
at the Revelation of Christ

WHEN CHRIST COMES AGAIN in the glory of his Father and with millions of angels, there will be a great global reckoning. "Every eye will see him, even those who pierced him, and all tribes of the earth will wail on account of him" (Rev. 1:7). It will be so terrifyingly different from all events in the history of the world that we all will be stunned and scarcely able to believe our eyes. One of the fears that could rightly arise in our hearts, even now, is this: Will there be grace in this terror? The aim of this chapter is to show an answer to this question that should intensify our love for the Lord's appearing.

Command to Hope in Grace

Peter's two epistles are permeated with references to Christ's second coming (1 Pet. 1:5, 7, 13; 2:12; 4:7, 12–13; 5:1, 4; 2 Pet. 1:16–19; 2:9; 3:1–13). He considered it a matter of great significance for the believers of his day, even though he reckoned with the strange possibility that it might be far in the future, since "with the Lord one day is as a thousand years, and a thousand years as one day" (2 Pet. 3:8). One of his most sweeping and joyfully hope-giving statements about the second coming is 1 Peter 1:13, which provides one of the deepest foundations for our love of Christ's appearing: "Set your hope fully on the *grace* that will be brought to you at the revelation of Jesus Christ."

Context of Waiting, Not Seeing, and Loving

To put the command in context, Peter says in 1 Peter 1:5 that believers are now "being guarded through faith for a salvation ready to be revealed in the *last time.*" The "last time" is the time of Jesus's coming. Peter makes this clear two verses later, when he tells the believers that their present sufferings are like purifying fire, which will refine them for the coming of Jesus. They are being tested so that the "genuineness of your faith—more precious than gold that perishes though it is tested by fire—may be found to result in praise and glory and honor *at the revelation of Jesus Christ*" (1 Pet. 1:7). That revelation is the coming of Christ, the bringer of the "salvation ready to be revealed in the last time."

Peter loves to describe the coming of Christ as the "revelation of Jesus Christ" (1 Pet. 1:5, 13; 4:13; 5:1). It reminds his readers that for now they cannot "see" Jesus, but in the day of his coming he will be revealed. They will see him. Peter himself had seen Jesus. He makes a point of telling us so. He was a "witness of the sufferings of Christ" (1 Pet. 5:1). Nevertheless, he now shares in the necessary patience of ordinary Christians, who must wait for the one they love. "Though you have not seen him, you love him. Though you do not now see him, you believe in him and rejoice with joy that is inexpressible and filled with glory" (1 Pet. 1:8).

In this temporary condition of not seeing Jesus, Peter intends to stir up the hope of the believers so that their love for Jesus would also be a love for his appearing. He points to "the prophets who prophesied about the grace" of God that would come to God's people through "the sufferings of Christ and the subsequent glories" (1 Pet. 1:10–11). Grace had come (in Christ's sufferings). Grace was coming (in Christ's glories). Even the angels long to look into God's great works of grace (1 Pet. 1:12).

Deep Foundation for Love

Then Peter says this: "Therefore, preparing your minds for action, and being sober-minded, set your hope fully on the *grace* that will be brought to you at the revelation of Jesus Christ" (1 Pet. 1:13). This is the statement that I said provides one of the deepest foundations for our love of Christ's appearing. That deep foundation is the grace of God. When Christ is revealed from heaven, his people will experience that event as grace. All that happens to them on that day will rest on this foundation: grace.

Glory of Grace

This word *grace* was so firmly established in Christian understanding that Peter did not define it in his letters. But we do well not to pass over its meaning too quickly, as if the glory of it were known and felt by all. In the New Testament, the apostle Paul makes the term clear and glorious. Of the 124 New Testament uses of the English word *grace*, eighty-four are in Paul.

The grace of God is essentially the disposition and act of God to give salvation to people who deserve his judgment. In other words, God's grace is doing good not to those who don't deserve it, but to those who deserve the opposite. All human beings have sinned (Rom. 3:9, 23). We are therefore not just undeserving. We are ill-deserving. We deserve God's wrath. We are "by nature children of wrath, like the rest of mankind" (Eph. 2:3). If God's only attribute were strict justice, we all would perish. In our sin and guilt, we are liable to eternal punishment (Matt. 25:46; 2 Thess. 1:9). Any suffering short of hell is less than we deserve.

But God's justice is not his only attribute. The hope of the human race is that "where sin increased, grace abounded all the more, so that, as sin reigned in death, grace also might reign through righteousness leading to eternal life through Jesus Christ our Lord" (Rom. 5:20–21). "The grace of God has appeared, bringing salvation for all people" (Titus 2:11). Grace made a way for God's justice to be upheld while guilty sinners, amazingly, are justified, instead of condemned. "[We] are justified by his grace *as a gift*, through the redemption that is in Christ Jesus" (Rom. 3:24). Being right with God is a free gift. That is what grace does.

This is possible because Christ became a curse for us (Gal. 3:13). The record of our debt was nailed to his cross (Col. 2:14). God "made him to be sin who knew no sin, so that in him we might become the righteousness of God" (2 Cor. 5:21). Now, "those who receive the abundance of grace and the free gift of righteousness reign in life through the one man Jesus Christ" (Rom. 5:17). That receiving is called *faith*. "Since we have been justified *by faith*, we have peace with God" (Rom. 5:1).

God's grace is such a deep foundation for our hope that its roots go back into eternity. "[God] saved us . . . not because of our works but because of his own purpose and *grace*, which he gave us in Christ Jesus before the ages began" (2 Tim. 1:9). The grace that saved us was given to us before creation. Paul describes this in Ephesians: "He predestined us for adoption to himself as sons through Jesus Christ, according to the purpose of his will, to the praise of the glory of his *grace*" (1:5–6, my translation). In other words, the eternal purpose of God's predestining his people for adoption was that we would praise the glory of his grace. That was God's plan for the ages before the ages began: the praise of the glory of God's grace.

Since grace has its deepest foundations in eternity past, we may be sure that it will carry us joyfully to eternity future. "God . . . loved us and gave us eternal comfort and good hope through *grace*" (2 Thess. 2:16). Eternal comfort. Through grace. Grace will see to it that our comfort and our hope never fail. "Being justified by his *grace* we . . . become heirs according to the hope of eternal life" (Titus 3:7). That life will bring the endless unfolding of newly satisfying dimensions of grace: "In the coming ages he [will] show the immeasurable riches of his *grace* in kindness toward us in Christ Jesus" (Eph. 2:7). It will take eternal ages to complete our joy because there are *immeasurable* riches of grace. Thus, the eternity of our never-bored, ever-refreshed life in Christ rests on the inexhaustible gift of God's grace. Eternal grace. Grace from eternity past to eternity future.

Let Yourself Try to Imagine

Now we return to 1 Peter 1:13: "Set your hope fully on the *grace* that will be brought to you at the revelation of Jesus Christ." Of all the dozens of realities Peter might have said are coming to us at the revelation of Christ, he says, "Grace is being brought to you." This is very good news for stumblers and doubters and worriers like us.

Let yourself imagine just slightly what that hour will be like. We do not know with detail or precision what the moment of his coming will be like. But only the slightest effort to imagine it overwhelms us. Suddenly, absolutely all doubt about his reality will vanish. Stark certainty will replace it. There will be nothing— absolutely nothing—imaginary about it. It will be raw reality. For the first time in our lives, sight will replace belief in the unseen. The magnitude of it will be such as to make our hearts feel like exploding. In ourselves, we will have no capacities for fathoming this event. It will stagger us.

The infinite canyon between his perfection and holiness mingled with his galactic power, on the one hand, and our ridiculously small weakness and moral evil and banal lives of trifling, on the other hand, will be overwhelmingly plain and terrifying. He will be "revealed from heaven with his mighty angels in flaming fire, inflicting vengeance on those who do not know God and on those who do not obey the gospel of our Lord Jesus" (2 Thess. 1:7–8). There is nothing warm and cuddly about these hours. They will bring stark terror and reprisal for all who are outside Christ. They will mark the end of all divine patience for those who did not embrace the gospel.

If There Is Any Hope, It Will Be Grace, Personal Grace

At this point, we will have one hope: grace. We will have no thought of merit. No thought of deserving or being a little better than others. We will have only a sense of absolute vulnerability and utter speechlessness, as when finally caught red-handed doing what you have gotten away with for years. No recourse. No escape. No plea. If there is any hope, it will be *grace*. So Peter puts into one word what is being brought to "you" at the revelation of Christ: grace.

You. Who are the "you" in verse 13? They are those whom God "caused . . . to be born again to a living hope through the resurrection of Jesus" (1 Pet. 1:3), and who "are being guarded through faith for a salvation ready to be revealed in the last time" (1:5), and whose tested faith has been refined through suffering (1:7), and who love and trust the unseen Christ (1:8).

For them, the day of Christ will not be destructive. It will be gracious. Personally gracious. I say *personally* gracious because of Peter's unusual expression that "grace is *being brought* to you." He does not say grace "is coming to you," but rather "is *being brought* to you" (τὴν φερομένην ὑμῖν χάριν). Someone is bringing it. It is not showing up impersonally as a kind of atmosphere or mood. It is coming in the hands of Jesus. Or, perhaps better, in the *heart* of Jesus. Jesus is coming with a gracious disposition toward his people.

That spectacular day will not be an impersonal event of shock and awe. It will be intensely personal. In ways we cannot fathom, the risen God-man will treat us personally. He knows our name. We will be dealt with as dear ones. "I will not leave you as orphans; I will come to you" (John 14:18). If we slip into thinking that he is coming with a sword to slay us, Peter's word is meant to correct our thinking: no, for us who are eagerly waiting, in his hand and in his heart, is grace. Grace is being brought to you.

Hitch Up Your Hips and Stay Sober

Not surprisingly, Peter precedes the command to "set your hope fully on . . . grace" with two participles to show us what will be needed to keep this hope lively before our minds. Literally, Peter says, "Having hitched up the hips of your mind [ἀναζωσάμενοι τὰς ὀσφύας τῆς διανοίας ὑμῶν], staying sober,"[1] hope fully in grace. In the first participle, Peter pictures them wearing long robes, and in order to run and not be entangled, they had to reach down and pull the back part of the robe up between their legs and tuck it into their belt in front so that the robe formed a kind of britches around their hips.

That, Peter says, is what you must do to your mind. In other words, do whatever it takes to keep the mind agile and responsive and active when dealing with spiritual reality—indeed when dealing with all reality. The mind will need to be hitched up for action if it is to take hold of the reality of grace, and keep it in view, and taste the glory of it as we ought, and feel the fullness of hope, and not waver when we sense the nearness of the Son of Man.

The other participle makes the same basic point: "stay sober" (νήφοντες). Drunkenness dulls the senses so that the mind is not as perceptive or responsive as it ought to be. That puts us in jeopardy of not seeing clearly and not acting wisely. The point is this: if there is a glorious promise that grace is being brought to us at the coming of Christ, that promise will do us no good if our minds are drunk with the world. We won't see it, and we won't believe it.

Peter wants believers to have a ready, alert, lively expectation of the coming of the Lord. The participle "is being brought to us" (φερομένην) is present tense, not future tense. It says, grace "*is* being brought to

---

1 This is the translation suggested by Robert H. Gundry, *Commentary on the New Testament: Verse-by-Verse Explanations with a Literal Translation* (Peabody, MA: Hendrickson, 2010), 939.

you," not "*will be* brought to you." The effect is to remind us that grace is on the way. Whether the grace arrives in months or centuries is not of the essence. Peter is open to both (1 Pet. 4:7; 2 Pet. 3:8). Our calling is not to speculate about how close it is, but to use our minds with agility and sobriety to "hope fully" in the grace of the second coming.

In other words, Peter is very aware that God calls his people to use means in order to prepare for Christ's coming. By *prepare*, I mean, in this case, to keep your hope alive, strong, and active so it will shape your life. By *means*, I am referring to the two commands: "hitch up the hips of your mind," and "stay sober." I wonder if any perceptive readers recognize the roots of these two means in the teachings of Jesus?

Hip-Hitching and Sobriety in the Teachings of Jesus

Both hip-hitching and sobriety were used by Jesus as instructions for how to be ready for the second coming. In Luke 12:40, Jesus says, "You also must be ready, for the Son of Man is coming at an hour you do not expect." To put this preparedness in a picture, Jesus compares his coming to a master returning home from a wedding feast. Would his servants be ready to open the door for him? So he tells them:

> Hitch around your hips [ὑμῶν αἱ ὀσφύες περιεζωσμέναι] and keep your lamps burning, and be like men who are waiting for their master to come home from the wedding feast, so that they may open the door to him at once when he comes and knocks. (Luke 12:35–36, my translation)

I translated the Greek as "hitch *around*" (περιεζωσμέναι) instead of "hitch up" (ἀναζωσάμενοι), as in 1 Peter 1:13, because there is a different preposition affixed to the word *hitch* (ζώννυμι). But the word *hips* (or *loins*, ὀσφῦς) is the same in both, and the idea is clearly the same. If you are going to be alert, doing what your master expects of you and ready for his coming, your mind and heart need to be "dressed for action." Jesus makes the point with a parable (a master returning home). Peter makes it with a metaphor (the mind kept agile and alert).

Similarly, Jesus, like Peter, uses sobriety as a picture of staying ready for his coming. He pictures the second coming as a master returning to his estate after some delay (Luke 12:45), and finding his manager fulfilling his calling—or not. Why would he not be? Drunkenness:

> The Lord said, "Who then is the faithful and wise manager, whom his master will set over his household, to give them their portion of food at the proper time? Blessed is that servant whom his master will find so doing when he comes. Truly, I say to you, he will set him over all his possessions. But if that servant says to himself, 'My master is delayed in coming,' and begins to beat the male and female servants, and to eat and drink and *get drunk*, the master of that servant will come on a day when he does not expect him and at an hour he does not know, and will cut him in pieces and put him with the unfaithful." (Luke 12:42–46)

The point is this: it is complete folly to use the "delay" of Jesus as an excuse to become careless with our minds. Drunkenness is a picture of mental obliviousness. If the manager were not drunk, he would not have been taken off guard by the coming of the master. Being sober is a picture of mental vitality in the service of the master. In this way, one is always ready, indeed eager, for the Lord's coming. For Jesus "will set him over all his possessions" (Luke 12:44). We will share in the ownership and rule of Jesus over all things.

Jesus sounds the alarm about drunkenness again in relation to the second coming. Having said that "the Son of Man [is] coming in a cloud with power and great glory" (Luke 21:27), Jesus warns his disciples:

> Watch yourselves lest your hearts be weighed down with dissipation *and drunkenness* and cares of this life, and that day come upon you

suddenly like a trap. For it will come upon all who dwell on the face of the whole earth. But stay awake at all times, praying that you may have strength to escape all these things that are going to take place, and to stand before the Son of Man. (Luke 21:34–36)

We hear again what I have called the "means" that Jesus and Peter tell us to use to prepare ourselves for the Lord's coming. "Watch yourselves . . . stay awake at all times, praying." This is the opposite of being "weighed down with dissipation and drunkenness and cares." Watching yourself with a view to sobriety is virtually the same as what Peter means by "hitch up your minds and be sober." We are called to mental and spiritual vigilance as we wait for the Lord.

Hitched Up and Sober for the Sake of Escape

These *means* are meant to help us live a kind of life that "escapes" destruction and stands accepted before the Son of Man. "Stay awake at all times, praying that you may have strength to *escape* all these things that are going to take place, and to *stand* before the Son of Man" (Luke 21:36). This word *escape* does not mean we don't experience the judgments of God that come on the world at the end of the age. Rather, it means that even from within them we are rescued from their ultimately destructive effects. That word *escape* in Luke 21:36 (ἐκφυγεῖν) is used two other times in Luke's writings, and both times it means to escape *out of* a crisis rather than being kept from entering the crisis (Acts 16:27; 19:16).

Peter makes the same point in 1 Peter 4:17–19:

It is time for judgment to begin at the household of God; and if it begins with us, what will be the outcome for those who do not obey the gospel of God? And "If the righteous is scarcely saved, what will become of the ungodly and the sinner?" Therefore let those who suffer according to God's will entrust their souls to a faithful Creator while doing good.

Christians do not escape the end-time judgments of God in the sense of never entering into suffering. Rather, we escape the destructive effects of suffering by experiencing them as purification, not punishment. This is Peter's point when he refers to these sufferings in chapter 1:

> In this you rejoice, though now for a little while, if necessary, you have been grieved by various trials, so that the tested genuineness of your faith—more precious than gold that perishes though it is tested by fire—may be found to result in praise and glory and honor at the revelation of Jesus Christ. (1 Pet. 1:6–7)

Similarly, in chapter 5, Peter comforts the believers not with escape from entering their sufferings, but with escape from the destructive effects of suffering:

> After you have suffered a little while, the God of all grace, who has called you to his eternal glory in Christ, will himself restore, confirm, strengthen, and establish you. To him be the dominion forever and ever. Amen. (1 Pet. 5:10–11)

Standing before the Son of Man—by Grace

So Jesus and Peter both teach that Christians are called to use means (agile, active, alert mental activity) for the sake of hoping fully in the grace of God and thus being able to stand before the Son of Man at his coming. The opposite of standing before the Son of Man is to be separated from the righteous and cast out forever from before the Lord:

> So it will be at the end of the age. The angels will come out and separate the evil from the righteous and throw them into the fiery furnace. In that place there will be weeping and gnashing of teeth. (Matt. 13:49–50; cf. 25:31–46)

Such a warning is sobering—indeed, frightening, if we are left to ourselves and our own capacities. Left to ourselves, the coming of the all-holy Christ is terrifying. Our minds run to every possible shortcoming we will feel at that day. This could easily undermine our love for the Lord's appearing. Peter's answer to that danger is a precious reminder in the form of a merciful command: hope fully in the *grace* being brought to you at the revelation of Christ (1 Pet. 1:13). Yes, we will bring shortcomings to that final day when we face Christ. Perfection awaits our final transformation in that face-to-face meeting (1 Cor. 13:9–12; 1 John 3:2). Until then, we need forgiveness every day (Matt. 6:12; Phil. 3:12; 1 John 1:8–10).

Therefore, Peter's precious word to help us love the Lord's appearing is that Jesus is bringing grace to us, not condemnation. The forgiveness that he purchased decisively on the cross will be as applicable to us on that day as on every other day of our lives. Grace will triumph over our sin on that day. This is why we love his appearing.

6

Will We Be Blameless at the Coming of Christ?

IN THE PREVIOUS CHAPTER, Peter promised that grace will be brought to Christ's people at the second coming (1 Pet. 1:13). Christ himself will administer it. We will be saved from wrath on that day (1 Thess. 1:10), not because of our merit, but because of God's grace—specifically, the grace needed on that day. Nevertheless, Peter directed us to use means so that we will be full of hope and ready for that day—especially the means of staying mentally alive and awake to Christ and the preciousness of his promises.

The apostle Paul states even more clearly that Christians are to use means to be ready for the second coming. In fact, he does so in a way that can be troubling. His words can even seem to undermine final salvation by grace through faith. He speaks about our preparation for that day in a way that, for some, makes their love for his appearing waver with uncertainty.

Pure and Blameless for the Day of Christ

I have in mind these three passages in particular:

> It is my prayer that your love may abound more and more, with knowledge and all discernment, so that you may approve what is

excellent, and *so be pure and blameless* [εἰλικρινεῖς καὶ ἀπρόσκοποι] *for the day of Christ,* filled with the fruit of righteousness that comes through Jesus Christ, to the glory and praise of God. (Phil. 1:9–11)

May the Lord make you increase and abound in love for one another and for all, as we do for you, *so that he may establish your hearts blameless in holiness* [ἀμέμπτους ἐν ἁγιωσύνῃ] *before our God and Father, at the coming of our Lord Jesus* with all his saints. (1 Thess. 3:12–13)

Now may the God of peace himself sanctify you completely, and may your whole spirit and soul and body be *kept blameless* [ἀμέμπτως] *at the coming of our Lord Jesus Christ.* (1 Thess. 5:23)

We are all keenly aware that we will bring imperfections and shortcomings to the day of Christ, and yet Paul treats our blamelessness on that day as in some sense dependent on real change in our lives here and now. These three passages make our blamelessness before Christ the aim of God's *sanctifying* work in our lives through the increase of our love for other people. Paul prays that God would work real transformation in our lives to the end that we might be found blameless at Christ's coming. That seems to undermine our peace and security, since none of us will be so transformed, it seems, as to be called *blameless* on that day.

Look with me carefully at each text.

Philippians 1:9–11

In Philippians 1:9–11, Paul is praying. That means he sees God as the one who will do what he is asking him to do, namely, to make us "pure and blameless for the day of Christ." These texts make our blamelessness in some sense dependent on *God's* sanctifying work in our lives. So, however much *we* are involved in working, *God* is the decisive worker in these texts. Paul is praying for him to act. Prayer is one of the means of preparation for the second coming.

But in order to fit us for the day of Christ, God causes our love to abound more and more with all discernment (1:9). Then, in verse 10, come the all-important words that connect the practical changes in our lives with our purity and blamelessness at the day of Christ. These key connecting words are "so that . . . and so." May God cause your love to abound with discernment, Paul prays, "*so that* you may approve [εἰς τὸ δοκιμάζειν] what is excellent, *and so* [ἵνα] be pure and blameless." These two connectors ("so that . . . and so") show that our blamelessness at the day of Christ is God's purpose for the practical changes he works in our lives—namely, that we abound in love with discernment and thus approve what is excellent.

How does our blamelessness on the day of Christ relate to the reality of justification by faith? The New Testament teaches that because of our union with Christ by faith, we have an imputed blamelessness, or righteousness (Rom. 4:4–12; 2 Cor. 5:21; Phil. 3:8–9). But what Paul focuses on here seems in tension with *imputed* blamelessness. Paul says that Christians will be found pure and blameless on the day of Christ because God has worked real transformative love in our minds and hearts. He is connecting our blamelessness before Christ with the abounding of our love. How does that relate to our justification?

1 Thessalonians 3:11–13

The second text to consider more closely is 1 Thessalonians 3:11–13. The thought is virtually identical with the thought of Philippians 1:9–11. Again, Paul is praying. It is a kind of bidirectional prayer. Paul addresses the Christians ("you"), but he asks God to act ("May *the Lord* make *you* increase . . ."). And what he asks God to do is cause the believers to "increase and abound in love for one another and for all" (1 Thess. 3:12). Then come those all-important words that make plain the logical connection between the love of the believers for other people and their blamelessness at the coming of Christ: "so that." May the Lord make you abound in love for others, Paul prays, "*so that* he may establish your hearts blameless in holiness before our God and Father, at the coming of our Lord Jesus."

This "blamelessness in holiness" is the purpose of God's sanctifying work to make us genuinely love other people. That love then is used by God, in some way, to establish us blameless in holiness at the second coming. Again, we will need to answer the question of how this connection between transformed hearts of love and final blamelessness relates to justification by faith.

1 Thessalonians 5:23

The third text to consider is 1 Thessalonians 5:23. For the third time, it is a prayer, again bidirectional. "May the *God* of peace himself sanctify *you*." Paul is asking God to act transformingly in the believers. Love is not mentioned this time. Paul cuts straight from God's act to our blamelessness. "Now may the God of peace himself *sanctify* you completely, and may your whole spirit and soul and body be *kept* blameless at the coming of our Lord Jesus Christ." Two facts are significant for our purposes. One is that God's act is an act of *sanctification*, not an act of *justification*: "May the God of peace himself *sanctify* you completely." The other is that Paul refers to our being "*kept* [τηρηθείη] blameless at the coming of our Lord." It seems to me that these two verbs, *sanctify* and *be kept*, are parallel in Paul's mind (same tense, aorist; same mood, optative), and that the process of sanctifying (*making* blameless) and *being kept* blameless are going on simultaneously, namely, now. Does this imply that we are already blameless in some sense, and that God's making us blameless (in another sense) keeps us that way to the day of Christ?

Perplexed

Unless I am mistaken, many serious Christians are perplexed by the kind of biblical teaching we have seen now in these three texts (Phil. 1:9–11; 1 Thess. 3:11–13; 5:23). How can Paul teach that we do not attain perfection in this life and yet that we will be blameless in purity and holiness at the second coming of Christ *because* God is making us genuinely loving people? How can he say, "Not that I have already obtained [resurrection] or am already perfect, but I press on to make it my own" (Phil. 3:12) and yet say that the way we live here and now will lead to being found blameless on the day of Christ?

There is a solution to this perplexity. It involves the relationship between justification by faith and the confirming fruit of faith, which is love. I hope, as Peter says, that you will hitch up the hips of your mind, and follow me in a fairly demanding train of thought.

Reconciled for the Sake of Blamelessness

A text in Paul that helps me take the first step is Colossians 1:21–23:

> You, who once were alienated and hostile in mind, doing evil deeds, [Christ] has now reconciled in his body of flesh by his death, in order to present you *holy and blameless and above reproach* [ἁγίους καὶ ἀμώμους καὶ ἀνεγκλήτους] before him, if indeed you continue in the faith, stable and steadfast, not shifting from the hope of the gospel.

So here is the same expectation of blamelessness we have seen previously. It's true that the second coming, or the day of Christ, is not explicitly named. But the words "present you . . . before him," and the fact that Paul deals with the same issue of blamelessness, make it almost certain that he has the same idea in mind as he did in the three texts we have considered—namely, blamelessness at the day of the Lord's coming.

But here, there is a striking difference. The logical connecting words ("*in order to* present you holy and blameless . . ."—an infinitive of purpose, παραστῆσαι) do not connect our blamelessness with God's *sanctifying* work in making us more loving, but with Christ's *reconciling* work on the cross. The flow of thought goes like this: Christ reconciled us to God at the cross, and the effect that Christ intends to achieve by that reconciliation is to present us on the day of Christ holy, blameless, and above reproach. So our blamelessness on that day is owing to Christ's reconciling work on the cross. Or, we could say, it is owing to God's *justifying* work, because that is how sinners are reconciled to God—by being *counted* righteous, that is, justified.

In other words, the focus of Colossians 1:21–23 is not mainly that God is working *in* us to make us blameless at the day of Christ.[1] The point is mainly that he has worked *for* us in Christ's death to make us blameless at the day of Christ. Our blamelessness at Christ's coming, whatever it means, will be owing to the fact that *Christ reconciled us to God by his death.* That is done. Finished. Reconciliation is not a process, like sanctification. It happened at the cross. In his death, Jesus absorbed the wrath of God for us, and now there is no condemnation, but rather reconciliation, acceptance, forgiveness, and adoption—forever (cf. Rom. 5:8–10; 8:1–3). If anyone stands before Christ blameless at his coming, it will be owing to the death of Jesus reconciling us to God.

Reconciled by Faith That Perseveres

Then the argument continues. Notice that there is a condition attached to this promise in Colossians 1:23. You will stand blameless before Christ at his coming, "if indeed you continue in the faith, stable and steadfast, not shifting from the hope of the gospel."

This is what Paul and all the apostles taught: genuine reconciling faith—justifying, saving faith—is not a flash in the pan at the point of conversion. It is a persevering faith. "The one who endures to the end will be saved" (Matt. 10:22). "We have come to share in Christ, if indeed we hold our original confidence firm to the end" (Heb. 3:14). If what, at first, looks like saving faith is eventually

---

1   The reason I say "mainly" is that I do not exclude the thought that God's reconciling (and justifying) work on the cross includes God's intention that, because of reconciliation, he will fulfill the new-covenant promise to work in us the blamelessness of experiential blamelessness (Jer. 31:33; Ezek. 36:27; Luke 22:20).

forsaken, we may conclude that the faith was counterfeit and evidence of no new birth.

We see this in the way John spoke of those who seemed to be Christians but forsook the faith: "They went out from us, but they were not of us; for if they had been of us, they would have continued with us. But they went out, that it might become plain that they all are not of us" (1 John 2:19). To be "not of us" means not truly born again, because "everyone who believes that Jesus is the Christ has been born of God" (1 John 5:1).

So when Paul says in Colossians 1:22–23 that those who are reconciled to God will stand before Christ blameless, "*if* indeed [they] continue in the faith," he is not implying that someone might have true saving faith and then lose it. Rather, he is saying that persevering faith is indeed necessary for final salvation, and those who forsake the faith were never truly born again—never truly reconciled to God.

Saving Faith Bears the Faith-Confirming Fruit of Love

Now, what links the necessity of persevering faith to our being blameless at the day of Christ? The link is that saving faith is the sort of faith that produces love for friend and foe. And love, Paul has shown, is the way God brings us blameless to the day of Christ: "May the Lord make you increase and abound in love . . . *so that* he may establish your hearts blameless . . . at the coming of our Lord Jesus" (1 Thess. 3:12–13).

If saving faith is real, it changes us. That is the New Testament teaching throughout. And that change is fundamentally the transformation of a proud, selfish heart into a humble, loving heart. Paul describes faith as the root of love in the Christian: "In Christ Jesus neither circumcision nor uncircumcision counts for anything, but only *faith working through love*" (Gal. 5:6). The faith that unites us to Christ, who is our righteousness, shows its reality by "working through love." The fruit of loving people is not the tree of trusting Christ. But the fruit does show the tree to be alive and real.

Paul's great behavioral aim in believers is love that originates in a heart of faith. "The aim of our charge is love that issues from . . . a sincere faith" (1 Tim. 1:5). James made the same point by saying, "So also faith by itself, if it does not have works [of love], is dead" (James 2:17). And the apostle John made the same point by saying, "We know that we have passed out of death into life, because we love the brothers" (1 John 3:14).

Therefore, love in the life of a believer is a nonnegotiable evidence of saving faith. Therefore, when Paul prays (in Phil. 1:9–11 and 1 Thess. 3:11–13) for God to cause such love in the lives of believers, he is asking God to confirm the believers in their true faith. Without this faith-confirming love, any "faith" we may have is not saving faith. "If I have all faith, so as to remove mountains, but have not love, I am nothing" (1 Cor. 13:2).

Love confirms that our faith is true, saving faith. It truly unites us to Christ, who is our perfect righteousness. Peter makes the idea of "confirmation" explicit in 2 Peter 1:10: "Brothers, be all the more diligent to *confirm* your calling and election, for if you practice these qualities you will never fall." The "qualities" he refers to climax in verse 7 with love. Love is the fruit of faith (Gal. 5:6; 1 Tim. 1:5), and therefore the confirmation of faith—and, behind that, the confirmation of our calling and election.

But love is not perfection. The very epistle that requires love most explicitly as the proof of our new birth is also the epistle that insists most explicitly that believers are not without sin. In his first epistle, John says, "We know that we have passed out of death into life, because we love the brothers. Whoever does not love abides in death. . . . Anyone who does not love does not know God" (1 John 3:14; 4:8). But in the same epistle, John also says, "If we say we have no sin, we deceive ourselves, and the truth is not in us. If we confess our sins, he is faithful and just to forgive us our sins and to cleanse us from all unrighteousness" (1 John 1:8–9). Therefore, the nonnegotiable evidence of faith that Paul prays for is not a sinless love. It is an authentic love that reveals the genuineness of saving faith—imperfect love confirming faith in a perfect Savior, whose sinlessness is counted as ours.

Perfect Blamelessness Confirmed by Imperfect Love

Now we can circle back to the three troubling texts (Phil. 1:9–11; 1 Thess. 3:11–13; 5:23) and suggest a solution to the perplexity. My suggestion is that the blamelessness of Christians at the day of Christ, which Paul is praying for, refers to the sinless perfection that we have because of justification by faith. It is an imputed blamelessness of sinless perfection, which we have because of our union with Christ by faith. But this sinless blamelessness is real only if it is confirmed in the believer's life by a genuine transformation from proud selfishness to humble love. This means that Paul is praying for love in the hearts of believers because this confirms their saving faith. It confirms that they are united to Christ and therefore are counted blameless by the imputation of his perfections.

What about those crucial connecting words that we emphasized earlier? Love, *so that* you will be pure and blameless on the day of Christ (Phil. 1:9–10). Love, *so that* your hearts will be established blameless in holiness at the coming of the Lord (1 Thess. 3:12–13). May God sanctify you *so that* (implied) you will be kept blameless at the coming of Christ (1 Thess. 5:23).

My suggestion is this: those connectors show that real, practical, lived-out love is a nonnegotiable necessity if we are to be found blameless on the day of Christ. But this is *not* because the blamelessness of that day *consists in* that love. Our love is not our blamelessness. Our love confirms the blamelessness that we have because our faith unites us to Christ, who reconciles us to God and is blameless. True faith works by love (Gal. 5:6). Therefore, love is the necessary confirmation of faith. And faith unites us to Christ our perfect righteousness. Therefore, love confirms our blameless-ness. There is no blamelessness without it. Therefore, Paul is not praying for something optional or peripheral. He is praying for what is necessary if we are to stand before the Son of Man. There must be real, though imperfect, love in us, confirming real and perfect blamelessness in Christ.

Illustration of Confirmation from King Solomon

For readers who may have difficulty picturing the difference be-tween a confirmed salvation and a caused salvation, let me give a picture from the life of King Solomon. Recall the story of how two harlots brought a baby to Solomon, each claiming that the baby was hers (1 Kings 3:16–27). They asked the king to act as judge between them. He said that a sword should be brought and that the baby should be divided, with half given to the one and half to the other. The true mother cried out, "Oh, my lord, give her the living child, and by no means put him to death" (1 Kings 3:26). Solomon said, "Give the living child to [this] woman; . . . she is his mother" (1 Kings 3:27).

What was Solomon looking for at this "judgment day"? He was not looking for any deeds that would *create* or *cause* motherhood; he was looking for deeds that would *confirm* motherhood. As the women stood before him, the reality of motherhood was already established. This was not in doubt. The judgment did not create the motherhood. Nor could any act done by either woman create the motherhood.

On the day when Christians are judged, God is not looking for deeds that purchased our pardon in his judgment hall. He is looking for deeds that proved we were already enjoying our pardon. The purchase of our pardon was the blood of Jesus, sufficient once for all to cover all our sins. And the means by which we own it is faith—faith alone. The deeds that will be brought forward confirm the faith because "faith apart from works is dead" (James 2:26).

Why Not *Blameless* the Way Elders Are?

A crucial question someone should ask me is, Why do you make it so complicated? Don't you realize that the words for *blameless* are all used in the New Testament for imperfect people in this world, even before the second coming? Why not let *blamelessness* at the second coming simply refer to Christians the way the word refers elsewhere to (imperfect) Christians now? Why do you insist that *blameless* before Christ at his coming refers to the imputed blamelessness we have in union with Christ?

This is a very good question because the premise is true. *Blamelessness* and its related words *are* ascribed to imperfect Christians in this life. For example, holiness is something we must have now, or we will not see the Lord (Heb. 12:14). Christians are to be "blameless and innocent [ἄμεμπτοι καὶ ἀκέραιοι], children of God without blemish [ἄμωμα] in the midst of a crooked and twisted generation" (Phil. 2:15). People are to serve as deacons only "if they prove themselves blameless [ἀνέγκλητοι]" (1 Tim. 3:10). "An overseer, as God's steward, must be above reproach [ἀνέγκλητον]" (Titus 1:7).[2] Paul always strove to keep his conscience clear (or "blameless," ἀπρόσκοπον, Acts 24:16). Zechariah and Elizabeth walked blamelessly (ἄμεμπτοι) in the commandments (Luke 1:6). Paul said to the Thessalonians, "You are witnesses . . . how . . . blameless [ἀμέμπτως] was our conduct toward you believers" (1 Thess. 2:10).

So the question being asked of me is, Why don't you think *blamelessness* at the coming of Christ refers to this kind of *imperfect* blamelessness rather than a perfect blamelessness that we have by union with Christ? Evidently, the *blamelessness* referred to in the preceding paragraph does not imply perfection, but something like "free from glaring reproach in the world, with a more or less mature habit of keeping short accounts by

2 This word translated "above reproach" is the same word that is translated "blameless" in 1 Tim. 3:10. It is translated "guiltless" in 1 Cor. 1:8 and is used in a pair with ἄμωμος, "without blemish," in Col. 1:22.

confessing sin, and walking in significant victory over temptation." Why not assume *that* is what Paul is asking for when he prays that we would be "blameless" for the day of Christ (Phil. 1:10; 1 Thess. 3:13; 5:23)?

The answer has two parts. First, not all Christians are in fact "imperfectly blameless" in the sense that is required, say, of elders and deacons. Second, Paul promises that God will see to it that all, not just some, Christians will stand blameless before Christ at his coming.

1. When Christ Comes, Not All Christians Have the Elder Qualification of Blamelessness

It is unlikely that Paul would say deacons (1 Tim. 3:10) and elders (Titus 1:7) must be "blameless" in order to qualify as officers in the church, if *all* believers are blameless. Moreover, Paul pictures some Christian teachers arriving at the day of Christ's judgment and suffering loss because they built on the foundation of Christ with human contrivances and doctrines that did not truly build up a holy, healthy church. Paul says that these Christians will be saved "as through fire," but what they built will be burned up. They will suffer loss:

> If anyone builds on the foundation [of Christ] with gold, silver, precious stones, wood, hay, straw—each one's work will become manifest, for the Day [of Christ's coming] will disclose it, because it will be revealed by fire, and the fire will test what sort of work each one has done. If the work that anyone has built on the foundation survives, he will receive a reward. If anyone's work is burned up, he will suffer loss, though he himself will be saved, but only as through fire. (1 Cor. 3:12–15)

We will say more about this text in chapter 11, but the point now is only that I do not think Paul would describe these teachers as "blameless" in the day of Christ *in the sense of being elder qualified and walking in maturity*. But since they are "saved," we know they stand before Christ "blameless" in the sense of being counted righteous for Christ's sake. They experienced a true new birth. They had authentic faith. Love for people marked their lives of service. But their ministries were significantly flawed, and aspects of their imperfect hearts blinded them from seeing the follies of building with wood, hay, and straw.

2. Glorious Promises to Help Us Love the Lord's Appearing

Here's the other part of my answer to why I think "blamelessness" at the day of Christ refers to perfect blamelessness in Christ, confirmed by imperfect love in us. Paul promises that God will bring this blamelessness about for all Christians. His very faithfulness guarantees it. This is a great encouragement to love the Lord's appearing.

After praying that God would sanctify the believers and keep them free from blame in every respect and in every aspect of their being (spirit, soul, and body), Paul says, with tremendous encouragement for us, that God's faithfulness will absolutely see to it:

> Now may the God of peace himself sanctify you completely, and may your whole spirit and soul and body be kept blameless at the coming of our Lord Jesus Christ. *He who calls you is faithful; he will surely do it.* (1 Thess. 5:23–24)

This is a glorious promise designed to help us love the Lord's appearing. God will keep you blamelessly![3] This *will* happen. You will be kept.

---

3 Yes, the word in Greek is an adverb (*blamelessly*), not an adjective (*blameless*). Most translations render it as an adjective—such as the ESV, which I have quoted—because the adverbial meaning seems so strange. As an adverb, it would modify an adjective or a verb. The adjective it could modify is "whole" ("your whole spirit and soul and body"), and the verb it could modify is "be kept." Both seem awkward: "blamelessly whole," or "blamelessly kept." The latter suggests that God acts blamelessly. The former suggests that the wholeness of spirit, soul, and body is to be seen in reference to their blamelessness—a blameless kind of wholeness. I am not sure how the adverb (blamelessly) is functioning here. One of the particulars that makes this text seem a bit awkward is the reference to the "body" as considered "blameless." But the fact that ἀμέμπτως (blamelessly)

You will stand before Christ at his coming without blame or fault. Not because you are perfect in yourself or your ministries, but because you are kept in Christ Jesus with his perfections counting as yours. Your sanctification confirms your faith. And your faith is the instrument by which you are in Christ. That is secure. God will do it.

Confidence of the Called at Christ's Coming

Paul gives us the same unshakable promise with even more forcefulness in 1 Corinthians 1:7–9:

> You [are waiting] for the revealing of our Lord Jesus Christ, who will sustain you to the end, guiltless in the day of our Lord Jesus Christ. *God is faithful, by whom you were called into the fellowship of his Son, Jesus Christ our Lord.*

In other words, Paul's prayers for our love to abound *so that* we will be found blameless at the day of Christ (Phil. 1:10; 1 Thess. 3:13) will be answered! God will bring us to the day of Christ guiltless. That is a promise to all true Christians, not just some (like the mature or the elder qualified). This promise is even more forceful than the one in 1 Thessalonians 5:24 because Paul not only roots it in the faithfulness of God, but also connects it to our calling. We know how Paul's mind works: "Those whom [God] predestined he also called, and those whom he called he also justified, and those whom he justified he also glorified" (Rom. 8:30). In other words, by connecting this promise to our calling, Paul says it is absolutely certain. We can add to the chain of certainty: "Those whom he called he also sustained guiltless in the day of Christ."

---

is an adverb may help us not stumble over that awkwardness. Paul is not applying blameless as an adjective to "body," as most translations imply. I conclude, therefore, that in general, the point is that God will act so that in the fullest possible way (ὁλόκληρον), no blame will attach to us in any way.

WILL WE BE BLAMELESS?   85

He Will Finish What He Began

Again, Paul makes the same promise in Philippians 1:6: "I am sure of this, that he who began a good work in you will bring it to completion at the day of Jesus Christ." The work that God began in every true believer is the work of faith and love and holiness. He will continue that work in all his elect infallibly. He will finish the work of sanctification to the point where all believers will give evidence at the day of Christ that their faith is real and that in Christ Jesus they stand complete.

Majesty of the Keeper

I will add one more promise from Jude to these hope-strengthening promises of God:

> Now to him who is able to keep you from stumbling and *to present you blameless* [ἀμώμους] *before the presence of his glory with great joy*, to the only God, our Savior, through Jesus Christ our Lord, be glory, majesty, dominion, and authority, before all time and now and forever. Amen. (Jude 24–25)

Even though this is a doxology, rather than a direct promise, it has the force of a promise. Jude is celebrating the glory of God's keeping us and presenting us blameless, which is the way he identifies Christians at the beginning of his epistle: "Jude, a servant of Jesus Christ and brother of James, To those who are called, beloved in God the Father and *kept for Jesus Christ*" (Jude 1). That is, kept *by God*. This is our identity: called and kept. Whom God calls he keeps.

Jude's closing doxology soars with the "glory, majesty, dominion, and authority" of God by celebrating his explicit double act: *keeping* us from stumbling and *presenting* us blameless before the presence of his glory with great joy. He will do it. Paul roots the promise in God's faithfulness. Jude roots it in his glory and majesty and dominion and authority. God's glory secures the keeping of his called ones—for what? For blamelessness and joy at the coming of Christ.

Untroubled Conscience, Intensified Love—for Christ's Appearing

My answer to the question of why I think the blamelessness Paul prays for us to have at the coming of Christ refers to the perfection of Christ counted as ours, rather than the kind of imperfect blamelessness required, for example, of elders and deacons, is that (1) not all true Christians will have that kind of blamelessness when Christ comes, yet (2) all true believers are promised that God will present them blameless on that day.

Therefore, the passages that I called troubling and perplexing (Phil. 1:9–11; 1 Thess. 3:11–13; 5:23) should not trouble us or perplex us, but rather intensify our love for Christ's appearing. They show us how we should pray (with Paul) for God's love-increasing work in our hearts that will confirm the fact that Christ has called us into his kingdom, and they point us to the multiple promises that God will infallibly confirm his called ones as blameless on the day of Christ.

"He who calls you is faithful; he will surely do it" (1 Thess. 5:24). "He who began a good work in you will bring it to completion at the day of Jesus Christ" (Phil. 1:6). The glory, majesty, dominion, and authority of God guarantee that his called ones will be kept from stumbling into unbelief and will be presented blameless before the presence of Christ's glory with great joy (Jude 24).

My prayer is that we will believe these promises, long for the prospect of that joy, and love the Lord's appearing.

7

We Will Be Perfected Mind, Heart, and Body

IN CHAPTERS 3 AND 4, I argued that the heart of the matter at the second coming will be the glory of Christ magnified in the marveling of his people. "He [will come] on that day to be glorified in his saints, and to be marveled at among all who have believed" (2 Thess. 1:10). In other words, the glory of Christ is the supreme objective reality of that great event, but without the amazed, worshiping, loving, marveling response of God's people, the ultimate purpose of God in history and redemption would be incomplete.

The reason for this is that God's ultimate purpose is for the glory of Christ to be magnified most fully by his people being most fully satisfied in him. His purpose is not merely that the glorification of his Son occur *alongside* the happiness of his people, but that the happiness of his people be *in* the glory of Christ so that the glorification of Christ would shine most brightly in the happiness of his people in him. God has so designed redemption that the happiness of man and the glorification of Christ reach their fullness precisely because the happiness of man is *in* the glory of Christ. Christ will be most glorified in his people because his people will be most satisfied in him.

How Can Emotionally Crippled Saints Marvel as We Ought?

We have not yet addressed the fact, however, that the marveling, worshiping, loving response of Christ's people can never be what it ought to be if we must meet the Lord on that day with the meager, sin-infected, weak, fallen emotional capabilities of our present condition—even our present redeemed, justified, and partially sanctified condition. Given the dimness of our present spiritual vision and the crippled condition of our emotional capacities, and the remaining corruption in our fallen hearts, there is no way that Christ will receive from us at his coming a fitting welcome of marveling and worshiping and loving. That is the problem I will address in this chapter.

But before I address that problem, we should realize that the same problem exists with the incompleteness of chapters 5 and 6. The point of those chapters was that there will be grace for Christian believers at the second coming. "Set your hope fully on the *grace* that will be brought to you at the revelation of Jesus Christ" (1 Pet. 1:13). True Christians will be found blameless on that day. The sanctifying work of God in our lives to transform us from proud, selfish people to humble, loving (but imperfect) people will be found to confirm the genuineness of our faith in Christ and our union with him. That union will be the gracious ground of blamelessness at his coming.

But the problem, as with chapters 3 and 4, is that no follower of Christ will ever be satisfied with a blamelessness that is *counted* as ours because of Christ unless we are also *transformed* in heart and mind and body to be sinlessly blameless and free from every defect and hindrance to our worship. To be sure, imputed blamelessness because of justification by faith is glorious and precious. There is no hope without it. But God's aim is not to have an eternally sinning people who are glad they are forgiven and counted blameless. God's aim is that we move from forgiven sinners to forgiven and sinless. If this does not happen, we will never be able to enjoy and worship and glorify God as we ought.

For the very essence of sin is the preference of other things over God. If we are to enjoy and glorify God as we ought, and as we desire, we must not only be *counted* perfect in Christ, but *made* perfect—mind, heart, and body—by Christ. That change will happen at the coming of Christ, which is what this chapter is about.

Interwoven Mysteries of Soul and Body Will Be Redeemed

One of the mind-boggling reasons we love the coming of Christ is that all deceased Christians will be raised from the dead with their new resurrection bodies (1 Cor. 15:23, 43), and all Christians who are alive at his coming will be transformed so that they have bodies like Christ's glorious resurrection body (Phil. 3:21). Not only that, but along with this physical wonder of bodily resurrection and transformation, there will also be a moral and spiritual transformation for those who are alive at his coming (1 John 3:2) so that we will never sin again. For those believers (including Old Testament saints) who have died before Christ's coming, that spiritual transformation happens in the presence of Christ before the second coming (Heb. 12:23).

Both physical resurrection and spiritual transformation are essential for God's ultimate purposes to be fulfilled. His people must undergo both bodily and moral perfecting. If, at the second coming, the glory of Christ is to be suitably magnified in the marveling of his people (2 Thess. 1:10), then their marveling must be set free from its sinful corruptions and limitations. It must be transformed and perfected. Christ is worthy of nothing less. To be sure, the glory of God's grace shines beautifully in counting imperfect believers as righteous. But there is more grace in Christ than justifying grace. There is also the mighty power of sanctifying, purifying grace (1 Cor. 15:10; 2 Cor. 9:8; 2 Thess. 1:11–12). For Christ to be glorified in our marveling at his coming, that grace too must be triumphant in our complete transformation. Otherwise, our marveling will be marred by sin.

Not only that, but if Christ is to be suitably glorified in his people at the second coming, their bodies must be glorified in a way that reflects the glory of Christ. Bodies that bear the flaws of the futility and corruption of the fall (Rom. 8:20–21) could never magnify Christ as they ought. This is not only because the raising and perfecting of our bodies will glorify the "power that enables him even to subject all things to himself" (Phil. 3:21). It is also because our bodies are the God-designed instruments of our minds and hearts, which make audible our praises and make visible the obedience of our love. The God-designed interweaving of soul and body (whose mysteries modern science can scarcely fathom) calls for redeemed bodies as well as redeemed souls if the praise and obedience of our souls is to find the bodily expression of which Christ is worthy.

There have always been false teachers who denigrate bodily existence as intrinsically defective and encumbering to the human spirit. The biblical view of the body is very different. The body is not only part of God's "very good" creation before the fall (Gen. 1:31), but it is destined to be raised, perfected, and made an eternal part of our worship and obedience. As with Christ, God's people will have transformed physical bodies forever. If our idea of eternity is a future of bodiless spirits in heaven, we should test our view by the biblical teaching that heaven comes down to a new earth where embodied people worship an embodied Christ (Rev. 21:1–2, 10). Therefore, the physical and spiritual transformation that happens at the second coming is essential for the completion of God's ultimate purpose for creation.

Let's deal first with the bodily resurrection and then with the moral transformation of our hearts and minds, both of which reach their completion at the second coming of Christ.[1]

---

1   It will become plain by the end of the chapter what I mean by the *completion* of our moral transformation at the second coming, even though the spirits of those who die in the Lord are "made perfect" in heaven when they die (Heb. 12:23).

Christ Raised His Own Body, and He Will Raise Ours

Jesus confronted the Sadducees, who did not believe in resurrection. "Sadducees came to him, who say that there is no resurrection" (Mark 12:18). His response to them was clear and blunt: "Is this not the reason you are wrong, because you know neither the Scriptures nor the power of God?" (12:24). Jesus not only believed in the resurrection of the dead, but he knew that God the Father had given him authority to make it happen. "As the Father has life in himself, so he has granted the Son also to have life in himself. And he has given him authority to execute judgment, because he is the Son of Man" (John 5:26–27). Thus, Jesus can say, "I am the resurrection" (John 11:25). And he promises that he will raise his people from the dead on the last day:

> All that the Father gives me will come to me, and whoever comes to me I will never cast out. For I have come down from heaven, not to do my own will but the will of him who sent me. And this is the will of him who sent me, that I should lose nothing of all that he has given me, but *raise it up on the last day*. For this is the will of my Father, that everyone who looks on the Son and believes in him should have eternal life, and *I will raise him up on the last day*. (John 6:37–40; cf. v. 54)

Jesus said that he himself will be the one who raises his people from the dead, just as he said he would raise his own body from the grave. "No one takes [my life] from me, but I lay it down of my own accord. I have authority to lay it down, and I have authority to take it up again" (John 10:18). "Destroy this temple, and in three days I will raise it up" (John 2:19). This does not contradict Jesus's repeated statement that he would "be raised [by God]" from the dead (Matt. 16:21; 17:23; 20:19). The whole Trinity was engaged at the resurrection of Jesus, including the Holy Spirit: "If the Spirit of him who raised Jesus from the dead dwells in you, he who raised Christ Jesus from the dead will also give life to your mortal bodies through his Spirit who dwells in you" (Rom. 8:11). The natural implication here is that God will raise us "through the Spirit," as he raised Jesus "through the Spirit."

Raised by the Trinity to Have a Body Like the Son's

Therefore, what we find is that Christians are raised from the dead not only through the Spirit (Rom. 8:11), but by God (the Father) and by Christ (the Son):

> The body is not meant for sexual immorality, but for the Lord, and the Lord for the body. And *God raised the Lord and will also raise us up by his power.* (1 Cor. 6:13–14)

> Our citizenship is in heaven, and from it we await *a Savior, the Lord Jesus Christ, who will transform our lowly body to be like his glorious body,* by the power that enables him even to subject all things to himself. (Phil. 3:20–21)

In both of those passages, the resurrection of *Christ* and *our* resurrection are connected. They are linked in 1 Corinthians 6:14 because God performs both resurrections. They are linked in Philippians 3:20–21 to make clear that our resurrection bodies will be like Christ's resurrection body. The *cause* of both resurrections will be the same—God. And the *effect* of both resurrections will be the same—"a body like the body of his glory" (σύμμορφον τῷ σώματι τῆς δόξης αὐτοῦ). Our resurrection and Christ's resurrection, Paul says, are part of one great harvest. "Christ has been raised from the dead, *the firstfruits of those who have fallen asleep*" (1 Cor. 15:20). The firstfruits defines and secures the whole harvest.

Christ's resurrection body was a real physical body, and was enough like his preresurrection body that he could be recognized, he could be touched, and he could eat fish. "'See my hands and my feet, that it is I myself. Touch me, and see. For a spirit does not have flesh and bones as you see that I have.' . . . They gave him a piece of broiled fish, and he took it and ate before them" (Luke 24:39, 42–43). That is how physical our resurrection bodies will be.

We Will Be Raised at His Coming

When does this happen? It happens at the second coming of Christ. We can see this in three passages. In 1 Corinthians 15:22–23, Paul says, "As in Adam all die, so also in Christ shall all be made alive. But each in his own order: Christ the firstfruits, then *at his coming those who belong to Christ.*" "At his coming." That is when those who belong to him will be raised. This is not the general resurrection of all humans, but only of Christians.[2]

A second text that locates our resurrection at the second coming is Philippians 3:20–21: "Our citizenship is in heaven, and from it we await a Savior, the Lord Jesus Christ, who will transform our lowly body to be like his glorious body, by the power that enables him even to subject all things to himself." When the Savior comes, the bodies of Christians will be transformed. Paul does not distinguish here between the bodies of Christians who are alive at the Lord's coming and the bodies of the Christians who have died. Both will receive new bodies like Christ's glorious body.

The third text that locates our resurrection at the second coming shows Paul's special concern for Christians who had died:

---

2 Sometimes the resurrection is spoken of in Scripture without making temporal distinctions explicit between when believers and unbelievers will be raised or when all will be judged. For example, Jesus says in John 5:28–29, "Do not marvel at this, for an hour is coming when all who are in the tombs will hear his voice and come out, those who have done good to the resurrection of life, and those who have done evil to the resurrection of judgment." I think this text, like so many others, telescopes future events that are separated by time, the way mountain ranges look like one mountain from a distant perspective. This prophetic perspective is common in Scripture and helps us account for events far and near sometimes being treated as one vision. See chapter 8, note 1.

> This we declare to you by a word from the Lord, that we who are alive, who are left until *the coming of the Lord*,[3] will not precede those who have fallen asleep. For *the Lord himself will descend from heaven* with a cry of command, with the voice of an archangel, and with the sound of the trumpet of God. And the dead in Christ will rise first. Then we who are alive, who are left, will be caught up together with them in the clouds *to meet the Lord in the air*, and so we will always be with the Lord. (1 Thess. 4:15–17)

Paul's immediate pastoral aim here was to encourage those who had lost Christian loved ones in death. The prospect and joy of the second coming were such a prominent hope for the believers that the question arose, Will the deceased believers miss out on the glorious appearance of Christ in the day of his coming? It is significant that Paul did not choose to comfort them with the truth of Philippians 1:23, that "to depart and be with Christ . . . is far better." Nor did he comfort them with the truth of 2 Corinthians 5:8, that "we would rather be away from the body and at home with the Lord." That is not what the surviving loved ones were wondering about.

They wondered, What about the second coming? What about the Lord's glorious appearing—the astounding descent on the clouds, the cry of command, the voice of the archangel, the trumpet of God, the Lord himself, personal, present, visible, vindicating in an instant every embattled act of faith? What about that? Will our loved ones be full participants on that day? One of my motives in writing this book is that many Christians today would find Paul's pastoral teaching here to be foreign to their way of thinking. They would not share the Thessalonian concern about participation in the Lord's coming. They would

---

3 When Paul says, "*we* who are alive," he is not teaching that he knows the second coming will happen within his lifetime. We know this because in the next chapter he says, "[Christ] died for us so that whether *we* are *awake* [=alive] or *asleep* [=deceased] we might live with him" (1 Thess. 5:10). In both texts, he is picturing himself as possibly being in the number of the living. But he knows he may not be, as he says in 5:10.

be content to know that "away from the body [is to be] at home with the Lord" (2 Cor. 5:8).

But Paul is at pains to explain that the dead will be at no disadvantage in experiencing the full glory of that great day. He denies that those who are alive at the coming of Christ will have any advantage over the dead. To make that plain, he focuses on the resurrection of the bodies of those who had died. The second coming of Christ is when that will happen:

> We who are alive, who are left until *the coming of the Lord*, will not precede those who have fallen asleep. . . . The dead in Christ will rise first. Then we who are alive, who are left, will be caught up together with them in the clouds to meet the Lord in the air. (1 Thess. 4:15–17)

This spectacular welcome by millions of God's people, from all the centuries, will be shared by every believer fully. To that end, all the dead will be raised at his coming.

Completing the Progress of Earth and Perfections of Heaven

But our focus in this chapter is not on the *events* of the Lord's coming so much as the *effects* of the events in the transformation of believers. Our concern is that Christ be glorified by us at his coming in a way that is worthy of his greatness and beauty and worth. This cannot happen if our bodies and souls are not transformed. The dullness of our spiritual vision, the weakness of our affections, and the remaining corruption in our fallen hearts must be changed if Christ is to be glorified in our marveling as he ought to be (2 Thess. 1:10). Body and soul were ruined in the fall. They must be redeemed. The redemption begins in this life through the death and resurrection of Jesus. It begins in us with new birth, and forgiveness of sins and justification, and advancing sanctification. But it comes to completion at the coming of Christ.

Even the joys of deceased believers in the presence of Christ, though greater than anything known in this life (Phil. 1:23), are incomplete. Those joys are designed to overflow in physical expression through glorious bodies with white-hot praise and joyful obedience. Though the essence of our praise and obedience is *inward*, nevertheless its completion is *outward*. Though the *spiritual* excellencies of Christ are the supreme source of our joy, nevertheless the *physical* manifestations of those excellencies through the material creation, including his glorious body and the new world, are part of God's plan for the fullest glorification of his Son.

To be sure, the perfecting of our spirits in heaven after death, and before the second coming, is a great and glorious and joyful experience far beyond any joy in this present world. The book of Hebrews describes the saints in heaven as "the spirits of the righteous *made perfect*" (Heb. 12:23). Believers in Jesus will never sin again after death. We will be spiritually and morally perfected. Therefore, Paul was no fool to say, "My desire is to depart and be with Christ" (Phil. 1:23), nor to say, "We would rather be away from the body and at home with the Lord" (2 Cor. 5:8).

But this was not his greatest desire—to be a disembodied, sinless spirit in heaven with Christ. That never-sinning experience with Christ in heaven will be vastly better than any experience on earth. Gloriously better. But it is not the goal. It is not God's best. It is not the completion of redemption. When Paul groaned with the miseries of this fallen age, he did not dream mainly of *escape* from a suffering body. He dreamed mainly of a redeemed body: "Not only the creation, but we ourselves, who have the firstfruits of the Spirit, groan inwardly as we *wait eagerly for adoption as sons, the redemption of our bodies*" (Rom. 8:23). This eager waiting was for the second coming.

Predestined to Be Conformed to the Son of God—Bodily

From all eternity, God's plan has been that the glory of his grace be praised (Eph. 1:4–6) through the hearts and bodies of a redeemed people. He planned that this heartfelt, embodied praise would be worthy of his Son's greatness. He secured this worthy praise by predestining his people to be conformed to Christ—to reflect and share the glory of his Son. "Those whom [God] foreknew he also predestined *to be conformed to the image of his Son*, in order that he might be the firstborn among many brothers" (Rom. 8:29). This conformity to the Son makes it possible for Christians to reflect and praise the glory of Christ as we ought.

This word "conformed" (συμμόρφους) is used in only one other place in the New Testament. "We await a Savior, the Lord Jesus Christ, who will transform our lowly body to be *conformed* [σύμμορφον] to the body of his glory by the power that enables him even to subject all things to himself" (Phil. 3:20–21, my translation). This means, then, that the predestined conformity to the image of the Son in Romans 8:29 includes conformity to Christ's *body*. This was part of the great eternal plan, because without glorious bodies like Christ's body, we could not reflect or express the glory of Christ the way we should.

We Will Shine Like the Sun at the Coming of Christ

At the appearing of Christ, the body of the lowliest, homeliest, most disfigured, most disabled, most despised and rejected believer will be like the glorious body of Christ. What will that be like? Here is the picture of the risen Christ painted for us with the words of the apostle John:

> I saw . . . one like a son of man, clothed with a long robe and with a golden sash around his chest. The hairs of his head were white, like white wool, like snow. His eyes were like a flame of fire, his feet were like burnished bronze, refined in a furnace, and his voice was like the roar of many waters. In his right hand he held seven stars, from his mouth came a sharp two-edged sword, and his face was like the sun shining in full strength. (Rev. 1:12–16)

When Paul says we will be conformed to the image of the Son (Rom. 8:29), and we will be transformed to have a body like Christ's glorious body (Phil. 3:21), he means, at least, what Jesus meant when he said, "The righteous will shine like the sun in the kingdom of their Father" (Matt. 13:43). Picture the average Christians you know, and imagine them shining like the sun—so bright you cannot look at them without new resurrection eyes. C. S. Lewis asks us to imagine this, both for believers and unbelievers, and what effect it might have on our lives:

> It is a serious thing . . . to remember that the dullest and most unin-
> teresting person you can talk to may one day be a creature which, if
> you saw it now, you would be strongly tempted to worship, or else
> a horror and a corruption such as you now meet, if at all, only in a
> nightmare. All day long we are, in some degree, helping each other
> to one or the other of these destinations. It is in the light of these
> overwhelming possibilities, it is with the awe and the circumspection
> proper to them, that we should conduct all of our dealings with
> one another, all friendships, all loves, all play, all politics. There are
> no *ordinary* people. You have never talked to a mere mortal. Na-
> tions, cultures, arts, civilizations—these are mortal, and their life
> is to ours as the life of a gnat. But it is immortals whom we joke
> with, work with, marry, snub, and exploit—immortal horrors or
> everlasting splendors.[4]

Like Christ—Alive Forevermore

Not only will our new bodies be unimaginably glorious; they will also be immortal. For Christ is immortal. "I died, and behold I am alive forevermore" (Rev. 1:18). "We know that Christ, being raised from the dead, will never die again; death no longer has dominion over him" (Rom. 6:9). And we are destined to be like him. So Jesus says, "Everyone

---

4   C. S. Lewis, "The Weight of Glory," in *C. S. Lewis: Essay Collection and Other Short Pieces* (London: HarperCollins, 2000), 105.

who lives and believes in me shall never die" (John 11:26). "God gave us eternal life, and this life is in his Son" (1 John 5:11).

Bodies of the Living Must Be Radically Changed

This immortal, new resurrection body will be radically different from the body that is laid to rest in the ground, or the body that is alive when Jesus comes. Whether we are alive or deceased when Jesus comes, we will undergo a profound change. Paul is eager to assure those who will be alive at the Lord's coming that they will experience no less a transformation than those who have died. That is why he says, "Behold! I tell you a mystery. *We shall not all sleep [= die], but we shall all be changed*" (1 Cor. 15:51). In other words, even the living will be changed. It is not only the dead who need changing (given the obvious decomposition they undergo), but all believers need a radical change.

The bodies we have now are not glorified. But they will be. They must be, or else we will not be suited for the glory of the new heavens and the new earth. Paul lays out the radical newness of the "changed" body—the resurrection body, which he says even the living will receive:

So is it with the resurrection of the dead. What is sown is perishable; what is raised is imperishable. It is sown in dishonor; it is raised in glory. It is sown in weakness; it is raised in power. It is sown a natural body; it is raised a spiritual body. (1 Cor. 15:42–44)

Imperishable. Glorious. Powerful. Spiritual. The phrase "spiritual body" is not an oxymoron. Jesus had said clearly that he was no mere "spirit" when he was raised from the dead. "A spirit does not have flesh and bones as you see that I have" (Luke 24:39). *Spiritual* does not mean ethereal and disembodied. It means mysteriously fitted for a new level of existence where the Holy Spirit has transformed all physicality to be his perfect habitat, with powers we cannot now even imagine. After his resurrection, Jesus seemed to come and go in ways that defy explanation (Luke 24:31; John 20:26). So will our "spiritual body" be inexplicable to our present way of thinking.

Being Conformed to Christ Is Moral as Well as Physical

Even though Philippians 3:20–21 and 1 Corinthians 15:50–53 focus on the transformation of our *bodies* at the coming of Christ, this transformation will also include our *hearts* and *minds*. This was surely implicit in Romans 8:29: "Those whom [God] foreknew he also predestined to be conformed to the image of his Son, in order that he might be the firstborn among many brothers." God's aim is not physical look-alikes. His aim is shared views of reality and common assessments of truth and beauty and greatness and worth—especially a shared vision and love of God. In other words, God's aim to change us into sinless conformity to Christ is both physical and spiritual.

This spiritual transformation comes to climax at the second coming, when we are perfected completely. The change begins in this life. "We all, with unveiled face, beholding the glory of the Lord, are being transformed into the same image from one degree of glory to another" (2 Cor. 3:18). Then, if we die, our spirits are perfected in heaven in the presence of Christ (Heb. 12:23). Then at the coming of Christ, the transformation is completed. He perfects our bodies and restores our perfected spirit to its resurrected body, where it finds its completed purpose of visible, audible, touchable expression.

We see the completion of our transformed souls at the coming of Christ in 1 John 3:1–3 and Colossians 3:3–5.

When He Appears, We Will Be Like Him

First, consider 1 John 3:1–3:

See what kind of love the Father has given to us, that we should be called children of God; and so we are. The reason why the world does not know us is that it did not know him. Beloved, we are God's children now, and what we will be has not yet appeared; but we know that *when he appears we shall be like him, because we shall see him as he is*. And everyone who thus hopes in him purifies himself as he is pure.

Remarkably, just as *progressive* transformation happens in this life by "beholding the glory of the Lord" (especially in his gospel, 2 Cor. 3:18; 4:4–6), so also *instantaneous* transformation will happen when we behold God in the coming of his Son, Jesus Christ. It is true that "when he *appears*" refers most naturally to "God" in this paragraph, not first to Christ. But John has told us what Jesus said: "Whoever has seen me has seen the Father" (John 14:9). And we know that John referred to *Jesus's* second coming in 1 John 2:28 with the same words that he uses to refer to *God's* appearance in 1 John 3:2 ("when he appears," ἐὰν φανερωθῇ). Therefore, it is likely that in 1 John 3:2 John is referring to the second coming as a manifestation of the risen Christ, and God in him.

When we see him face-to-face, "we will be like him." The transformation will be complete when the vision of the glory of Christ is complete. The reason I think this transformation includes the moral and spiritual transformation of our hearts and minds is the way John connects verses 2 and 3. After referring to our hope of seeing Christ at his coming and being changed into his likeness, John says, "And everyone who thus hopes in him purifies himself as he is pure" (1 John 3:3). The logic is this: if we hope to be changed to be like him at his coming, then we will be about that change now. And the change he names is *purity*. I infer, therefore, that the change that will be completed at the second coming is moral as well as physical. We will be made free from all bodily and moral and spiritual defect.

You Will Appear with Him in Glory

Paul expresses the same logic in Colossians 3:3–5:

> You have died, and your life is hidden with Christ in God. When
> Christ who is your life appears, then you also will appear with him in
> glory. Put to death therefore what is earthly in you: sexual immorality,
> impurity, passion, evil desire, and covetousness, which is idolatry.

When Christ comes, believers will be shown to be who we really are.
The whole creation is waiting for this, Paul says in Romans 8:19:
"The creation waits with eager longing for the revealing of the sons
of God." In that day, we will be glorified as he is glorious. Then,
in the connection between verses 4 and 5 of Colossians 3, comes
the same logic as in 1 John 3:2–3: *Therefore*, because you will be
perfectly glorified at the coming of Christ, put to death impurity
(Col. 3:5). In other words, since you are destined to be perfected
in purity at the coming of Christ, seek to be done with all impurity
now. Which means that the appearing of Christ in glory will bring
about not only the physical but also the moral perfection of his
people. What has been progressive in this life will be completed at
the Lord's appearing.

Every Hindrance to Marveling Removed

In conclusion, I return to the concern raised at the beginning of this
chapter. If the heart of the matter at Christ's coming is the glory of
Christ magnified in the marveling of his people (2 Thess. 1:10), how
will this marveling be worthy of Christ's greatness if our capacities
for marveling are crippled by the dullness of our spiritual vision, the
weakness of our affections, and the remaining corruption in our fallen
hearts? And how will we marvel at the glory of justifying *and sanctifying*
grace if our sinning is only forgiven and not abolished?

The answer is that "we *shall all be changed*, in a moment, in the twinkling of an eye, at the last trumpet. For the trumpet will sound, and the dead will be raised imperishable, and *we shall be changed*" (1 Cor. 15:51–52). We will be conformed fully to Christ. That will include sinless hearts and flawless bodies. None of our powers to marvel will be hindered by dullness, weakness, sin, or physical impediments. No restraint on the joy of worship will exist. No restraint on the bodily expression of that worship will exist. The glory of Christ will be the supreme reality of that day, and he will be glorified in the unfettered joy of our marveling.

Therefore, we need not worry about the inadequacies that burden us now, as if they will frustrate our joy and praise on that day. They will not. This is a glorious promise. And another reason to love the appearing of the Lord.

8

Jesus Will Deliver Us from
the Wrath of Jesus

THE NEW TESTAMENT DOES NOT treat the coming day of judgment as if Christians do not need deliverance on that day. Instead, it promises terrifying wrath and precious protection. The second coming of Christ will bring both the judgment and the deliverance. As fearsome as that day will be, it will not consume those who are in Christ. Christians are those who have "turned to God from idols to serve the living and true God, and to wait for his Son from heaven, whom he raised from the dead, *Jesus who delivers us from the wrath to come*" (1 Thess. 1:9–10). We serve the living God. We see wrath coming. We wait eagerly for our deliverer, Jesus Christ. And, with trembling, we love his appearing.

Day of Judgment

Most often when the New Testament refers to a "day of judgment," it is referring to an unspecified period of time in which God will perform and complete his just reckoning with those who have suppressed the truth of his glory and turned away from his offers of mercy. The term *day* does not limit the time of judgment to a 24-hour day. We can see this most clearly in the remarkable phrase in the doxology of

2 Peter 3:18: "To him be the glory both now and to the *day of eternity.*" Peter may have been influenced to use this phrase ("day of eternity") because ten verses earlier he had said, "With the Lord one day is as a thousand years, and a thousand years as one day" (2 Pet. 3:8). So this "day" appears to be forever, or timeless.

Therefore, when I speak of our "deliverance from the wrath to come," or our salvation on the "day of judgment," I leave room in that time of wrath and that "day" of judgment for all the biblical acts of God that fall into the category of final judgments, regardless of how much time may separate them. Commonly the biblical authors speak of several separate future events as one cluster, with no time specified between the events—as if we saw several mountain ranges indistinctly as one mountain range.[1] I am not attempting to distinguish all those different acts of judgment, because the New Testament so often speaks generally about coming judgment rather than pausing to distinguish aspects of the judgment that might be separated by some time.

Consider, for example, the various events associated in the New Testament with the day of judgment:

---

1   For example, when Isaiah gave voice to the Messiah's words that Jesus quoted in Luke 4:18–19, he did not distinguish "the year of the Lord's favor" and "the day of vengeance of our God." He wrote, "The Spirit of the Lord GOD is upon me, because the Lord has anointed me to bring good news to the poor; he has sent me to bind up the brokenhearted, to proclaim liberty to the captives, and the opening of the prison to those who are bound; *to proclaim the year of the LORD's favor, and the day of vengeance of our God*" (Isa. 61:1–2). When Jesus quoted this as fulfilled in his ministry, he stopped just before the words "and the day of vengeance of our God." That "day" of vengeance" was part of the Messiah's coming, but not his first coming. What Isaiah saw as one cluster of events involved a separation of centuries. Similarly, when Isaiah predicted the coming of Christ, he saw the birth of the child and the rule of the king in one mountain glimpse: "For to us a child is born, to us a son is given; and the government shall be upon his shoulder, and his name shall be called Wonderful Counselor, Mighty God, Everlasting Father, Prince of Peace. Of the increase of his government and of peace there will be no end, on the throne of David and over his kingdom, to establish it and to uphold it with justice and with righteousness from this time forth and forevermore. The zeal of the LORD of hosts will do this" (Isa. 9:6–7). This "prophetic perspective," as Ladd called it, is helpful in understanding how the New Testament writers saw the relationship between near and distant events in the future. George Eldon Ladd, *A Theology of the New Testament* (Grand Rapids, MI: Eerdmans, 1974), 198. For more on the "prophetic perspective," see chapter 7, note 2.

If anyone will not receive you or listen to your words, shake off the dust from your feet when you leave that house or town. Truly, I say to you, it will be more bearable on the *day of judgment* for the land of Sodom and Gomorrah than for that town. (Matt. 10:14–15)

Woe to you, Chorazin! Woe to you, Bethsaida! For if the mighty works done in you had been done in Tyre and Sidon, they would have repented long ago in sackcloth and ashes. But I tell you, it will be more bearable on the *day of judgment* for Tyre and Sidon than for you. (Matt. 11:21–22)

As [Paul] reasoned about righteousness and self-control and *the coming judgment*, Felix was alarmed and said, "Go away for the present. When I get an opportunity I will summon you." (Acts 24:25)

Do you presume on the riches of his kindness and forbearance and patience, not knowing that God's kindness is meant to lead you to repentance? But because of your hard and impenitent heart you are storing up wrath for yourself on *the day of wrath when God's righteous judgment will be revealed.* (Rom. 2:4–5)

The Lord knows how to rescue the godly from trials, and to keep the unrighteous under punishment until the *day of judgment.* (2 Pet. 2:9)

But by the same word the heavens and earth that now exist are stored up for fire, being kept until the *day of judgment* and destruction of the ungodly. (2 Pet. 3:7)

By this is love perfected with us, so that we may have confidence for the *day of judgment,* because as he is so also are we in this world. (1 John 4:17)

[They will call] to the mountains and rocks, "Fall on us and hide us from the face of him who is seated on the throne, and from the wrath of the Lamb, for *the great day of their wrath has come*, and who can stand?" (Rev. 6:16–17)

He Will Deliver Us from the Wrath to Come

Against this backdrop of coming judgment, the second coming of Christ is pictured as a rescue of his people. He is coming to save us from God's wrath. "[We] wait for his Son from heaven, whom he raised from the dead, Jesus who *delivers us from the wrath to come*" (1 Thess. 1:10). The predictions of the day of judgment foresee a peril looming. Paul says it is divine wrath and that Christ is coming to rescue us from that peril. Peter says that God's people "are being guarded through faith *for a salvation* ready to be revealed in the last time" (1 Pet. 1:5). Hebrews 9:28 says, "Christ, having been offered once to bear the sins of many, will appear a second time, not to deal with sin but *to save those who are eagerly waiting for him*." Romans 5:9–10 portrays the death of Christ not only as the accomplishment of our past justification, but also as the guarantee of this future rescue from the wrath of God:

> Since, therefore, we have now been justified by his blood, *much more shall we be saved by him from the wrath of God.* For if while we were enemies we were reconciled to God by the death of his Son, much more, now that we are reconciled, *shall we be saved by his life.*

Paul makes plain in 1 Thessalonians 5 that this peril of God's wrath comes at "the day of the Lord"—the appearing of Christ:

> You yourselves are fully aware that *the day of the Lord* will come like a thief in the night. While people are saying, "There is peace and security," *then sudden destruction will come upon them* as labor pains come upon a pregnant woman, and they will not escape. But you

are not in darkness, brothers, for that day to surprise you like a thief. For you are all children of light. . . . For *God has not destined us for wrath*, but to obtain salvation through our Lord Jesus Christ, who died for us so that whether we are awake or asleep we might live with him. (5:2–5, 9–10)

Verse 9 clarifies that the "sudden destruction" of verse 3 is divine wrath. But it will not overtake the "children of the light" destructively (thief-like). "For God has not destined us for wrath." We are eagerly waiting "for his Son from heaven . . . who delivers us from the wrath to come" (1 Thess. 1:10).

Jesus Delivers from the Wrath of Jesus

But if we are not careful, we may conceive of our deliverance from wrath at the second coming in a way that badly distorts the reality. It would be a distortion if we thought of God pouring out wrath and his Son mercifully keeping us from the Father's wrath. It would be a serious mistake to pit the mercy of the Son against the wrath of the Father in this way—as if God were the just punisher and Christ the merciful rescuer.

It is quite otherwise. It is not as though divine judgment gets underway and Jesus shows up to intervene. Jesus himself sets the judgment in motion and carries it out. Jesus is the judge. Jesus brings the judgment. The surprising implication is that when Paul says, "Jesus . . . delivers us from the wrath to come" (1 Thess. 1:10), he means, "Jesus delivers us from the wrath of Jesus." This will become obvious as we look at several biblical passages.

"Their Wrath"

In the book of Revelation, John speaks not only of the wrath of God at the coming of Christ, but also the wrath of the Lamb:

The kings of the earth and the great ones and the generals and the rich and the powerful, and everyone, slave and free, hid themselves in the caves and among the rocks of the mountains, calling to the mountains and rocks, "Fall on us and hide us from the face of him who is seated on the throne, and from *the wrath of the Lamb*, for the great day of *their wrath* has come, and who can stand?" (6:15–17)

There is no sense of God being wrathful and the Lamb being weak. To be sure, this Lamb had been slain. But now he has "seven horns" (Rev. 5:6). He is not to be trifled with. His coming will be terrifying to all who have not embraced his first lamb-like work of sacrificial suffering (Rev. 5:9–10). The wrath is "*their* wrath" (Rev. 6:17).

The Father Has Given Judgment to the Son

It is "their wrath" and *their* judgment because the incarnate Son—the Son of Man—is acting in the authority of the Father:

The Father judges no one, but has given all judgment to the Son, that all may honor the Son, just as they honor the Father. . . . For as the Father has life in himself, so he has granted the Son also to have life in himself. And he has given him authority to execute judgment, because he is the Son of Man. (John 5:22–23, 26–27)

There is a special fitness in Jesus being the judge of the world. He is the one who came into the world, loved the world, and gave himself for the salvation of the world. There is a special fitness that the one who was judged by the world, and executed by the world, will judge the world.

The World Will Be Judged by a Man

Paul seems to have this same fitness in mind when he says that a man has been appointed as the judge of the world by being raised from the dead:

Now [God] commands all people everywhere to repent, because he
has fixed a day on which he will judge the world in righteousness by
a man whom he has appointed; and of this he has given assurance
to all by raising him from the dead. (Acts 17:30–31)

Peter, in preaching to the household of Cornelius, says the same:
"[Christ] commanded us to preach to the people and to testify that *he
is the one appointed by God to be judge of the living and the dead*" (Acts
10:42). Paul echoes the same conviction in 2 Timothy 4:1–2: "I charge
you in the presence of God and of Christ Jesus, *who is to judge the living
and the dead*, and by his appearing and his kingdom: preach the word."
James, too, saw the coming Christ as the coming judge: "Establish your
hearts, for the coming of the Lord is at hand. . . . Behold, the Judge is
standing at the door" (James 5:8–9).

Jesus, the Master, Will Cut Him in Pieces

Perhaps most striking of all the pictures of Christ's coming in wrath
as judge are the pictures that Jesus painted in his parables. For example, he portrays himself as a "master" who puts his servant over
his household. Then he pictures the master coming after being away
for some time:

If that wicked servant says to himself, "My master is delayed," and
begins to beat his fellow servants and eats and drinks with drunkards,
the master of that servant will come on a day when he does not expect
him and at an hour he does not know and *will cut him in pieces and
put him with the hypocrites.* In that place there will be weeping and
gnashing of teeth. (Matt. 24:48–51)

It is a parable. But a parabolic picture of Jesus cutting in pieces the
unfaithful servant is a dreadful picture of judgment. And Jesus himself
is the judge.

Jesus Orders the Slaughter

Similarly, in the parable of the ten minas, Jesus pictures himself as a nobleman returning from a far country after having received a kingdom (Luke 19:12–15). Before he left, a delegation of "his citizens" had said, "We do not want this man to reign over us" (Luke 19:14). When he returns and takes account from all his managers, he turns to this rebellious delegation and says, "But as for these enemies of mine, who did not want me to reign over them, bring them here and slaughter them before me" (Luke 19:27). This is the wrath of the Lamb.

Jesus Dispatches the Angels of Destruction

Here is one more parable that shows Jesus as the judge and as the Lamb of wrath. The parable of the weeds pictures a man sowing good seed in his field but an enemy at night sowing bad seed. Wheat and weeds come up together. The master of the harvest says, "Let both grow together until the harvest, and at harvest time I will tell the reapers, 'Gather the weeds first and bind them in bundles to be burned, but gather the wheat into my barn'" (Matt. 13:30).

Then Jesus gives the interpretation (Matt. 13:36–43). The good seed was sown by the Son of Man. The bad seed by the devil. Jesus describes the harvest like this:

> The Son of Man will send his angels, and they will gather out of his kingdom all causes of sin and all law-breakers, and throw them into the fiery furnace. In that place there will be weeping and gnashing of teeth. Then the righteous will shine like the sun in the kingdom of their Father. He who has ears, let him hear. (Matt. 13:41–43)

The Son of Man dispatches the angels in judgment and wrath. But he brings forth the righteous to shine like the sun.

Perplexity of a Coming in Mercy and a Coming in Wrath

None of these parable-pictures surprised the disciples. This is what the Messiah was expected to do to the enemies of Israel. John the Baptist expresses the common Jewish expectation that all the disciples shared at first:

> John answered them all, saying, "I baptize you with water, but he who is mightier than I is coming, the strap of whose sandals I am not worthy to untie. He will baptize you with the Holy Spirit and fire. His winnowing fork is in his hand, to clear his threshing floor and to gather the wheat into his barn, but the chaff he will burn with unquenchable fire." (Luke 3:16–17)

This picture of Messiah's salvation (into his barn) and judgment (into fire) was not different from what Jesus described. But what was surprising, and at first unintelligible for John and the disciples, was that this wrath and judgment by the Messiah would not happen here and now. That there would be a significant time gap between the first and second comings was not what they were expecting and was virtually unintelligible until it began to sink in that Jesus had given them significant pointers.

What pointers? Jesus pictures the wicked servant justifying his mistreatment of his fellow servants by saying, "My master is *delayed*" (Matt. 24:48). In the parable of the ten virgins, Jesus says, "The bridegroom was *delayed*" (Matt. 25:5). In the parable of the talents, Jesus says, "Now *after a long time* the master of those servants came and settled accounts with them" (Matt. 25:19). In the parable of the ten minas, Jesus says that the nobleman "went into a *far* country to receive for himself a kingdom" (Luke 19:12). He says this "because they supposed that the kingdom of God was to appear immediately" (Luke 19:11). And when he describes some events before his second coming, he says, "You will hear of wars and rumors of wars. See that you are not alarmed, for this must take place, *but the end is not yet*" (Matt. 24:6).

Sorting Out the Prophetic Perspective of Jesus's Coming

Jesus had given significant pointers that what John the Baptist and the disciples expected to happen in one single coming of the Messiah would in fact happen in two. And the second coming would be indefinitely "delayed" so that no one would know the day or hour except God the Father (Matt. 24:36). Jesus was sorting out for them, to some degree, the "prophetic perspective" I referred to earlier, which speaks of several separate future events as one cluster, with no time specified between the events— as if we saw several mountain ranges indistinctly as one mountain range.[2]

Jesus, the Judge and Deliverer from Judgment

What we have seen is that the "day of judgment," or "day of wrath," will be the day of *Jesus's* judgment and *Jesus's* wrath, acting by the appointment of God the Father. Therefore, when Paul says that Jesus "delivers us from the wrath to come" (1 Thess. 1:10), we are not to think of the Son rescuing us from the wrath of the Father, but of Jesus rescuing us from his own wrath, which is also the Father's. He and the Father are one (John 10:30). The coming wrath is "their wrath" (Rev. 6:17). And Jesus, acting on behalf of the Father, is the deliverer at his second coming.

Loving the Lord's Appearing—as Judge

One may ask, "Are we to love the appearing of the Lord Jesus as deliverer *and* as judge?" It is a precious thought that we will be delivered from wrath. We know we deserve wrath. We were "children of wrath, like the rest of mankind" (Eph. 2:3). It is amazing grace that when the wrath

2   See chapter 8, note 1.

of God comes, we will not be consumed. But when we think about God judging "those who do not know God and . . . those who do not obey the gospel of our Lord Jesus" (2 Thess. 1:8), what should we feel?

We should hear the summons of David in Psalm 31 and let our hearts be guided by his words:

> Love the LORD, all you his saints!
>> The LORD preserves the faithful
>> but abundantly repays the one who acts in pride. (31:23)

We do not delight in the pain of the punished for itself. We delight in the justice of God and the righteousness of Christ. We delight that this is not a universe where evil triumphs but where every wrong will be set right, either by condemnation on the cross of Christ or by just recompense in hell.

We take heart even now and rejoice that we do not bear the final burden of needing to avenge ourselves. We are glad that we may defer the impossible weight of settling all accounts. The coming just judgment of God brings to the soul even now a liberation from grudge-holding and from the poisonous burden of revenge. Here is the way Paul describes the joyful effect of God's future judgment:

> Beloved, never avenge yourselves, but leave it to the wrath of God, for it is written, "Vengeance is mine, I will repay, says the Lord." To the contrary, "if your enemy is hungry, feed him; if he is thirsty, give him something to drink; for by so doing you will heap burning coals on his head." Do not be overcome by evil, but overcome evil with good. (Rom. 12:19–21)

So, yes, we should love the Lord's appearing, even when we think of him as a coming judge. The absolute certainty that he knows everything that needs to be known and that he will show no partiality on behalf of the wicked sets us free to love our enemies and leave all retribution to the Lord.

What then will it look like for Jesus to come in wrath and in deliverance from wrath? That is the question we turn to in the next chapter.

9

In Flaming Fire, with Vengeance and Relief

HOW IS JESUS BOTH the judge and the deliverer? How is he both rescuer and punisher? The clearest picture of this double role of Jesus at his coming is found in 2 Thessalonians 1:5–10. In verse 4, Paul commends the church because of "your steadfastness and faith in all your persecutions and in the afflictions that you are enduring." Now in verse 5, he interprets these afflictions as God's way of making the believers "worthy of the kingdom of God." Then in verses 6–10, he justifies that divine strategy by pointing to God's reversal of their fortunes at the second coming:

> This is evidence of the righteous judgment of God, that you may be considered worthy of the kingdom of God, for which you are also suffering—since indeed God considers it just to repay with affliction those who afflict you, and to grant relief to you who are afflicted as well as to us, in the revelation of our Lord Jesus from heaven with his angels of power in flaming fire, inflicting vengeance on those who do not know God and on those who do not obey the gospel of our Lord Jesus. They will suffer the punishment of eternal destruction,

away from the presence of the Lord and from the glory of his might, when he comes on that day to be glorified in his saints, and to be marveled at among all who have believed, because our testimony to you was believed. (My translation)

Paul does not know when "the revelation of the Lord Jesus from heaven" (2 Thess. 1:7) will happen. He does not know if it will happen in his lifetime. He has already signaled in 1 Thessalonians 5:10 that he may or may not die: "[Christ] died for us so that *whether we are awake or asleep* we might live with him." Therefore, when he describes the coming of the Lord Jesus possibly in the lifetime of the Thessalonian believers, he happily includes himself with them. God considers it just to "grant relief to you who are afflicted *as well as to us.*"

Wrath and Rescue Together

Paul shows in 2 Thessalonians 1:6–10 that judgment and deliverance happen together at the second coming of Christ. They happen "in the revelation of our Lord Jesus from heaven with his angels of power in flaming fire" (2 Thess. 1:7–8). Or to say it another way, they happen "when he comes on that day to be glorified in his saints, and to be marveled at among all who have believed" (2 Thess. 1:10).

First, consider the judgment in these verses coming from both God and Jesus. Verse 6 says that "*God* considers it just to repay with affliction those who afflict you." This is *God's* decision. God's wrath. But the actual experience of that divine wrath happens "in the revelation *of our Lord Jesus* from heaven . . . in flaming fire, inflicting vengeance" (2 Thess. 1:7–8). Jesus is the one who "inflicts vengeance." God is pictured as "repaying with affliction" through Jesus's infliction of vengeance. Then in verse 9, this "repayment with affliction" and this "inflicting of vengeance" are described as "eternal destruction, away from the presence of the Lord and from the glory of his might." That is a description of "the wrath to come," from which we are awaiting deliverance by Jesus (2 Thess. 1:10). It is the wrath of Jesus and the wrath of God.

Then consider the deliverance in these verses. Simultaneous with the wrath is the rescue from it. This rescue is described first in verse 7. After saying that God considers it just to repay the persecutors with affliction, Paul says that God also considers it just "to grant relief to you who are afflicted as well as to us." This too, along with the wrath, happens in the revelation of the Lord Jesus from heaven with his mighty angels in flaming fire. This is crucial to see: *both* the divine repayment with affliction *and* the divine rescue with relief happen in the same event, namely, "in the revelation of our Lord Jesus from heaven . . . in flaming fire."

How the Rapture Fits In

This simultaneous vengeance and relief are crucial to see, in part, so that we do not make the mistake of thinking of a two-stage *second* coming: one stage (sometimes called the rapture) to take the church back to heaven during a time of tribulation, and another stage to bring judgment on the world.[1] This text pictures the rescue and the judgment as unmistakably simultaneous. There is indeed a rapture, but it refers to being caught up to meet the Lord in the air as he comes in judgment and rescue (1 Thess. 4:17). It is a great welcoming of the Lord Jesus to earth for the establishment of his kingdom. There is no return to heaven while the world goes on. The "relief" that 2 Thessalonians 1:7 promises "in the revelation of our Lord Jesus" includes that very rapture. Robert Gundry draws out the point I am making:

2 Thessalonians 1:3–10 puts the "relief" of Christians from their persecution at the very same coming of Christ at which the wicked

---

1 For more of my understanding of why a pretribulational rapture is mistaken, see John Piper, "Definitions and Observations of the Second Coming of Christ," Desiring God, August 30, 1987, https://www.desiringgod.org/.

are judged "with flaming fire." And in Revelation 19:1–21 the coming of Christ excites a fourfold "Hallelujah!" on the very occasion
of his "striking the nations with the sword of his mouth." What's
blessed for some is judgmental for others. No need here to separate
different comings of Jesus from each other.[2]

In One Coming, Repayment and Relief

So the point so far is that, at the second coming, Jesus proves to be both
a bringer of wrath and a rescuer from wrath. There is judicial repayment and merciful relief in one glorious coming—"in the revelation of
our Lord Jesus from heaven with his angels of power in flaming fire"
(2 Thess. 1:7–8). Jesus inflicts vengeance with the result that unbelievers
"suffer the punishment of eternal destruction" (2 Thess. 1:8–9). And
Jesus grants relief with the result that believers marvel at the glory of
Christ in his coming (2 Thess. 1:7, 10). There is much to be delivered
from and much to be delivered for.

Have the Generations Who Have Died
Missed Out on the Marveling?

The question inevitably rises: Since Paul and all his contemporaries at
Thessalonica have died, along with many generations of faithful believers
after them, is 2 Thessalonians 1:5–10 relevant for them? The answer is
yes. Of course, it will always apply most immediately and fully to every
living generation of believers, filling us with love and longing for the appearing of the Lord Jesus. But it is profoundly relevant for those who have
died in Christ. I say this because Paul deals with this question, and his
answer is unmistakable: yes, Jesus's wrath and Jesus's rescue at the second
coming are relevant for "those who have fallen asleep" (1 Thess. 4:15).

Paul explains why this is so in 1 Thessalonians 4:13–18. The question
there deals directly with the issue of believers who have died. "We do

---

2   Bob Gundry, *First the Antichrist: Why Christ Won't Come before the Antichrist Does* (Grand Rapids,
    MI: Baker, 1996), loc. 1719–24, Kindle.

not want you to be uninformed, brothers, about those who are asleep, that you may not grieve as others do who have no hope" (1 Thess. 4:13). We dealt briefly with this text in chapter 7. One amazing thing about this text is that Paul does not comfort the survivors of deceased saints at this point by saying that they are now with the Lord, as he might have done by using the words of Philippians 1:23 and 2 Corinthians 5:8.

Evidently, that was not the concern of the surviving Christians. Their concern was, "What about our loved ones' participation in the second coming? You have taught us that it will be the most glorious event imaginable, and that to experience it will be stupendous—the Lord descending, a cry of command, the voice of an archangel, the trumpet of God, mighty angels, flaming fire, relief from misery, vengeance on the adversaries, the majesty of the Lord, and hearts overflowing with marveling at his glory. You have described it as an event for the *living*, and now our loved ones are dead." That was the concern. Have they missed out?

Paul answered, "Not only have they not missed out, but they will, so to speak, have the front-row seats, showing up first with their resurrection bodies." That's a loose paraphrase of 1 Thessalonians 4:16–17: "The dead in Christ will rise first. Then we who are alive, who are left, will be caught up together with them in the clouds to meet the Lord in the air." This way of speaking is intended to say, "No! They will *not* miss out. They are at no disadvantage."

This has implications for every generation of believers who die in the Lord, not having yet experienced the Lord's coming. No Christian should approach his own death thinking, "I had so hoped to see the Lord's coming in my lifetime; now I will miss out on that great day. Now I will receive my resurrection body after those who are alive marvel at the Lord's glorious coming." That is not true. The experience of marveling at and glorifying Christ at his coming (2 Thess. 1:10) will be just as fully enjoyed by those who have died as by those who are alive at his coming. Therefore, our love for the Lord's appearing should carry us through death into Christ's presence just as much as it carries us from today forward with longing for his coming. Even in heaven, after death, before the second coming, we will pray, "Maranatha"—"Our Lord, come!" (1 Cor. 16:22). In that day, while in heaven with Christ, we will love the Lord's appearing more than we ever have.

The Day of the Lord Has Not Yet Come

What Paul does next, in the second chapter of 2 Thessalonians, is so unusual that we can easily miss the radically personal way his description of the last days is designed to intensify our love of the Lord's appearing. Paul is doing more than trying to persuade people that the day of the Lord has not yet come so that they will stop quitting their jobs and get back to work. To be sure, he is doing that. But as we will see, he is doing something more and deeper for the sake of our love for Jesus's appearing.

> Now concerning the coming of our Lord Jesus Christ and our being gathered together to him, we ask you, brothers, not to be quickly shaken in mind or alarmed, either by a spirit or a spoken word, or a letter seeming to be from us, to the effect that the day of the Lord has come. Let no one deceive you in any way. For that day will not come, unless the rebellion comes first, and the man of lawlessness is revealed. (2 Thess. 2:1–3)

The error Paul is trying to correct is that the day has come. But, he argues, it has not.

Get Back to Work

In 2 Thessalonians 3, we see the very practical effect of the error he is trying to correct: people are quitting their jobs and living in idleness. So, besides correcting the mistake about the Lord's coming, he tells the church how to respond to the idlers. "Keep away from any brother who is walking in idleness" (2 Thess. 3:6). Instead, "imitate us" (2 Thess. 3:7)—Paul, Silvanus, and Timothy (2 Thess. 1:1). "When we were with you," he says, "we were not idle" (2 Thess. 3:7). "We [did not] eat anyone's bread without paying for it" (2 Thess. 3:8). We "worked night and day" (2 Thess. 3:8) not to burden any of you. Though we could have demanded an apostolic right (the laborer deserves his wages), we chose to lead by example, not by demands (2 Thess. 3:9).

Then he gets specific and firm: "If anyone is not willing to work, let him not eat" (2 Thess. 3:10). "Do [your] work quietly and . . . earn [your] own living" (2 Thess. 3:12). No matter how long the affliction lasts, and the Lord's coming is delayed, "do not grow weary in doing good" (2 Thess. 3:13). Fill your lives—short or long—with gainful or volunteer employment. Don't be idle.

Bad eschatology had led to bad behavior. They were wrong about the second coming and had gone wrong about the duties of ordinary life. A kind of hysteria had gripped some in the church so that Paul says, "[Do not] be quickly shaken in mind" (2 Thess. 2:2). Don't lose your rational grip on reality.

Getting to the Root of Why People Are Deceived

What is striking about what Paul does next, however, is the amount of space and detail he devotes to the "rebellion" and "the man of lawlessness." If his purpose were simply to tell them that the day of the Lord had not come, he could have stopped effectively at 2 Thessalonians 2:3: "Let no one deceive you in any way. For that day will not come, unless the rebellion comes first, and the man of lawlessness is revealed." Point made. Case closed. So get back to work! This is especially true in view of verse 5: "Do you not remember that when I was still with you I told you these things?" In other words, he does not need to rehearse the issue of "the rebellion" and "the man of lawlessness." They know these things. Now that he has reminded them of the key fact in verse 3, why isn't that enough? What's the aim of verses 4–12?

My answer is that he wants to get to the heart of how Christians can avoid being deceived by the "mystery of lawlessness" (2 Thess. 2:7) and the "deception of unrighteousness" (2:10, my translation) and the "activity of Satan with all power and false signs and wonders" (2:9). He wants to make clear that the root issue is a failure to "welcome a love of the truth" (2 Thess. 2:10, my translation). Or to say it another way, the root issue is replacing love for the truth with "pleasure in unrighteousness" (2 Thess. 2:12).

In other words, these verses about "the rebellion" and "the man of lawlessness" focus on their insidious deceptiveness and how not to be taken in by it. It turns out that the decisive issue is not just what we *know*, but what we *love*. People are sucked into end-time deceit not just because they don't *have* truth, but because they don't *love* truth (2 Thess. 2:10). This, we will see, relates directly to our *love* for the Lord's appearing.

One Coming of Christ in 1 and 2 Thessalonians

Paul's argument begins in 2 Thessalonians 2 with a reference to "the coming [παρουσίας] of our Lord Jesus Christ" (2:1). Paul uses this Greek word for "coming" (παρουσίας) six times in the Thessalonian letters for the second coming of Christ (1 Thess. 2:19; 3:13; 4:15; 5:23; 2 Thess. 2:1, 8). It is the common New Testament word for his coming again. In Paul's letters, it is not a reference to Christ's coming in a spiritual way during the ordinary course of history. It is the coming that brings about the resurrection from the dead. "We who are alive, who are left until the *coming* [παρουσίαν] of the Lord, will not precede those who have fallen asleep. . . . We . . . will be caught up together with them in the clouds to meet the Lord in the air" (1 Thess. 4:15, 17).

This reference to being "caught up together with them" is what Paul has in mind in 2 Thessalonians 2:1 with the words "our being gathered together to him." Thus the "coming" of 2 Thessalonians 2:1 and the "coming" of 1 Thessalonians 4:13–18 are the same coming. Another link between the gathering together to him in 2 Thessalonians 2:1 and the coming of Christ in 1 Thessalonians 4:15–17 is that the word for "our being *gathered*" (ἐπισυναγωγῆς) is a form of the word used by Jesus concerning his second coming in Matthew 24:31, where he says that the Son of Man "will send out his angels with a loud trumpet call, and they will *gather* [ἐπισυνάξουσιν] his elect from the four winds." This "gathering" by a loud trumpet call is similar to the "sound of the trumpet of God" in 1 Thessalonians 4:16, which raises the dead and gathers the living and the dead to meet Christ.

Therefore, the "coming of our Lord Jesus" that Paul says happens in "the day of the Lord" (2 Thess. 2:1–2) is the one coming that Paul has in mind all the way through 1 and 2 Thessalonians. Therefore, when he says in 2 Thessalonians 2:8, "The lawless one will be revealed, whom the Lord Jesus will kill with the breath of his mouth and bring to nothing by the appearance of his coming [παρουσίας]," this is a reference to the same coming that raises the dead (1 Thess. 4:17) and in which Jesus "is revealed from heaven with his mighty angels in flaming fire" (2 Thess. 1:7–8).

What Is the Rebellion?

Before any of that can happen, Paul says that two things must occur: "the rebellion comes first, and the man of lawlessness is revealed" (2 Thess. 2:3). What is the "rebellion" (ἀποστασία)? The word refers to a turning away from something formerly believed. It is used one other time in the New Testament and refers to Jews being taught to "forsake Moses" (ἀποστασίαν διδάσκεις ἀπὸ Μωϋσέως, Acts 21:21). The rebellion Paul has in mind, therefore, refers to professing Christians turning away from Christ.

Paul is referring to something climactic. Something decisive and epoch-making. Something recognizable as utterly sweeping and catastrophic in the church and the world. I say this because apostasy was already a regular part of Christian experience. Jesus had said it would be. Apostasy was pictured by Jesus as an ordinary part of the gospel's spread:

> These are the ones sown on rocky ground: the ones who, when they hear the word, immediately receive it with joy. And they have no root in themselves, but endure for a while; then, when tribulation or persecution arises on account of the word, immediately they fall away. (Mark 4:16–17)

If such ordinary experience of apostasy were all Paul had in mind, his argument wouldn't work. For his argument to make sense, the "rebellion" must be referring to something climactic, recognizable as historically unusual.

Jesus's Prediction That Many Will Fall Away

Jesus's teaching gives us a glimpse into this rebellion. We have already seen close links between Paul's language about the second coming and Jesus's language (παρουσία, Matt. 24:3, 27, 37, 39; 2 Thess. 2:1; 1 Thess. 4:15; ἐπισυναγωγῆς, 2 Thess. 2:1; cf. Matt. 24:31). There are other links surrounding the idea of rebellion and lawlessness. Consider Matthew 24:9–13:

> Then [after the beginning of the global birth pangs that run through history, v. 8; cf. Rom. 8:22] they will deliver you up to tribulation and put you to death, and you will be hated by all nations for my name's sake. And then *many will fall away* and betray one another and hate one another. [Of course, this happens all through history, but the word *then* seems to show that Jesus is thinking of a climactic gathering storm.] And many false prophets will arise and lead many astray. And because *lawlessness* will be increased, the love of many will grow cold. But the one who endures to the end will be saved.

We need not deny that these kinds of things (tribulation, martyrdom, hatred toward believers, false prophets, lawlessness, lovelessness)
happen all through history, but it is difficult to escape the impression
that Jesus is pointing to a climactic experience of them.[3] The word
then in verses 9 and 10 points to a growing crescendo. Similarly, the
reference to lawlessness being "increased" (or "multiplied") seems
pointless as a mere reference to the ongoing historical ups and downs
of lawlessness. Therefore, the reference to "many" who "will fall away"
(Matt. 24:10, σκανδαλισθήσονται; cf. Matt. 13:21) looks like a
crescendo of apostasy and rebellion, like the one Paul refers to in
2 Thessalonians 2:3.

This is confirmed by the remarkable link between the references to
"lawlessness" in 2 Thessalonians 2:3, 7, 8, 9 and in Matthew 24:12. Jesus
says that "because lawlessness will be increased, the love of many will

3   I think it is a mistake to limit the focus of Matt. 24 to the historical events leading up to and
    including the destruction of Jerusalem in AD 70. See chapter 16. The problem is not with seeing
    references to these first-century events. The problem is *limiting* Jesus's thoughts to these events.
    I agree with Ladd when he writes:

    From the totality of [Jesus's] teaching one thing is clear: Jesus spoke both of the fall of
    Jerusalem and of his own eschatological parousia. Cranfield has suggested that in Jesus'
    own view the historical and the eschatological are mingled, and that the final eschatological
    event is seen through the "transparency" of the immediate historical. The present author
    has applied this thesis to the Old Testament prophets and found this foreshortened view
    of the future to be one of the essential elements in the prophetic perspective. In Amos, the
    Day of the Lord is both an historical (Amos 5:18–20) and an eschatological event (Amos
    7:4; 8:8–9; 9:5). Isaiah describes the historical day of visitation on Babylon as though it
    was the eschatological Day of the Lord (Isa. 13). Zephaniah describes the Day of the Lord
    (Zeph. 1:7, 14) as an historical disaster at the hands of an unnamed foe (Zeph. 1:10–12,
    16–17; 2:5–15); but he also describes it in terms of a worldwide catastrophe in which all
    creatures are swept off the face of the earth (Zeph. 1:2–3) so that nothing remains (Zeph.
    1:18). This way of viewing the future expresses the view that [in Cranfield's words] "in the
    crises of history the eschatological is foreshadowed. The divine judgments in history are,
    so to speak, rehearsals of the last judgment and the successive incarnations of antichrist
    are foreshadowings of the last supreme concentration of the rebelliousness of the devil
    before the End" [C. E. B. Cranfield, *The Gospel according to St Mark: An Introduction and
    Commentary* (Cambridge, UK: Cambridge University Press, 1959), 404]. George Eldon
    Ladd, *A Theology of the New Testament*, rev. ed., ed. D. A. Hagner (Grand Rapids, MI:
    Eerdmans, 1993), 199.

grow cold." This reference to "many" who are infected with lawlessness, no doubt, overlaps with the "many" who fall away (Matt. 24:10), and the "many" who are led astray (24:11; cf. 24:5). This is a picture of a significant rebellion. Paul picks up this idea of lawlessness and refers to a "mystery of lawlessness . . . already at work" (2 Thess. 2:7), preparing the ground for the final "man of lawlessness" (2:3; cf. "lawless one," 2:8, 9). Linking Jesus and Paul even closer, both attribute the "rebellion" or the "falling away" to deceptive "signs and wonders" (Matt. 24:24; 2 Thess. 2:9).

So I conclude that when Paul says "the rebellion comes first," before the coming of Christ, he is referring to a climactic, decisive, epoch-making, catastrophic rebellion against God, Christ, and his people, from inside and outside the visible church—all nations hating the church from outside (Matt. 24:9), love growing cold from inside (24:12). In Paul's mind, that is a discernible, limited season of dramatic apostasy—a period that has not yet happened.

Man of Lawlessness

The other event Paul says must happen before Christ's coming is this: the man of lawlessness must be revealed. "That day will not come, unless the rebellion comes first, *and the man of lawlessness is revealed*" (2 Thess. 2:3). Paul tells us at least seven things about the man of lawlessness.

1. He is a "man," a human (2 Thess. 2:3). Not an angel. Not a demon.

2. He is quintessentially lawless. He is called "the man of lawlessness" (2 Thess. 2:3). He considers himself above any law outside himself.

3. Since there is only one being who is above all law in that sense—namely, God—this is what the man of lawlessness claims: that he is God. "[He] opposes and exalts himself against every so-called god or object of worship, so that he takes his seat in the temple of God, *pro-*

claiming himself to be God" (2 Thess. 2:4). This is the final and climactic antichrist, that is, the substitute Christ who is against Christ. Paul never uses the term *antichrist*. Only John does (1 John 2:18, 22; 4:3; 2 John 7). But he has the same conception of the man of lawlessness as John does of the antichrist.

Just as John says that in the last hour "antichrist is coming" (1 John 2:18), he is aware that in his own day many have already come who have "the spirit of the antichrist" (4:3). One could say, in this sense, that "many antichrists have come" (1 John 2:18). Similarly, Paul says that even though the "man of lawlessness" is coming, "the mystery of lawlessness is already at work" (2 Thess. 2:7). Paul intends us to see that even though the traits of the end time will be at work earlier in history, the crisis at the end, with the rebellion and the man of lawlessness, will be identifiable. There will be a point, as Jesus says, when we should "straighten up and raise your heads, because your redemption is drawing near" (Luke 21:28).

4. The man of lawlessness is born for destruction. Paul calls him "the son of destruction" (2 Thess. 2:3). His spiritual DNA, so to speak, destines him for ruin. He has no future but is quintessentially lawless and doomed. So there is no thought of the serious endangerment of Christ or his kingdom. The man of lawlessness has lost the battle before he starts.

5. As a man, he is coming, nevertheless, by the power of Satan. "The coming of the lawless one is by the activity of Satan" (2 Thess. 2:9). Orchestrating this conflict between the man of lawlessness and Christ is the archenemy of God.

6. Therefore, as a man, he will, nevertheless, have supernatural power. Paul calls it "all power" (2 Thess. 2:9). With it he will work signs and wonders. When the ESV calls them "false signs and wonders" we should not read that to mean they don't really happen. It means they really happen in the service of falsehood. They are real miracles that aim to deceive (cf. Deut. 13:1–3; Matt. 24:24).

7. Therefore, the man of lawlessness will be unparalleled in his ability to deceive. "The coming of the lawless one is . . . with all wicked deception for those who are perishing" (2 Thess. 2:9–10). Or more literally, "in all deception of wickedness," because we are going to see below that the way he deceives is by making wickedness seem pleasurable (2 Thess. 2:11).

Things Will Be Clearer as They Approach

We do not need to know precisely what Paul means when he says in 2 Thessalonians 2:4 that the man of lawlessness "takes his seat in the temple of God." We may be sure that it is not a limited reference to the desecration of the Jewish temple in AD 70. We can be sure of this because of what Paul says in verse 8: "And then [when he is no longer restrained] the lawless one will be revealed, whom the Lord Jesus will kill with the breath of his mouth and bring to nothing *by the appearance of his coming*." This coming (παρουσίας) is the coming of verse 1, when Christ gathers his elect from the four winds (see Matt. 24:31). It is the coming of 2 Thessalonians 1:7–8, when he comes "with his mighty angels in flaming fire." It is the coming of 1 Thessalonians 2:19 and 3:13 and 4:15, when the saints will be raised, and we will rise to meet him in the air. This rebellion and this man of lawlessness are at the end of the age. They are ended and undone (ἀνελεῖ . . . καὶ καταργήσει) by the glorious appearing of the coming of the Lord (τῇ ἐπιφανείᾳ τῆς παρουσίας αὐτοῦ).

Where the man of lawlessness takes his seat—whether in Jerusalem, or the Vatican, or Geneva, or Salt Lake City, or Colorado Springs—is not of the essence. It will be in the place of the global focus of false worship. And it will be with the claim to be above all law—to be God. For those who have eyes to see, the signs will be clearer in that day than they are now. "You are not in darkness, brothers, for that day to surprise you like a thief. For you are all children of light, children of the day" (1 Thess. 5:4–5).

Warnings and Encouragements

What we have seen is that in both chapter 1 and chapter 2 of 2 Thessalonians, Paul gives warning and encouragement. The warning of chapter 1 is that the Lord Jesus is coming "with his mighty angels in flaming fire, inflicting vengeance on those who do not know God and on those who do not obey the gospel of our Lord Jesus" (2 Thess. 1:7–8). Be warned. You do not want to be on the receiving end of that fire. The encouragement of chapter 1 is that by that fiery coming, the Lord will "grant relief" to those who suffer for their faithfulness to Christ (2 Thess. 1:7), and will display his glory for the marveling of all who have believed (2 Thess. 1:10).

The warning of chapter 2 is that the seeds of end-time apostasy are already being sown by the "mystery of lawlessness" (2 Thess. 2:7). This apostasy will come by the activity of Satan with tremendous power ("all power" 2 Thess. 2:9), and God himself will hand over to a "strong delusion" those who do not "love the truth" (2:10–11). By every means possible, prepare yourself not to be part of this "rebellion." The encouragement of chapter 2 is that the Satan-empowered embodiment of this rebellion, the man of lawlessness, will be destroyed by the appearance of the coming of the Lord Jesus (2 Thess. 2:8). There need be no fear that he stands a chance to upend the saving plans of the Son of God.

Hearts That Do Not Welcome a Love for the Truth

What should the effect of these warnings and encouragements be as we ponder "the appearance of his coming [τῇ ἐπιφανείᾳ τῆς παρουσίας αὐτοῦ]"? One answer is this: greater love for the Lord's appearing. Paul doesn't say so in just those words. But look carefully with me at the concluding verses of Paul's paragraph about the rebellion and the lawless one and the mystery of lawlessness:

The coming of the lawless one is . . . with all deception of unrighteousness for those who are perishing, because they did not welcome a love of the truth in order to be saved. Therefore God sends them a strong delusion, so that they may believe what is false, in order that all may be condemned who did not believe the truth but had pleasure in unrighteousness. (2 Thess. 2:9–12, my translation)

This is an extremely important passage for getting to the root of why people will be swept away in the apostasy. Why will they be deceived? The answer of verse 10 is, "because they did not welcome a love of the truth [τὴν ἀγάπην τῆς ἀληθείας οὐκ ἐδέξαντο]." This is an unusual manner of expression: "welcome a love." The idea is that they did not just fail to love the truth but, more deeply, they did not *want* to love it. Truth was not welcome in their hearts. In other words, these hearts already shared in the mystery of lawlessness, because that is what lawlessness is: I am my own truth and do not even like the idea of receiving truth from outside.

Then verses 11–12 take us even deeper into the meaning of what they actually did love instead of the truth. "God sends them a strong delusion, so that they may believe what is false, in order that all may be condemned who *did not believe the truth but had pleasure in unrighteousness.*" Granted, God gives up these truth rejecters to strong delusion, but why, in the end, did they reject the truth? What did they love instead? Answer: they "had pleasure in unrighteousness" (2 Thess. 2:12). It's a pleasure issue. Which is the same as saying that it is in some measure a love issue. That is, what do you find most pleasure in: truth or unrighteousness? Which do you love? Verse 9 says that the deception of the lawless one is a "deception of unrighteousness." In other words, he deceives by causing people to find more "pleasure in unrighteousness" than in truth.

It is difficult not to see a connection between Paul's thinking here and Jesus's end-time prediction, "Because lawlessness will be increased, the love of many will grow cold" (Matt. 24:12). Lawless hearts will not welcome love for the truth. Love for truth (and for people) disappears from hearts that find pleasure in being their own god—hearts that become their own law, and thus love unrighteousness.

Crucial Strategy against the Mystery of Lawlessness

My conclusion is that love for the appearing of the Lord Jesus (2 Tim. 4:8) is an essential part of loving the truth that Paul has in mind in 2 Thessalonians 2:10, 12. Therefore, stirring up an unwavering love for the Lord's appearing is a crucial strategy for protecting ourselves and our churches from the mystery of lawlessness, which is "already at work" (2 Thess. 2:7). The effect of the *warnings* of 2 Thessalonians 1 and 2 should be that we take every step possible to keep our love for the Lord's appearing from growing cold. And the effect of the *encouragements* of 2 Thessalonians 1 and 2 should be that we see the fierce and flaming arrival of Jesus as the triumph over all our adversaries. Let us marvel even now at the coming of this triumphant Christ, and let us find more pleasure in him than in anything this world can offer. Let us love his appearing.

10

Repaying Each for What He Has Done

IN THIS CHAPTER AND THE NEXT, I am trying to answer the question, How does a *judgment according to works* at the Lord's coming help us love his appearing? To answer this question, we need to clarify that there is such a judgment when Jesus comes and how our works function on that day. In chapter 10 we will ask, Do works function to confirm our faith? Do they win rewards? And then, in chapter 11, we need to answer the question, In view of such a judgment, how does this reality help us to love the Lord's appearing?

Should We Rejoice or Fear?

When Christians learn from Jesus that at his coming "he will repay each person according to what he has done" (Matt. 16:27), are we inclined to love his appearing because of this news? Or does it make us shrink back from his coming with fear? Or what about his words in Revelation 22:12, "Behold, I am coming soon, bringing my recompense with me, to repay each one for what he has done"? Is this a cause for rejoicing in the Lord's coming? Presumably, Paul is referring to the same event when he says, "We must all appear before the judgment seat of Christ, so that each one may receive what is due for what he has done in the body, whether good or evil" (2 Cor. 5:10).

Christians Suffering Loss at the Appearing of Christ

I suppose that if we could assume every Christian would hear the same unqualified commendation on that day—"Well done, good and faithful servant" (Matt. 25:21, 23)—then the prospect of a judgment according to our deeds would be joyful rather than worrisome. But what about Paul's words in 2 Corinthians 5:10, that all of us will receive our rewards, or not, according to what we have "done in the body, whether good *or evil*"? "Or evil." What if we are truly Christian but have fallen far short of walking in a fruitful way?

That is the picture of Christ's servants in 1 Corinthians 3:11–15:

> No one can lay a foundation other than that which is laid, which is Jesus Christ. Now if anyone builds on the foundation with gold, silver, precious stones, wood, hay, straw—each one's work will become manifest, for the Day [of Christ's coming judgment and rescue] will disclose it, because it will be revealed by fire, and the fire will test what sort of work each one has done. If the work that anyone has built on the foundation survives, he will receive a reward. If anyone's work is burned up, he will suffer loss, though he himself will be saved, but only as through fire.

In this context, Paul is dealing most directly with those who build on Christ as the true foundation of the church (1 Cor. 3:10–11). So the building materials refer, most immediately, to the teachings one is building with. Therefore, "wood, hay, [and] straw" most likely refer to defective teachings. He's probably not referring to blatant, gospel-denying heresy, which elsewhere calls down Paul's anathema (Gal. 1:8–9). Rather, he is probably referring to teaching that is in some lesser way erroneous, or distorted, or unwise, or irrelevant, or misapplied, or poorly explained, or superficial, or twisted to fit unbiblical church traditions or worldliness.

But it is doubtful that one could build consistently with such defective teaching and not have significant issues of worldliness in the mind and heart as well. "Out of the abundance of the heart the mouth speaks" (Matt. 12:34). Therefore, the principle of judgment here applies to defective attitudes and actions in general, not just to teaching and teachers. This is confirmed when we realize that the church is built up in some measure by all believers, and that this upbuilding is done *in love* (Eph. 4:16), not just *in truth* (4:15). Defective love is just as flammable as defective teaching.

Will Each Hear, "Well Done"?

Will the person of 1 Corinthians 3:15 hear Jesus say, "Well done, good and faithful servant"? According to Paul, the truth and worth of a person's teaching or deeds "will be revealed by fire, and the fire will test what sort of work each one has done. . . . If anyone's work is burned up, he will suffer loss, though he himself will be saved, but only as through fire" (1 Cor. 3:13, 15).

I take these words "suffer loss" to be Paul's best explanatory comment about his meaning in 2 Corinthians 5:10 when he says, "We must all . . . receive what is due for what he has done in the body, whether good *or evil*." I take Paul to mean that the judgment that befalls a Christian for the "evil" in his life is this "suffering loss" in 1 Corinthians 3:15. "If anyone's work is burned up, he will suffer loss."

The "loss" that such a Christian suffers is the loss of a possible reward that he might have had, but will not receive. That seems clear from verse 14: "If the work that anyone has built on the foundation survives, he will receive a reward." So the alternatives are these: "receive a reward" or "suffer loss." It makes sense to conclude that "suffer loss" refers to the loss of rewards that might otherwise have come. So, based on the ministry described in 1 Corinthians 3:10–15, it would be right to say that some Christians will not hear the words, "Well done, good and faithful servant" (Matt. 25:21, 23)—at least, not spoken with the same commendation as to other, more faithful disciples. Those words are spoken to servants who built ten talents out of five, and four talents out of two (Matt. 25:20–23).

Doesn't Failure in Holiness Mean Faith Is Unreal?

However, one may ask, Would not a failure to live a life of love show that one is not born again, and so not united to Christ, and so not a Christian at all? This question is especially relevant in view of what we saw in chapters 6 and 7. The aim of those chapters was to discover what the New Testament means when it says that Christians will "be pure and blameless for the day of Christ" (Phil. 1:10), and that God will "establish your hearts blameless in holiness . . . at the coming of our Lord Jesus" (1 Thess. 3:13), and that God will "sustain you to the end, guiltless in the day of our Lord Jesus Christ" (1 Cor. 1:8), and that God will "present you blameless before the presence of his glory with great joy" (Jude 24).

One of the conclusions of chapters 6 and 7 was that

love is a nonnegotiable necessity if we are to be found blameless on the day of Christ. But this is *not* because the blamelessness of that day *consists in* that love. Our love is not our blamelessness. Our love *confirms* the blamelessness that we have because our faith unites us to Christ, who reconciles us to God and is blameless. True faith works by love (Gal. 5:6). Therefore, love is the necessary confirmation of faith. And faith unites us to Christ our perfect righteousness. Therefore, love confirms our blamelessness. There is no blamelessness without it. . . . There must be real, though imperfect, love in us, confirming real and perfect blamelessness in Christ.

We also saw previously that

this sinless blamelessness is real only if it is confirmed in the believer's life by a genuine transformation from proud selfishness to humble love. . . . Paul is praying for love in the hearts of believers because this confirms their saving faith. It confirms that they are united to Christ and therefore are counted blameless by the imputation of his perfections.

So the answer to the question is yes, a failure to live a life of love would show that one is not born again, and so not united to Christ, and so not truly a Christian.

Imperfection of Walking in the Light

Perhaps the clearest texts on this question are 1 John 3:14 and 4:8: "We know that we have passed out of death into life, because we love the brothers. Whoever does not love abides in death. . . . Anyone who does not love does not know God, because God is love." But as we pointed out in chapter 6, the very book (1 John) that most forcefully connects loving others with being true Christians is also the book that says, more clearly than any other, that this life of love, which confirms our new birth, remains defective in this earthly lifetime:

> If we walk in the light, as he is in the light, we have fellowship with one another, and the blood of Jesus his Son cleanses us from all sin. If we say we have no sin, we deceive ourselves, and the truth is not in us. If we confess our sins, he is faithful and just to forgive us our sins and to cleanse us from all unrighteousness. If we say we have not sinned, we make him a liar, and his word is not in us. (1:7–10)

What is startling and relevant for us about this text is that John says "walking in the light" is necessary if the blood of Jesus is going to cleanse us from all sin: "*If* we walk in the light, as he is in the light . . . the blood of Jesus his Son cleanses us from all sin" (1 John 1:7).

In other words, we are not forgiven and saved if we do not walk in the light. He is not saying that *walking* brings us into salvation but rather that it confirms that we are saved. It is a *necessary* confirmation. Yet this walking in the light is not sinlessness.

If we say we have no sin (as we walk in the light!), we deceive ourselves. In John's thinking, walking in the light includes walking in love. "Whoever loves his brother abides in the light" (1 John 2:10). Therefore, John (with all the rest of the New Testament) teaches that a life of love (imperfect as it always will be in this life) is necessary as a confirmation of our being born again and having our sins cleansed through faith (1 John 5:1).

This means that the person in 1 Corinthians 3:15 who "will be saved, but only as through fire" was born again and lived a life of love sufficiently to confirm his union with Christ. There will always be something to which God can say, "Well done," whether those very words will be used or not. Our defective teaching, or defective love, will be not of such a nature that it nullifies our faith in Christ or our love for people. At the day of judgment, Christ will be the infallible judge of our motives. So we take care to heed his counsel: "Do not pronounce judgment before the time, before the Lord comes, who will bring to light the things now hidden in darkness and will disclose the purposes of the heart" (1 Cor. 4:5).

Judgment of Salvation "according to Works"

What we have seen, then, is that the totality of our lives (deeds and heart motives) has a double function in the judgment at the Lord's coming. On the one hand, our lives of love *confirm* the genuineness of our saving faith. This is why Paul says that God will "render to each one *according to his works*: to those who by patience in well-doing seek for glory and honor and immortality, *he will give eternal life*" (Rom. 2:6–7). The gift of eternal life *accords with* our works of love.

This in no way contradicts the fact that eternal life is a *free gift of grace*. Eternal life is not earned by good works. "The *free gift of God* is eternal life in Christ Jesus our Lord" (Rom. 6:23; cf. 5:21). When Paul says that eternal life comes to us "according to" our works, this is not the same as saying that eternal life is *deserved* or *earned* by our works. Rather, Paul is saying that the works *confirm* our faith (Gal. 5:6). They confirm that we are new creatures in Christ (Eph. 2:8–10). Paul is clear and explicit about this:

> [God] saved us, *not because of works* done by us in righteousness [οὐκ ἐξ ἔργων τῶν ἐν δικαιοσύνῃ], but according to his own mercy, by the washing of regeneration and renewal of the Holy Spirit, whom he poured out on us richly through Jesus Christ our Savior, so that being justified by his grace we might become *heirs according to the hope of eternal life.* (Titus 3:5–7)

Not only is our salvation "not because of works," but it is the other way around. We are saved *that we may do good works*: "[Christ] gave himself for us to redeem us from all lawlessness and to purify for himself a people for his own possession *who are zealous for good works*" (Titus 2:14). Or as Paul says in Ephesians 2:8–10:

> By grace you have been saved through faith. And this is not your own doing; it is the gift of God, *not a result of works,* so that no one may boast. For we are his workmanship, created in Christ Jesus *for good works.*

In other words, we are saved not *by* works but *for* works. Works are not the cause of our becoming new creatures. They are the result. And as a result, they confirm our newness the way good fruit confirms the good tree (cf. Matt. 7:17–19).

Now back to the double function of our works when Christ comes in judgment. I have just described one of those two functions, namely, our lives of love confirm the genuineness of our saving faith (1 John 3:14). Our works of love in this life confirm our acceptance (2 Pet. 1:10); they do not merit it. They confirm living faith, because "faith apart from works is dead" (James 2:26).

Christ Is Coming to Distribute Rewards

The other function of our deeds on the day of Christ's coming will be to function as the criteria Christ will use in measuring out rewards that differ from Christian to Christian. We already looked at 2 Corinthians 5:10: "We must all . . . receive what is due for what he has done in the body, whether good *or evil*." We also looked at 1 Corinthians 3:15: "If anyone's work is burned up, he will suffer loss." Those passages clearly imply that at the judgment, rewards will be decided by Christ and will differ from Christian to Christian.

Jesus connected this kind of judgment to his second coming:

> Jesus told his disciples, "If anyone would come after me, let him deny himself and take up his cross and follow me. For whoever would save his life will lose it, but whoever loses his life for my sake will find it. For what will it profit a man if he gains the whole world and forfeits his soul? Or what shall a man give in return for his soul? For the Son of Man is going to come with his angels in the glory of his Father, and *then he will repay each person according to what he has done*." (Matt. 16:24–27)

The word *repay* (Matt. 16:27) could easily sound like a kind of transaction that suggests Jesus was put in debt by the work of the disciples, and now he must pay up like a just employer. I don't think Jesus saw his ministry or the judgment that way. Both the wider teaching of the New Testament and the teaching of Jesus itself keep us from construing *repay* as a transaction in which Jesus is paying back what he owes.[1]

Repay *Does Not Mean "Settle a Debt"*

Repay does not mean "settle a debt." God is not "served by human hands as though he needed anything, since he himself gives to all mankind life and breath and everything" (Acts 17:25), so he cannot be put in debt to any man. It's the other way around: all men are debtors to his all-supplying grace. So Paul asks rhetorically, "Who has given a gift to [God] that he might be repaid?" The answer is *nobody*, because "from him and through him and to him are all things" (Rom. 11:35–36).

And Jesus himself said, "Even the Son of Man came not to be served but to serve, and to give his life as a ransom for many" (Mark 10:45). Jesus's whole ministry, then and now, is not to recruit needed laborers, be served, and then pay them what he owes. On the contrary, he said, "So you also, when you have done all that you were commanded, say, 'We are unworthy servants; we have only done what was our duty'" (Luke 17:10). In other words, he owes us nothing.

In fact, the word *repay* (ἀποδίδωμι) has a broad range of meanings. It does not carry the intrinsic meaning of "pay what you owe." Here's a sample of this broad usage:

[Jesus] rolled up the scroll and *gave it back* to the attendant and sat down. (Luke 4:20)

The apostles were *giving* their testimony to the resurrection of the Lord Jesus. (Acts 4:33)

---

1   For example, Luke 17:7–10 shows that we cannot put Jesus in our debt: "You also, when you have done all that you were commanded, say, 'We are unworthy servants; we have only done what was our duty.'"

There is no cause that we can *give* to justify this commotion. (Acts 19:40)

For the moment all discipline seems painful rather than pleasant, but later it *yields* the peaceful fruit of righteousness. (Heb. 12:11)

The main reason we should not think of rewards as earned or deserved payback for good deeds is that the only good deeds that have moral beauty in God's eyes are "works of *faith*" (cf. 1 Thess. 1:3; 2 Thess. 1:11). Apart from faith, we cannot please God (Heb. 11:6). Therefore, Paul's aim in his ministry is "the obedience of faith" (Rom. 1:5; 16:26). In other words, the only good deeds that receive Christ's reward are the deeds that we *trust* God to work through us by the power of his *grace*. "[God's] grace toward me was not in vain. On the contrary, I worked harder than any of them, though it was not I, but the grace of God that is with me" (1 Cor. 15:10).

Paul prays that *God* will "fulfill every resolve for good and every work of *faith* by *his power* . . . according to the *grace* of our God and the Lord Jesus Christ" (2 Thess. 1:11–12). By his *power*. According to his *grace*. Through our *faith*. The life of love that God rewards is a life that he himself works in us. It is repayment only in the sense that there is a real correspondence between the goodness and beauty of our deeds and the rewards he gives.

Praise and Glory and Honor for Faith, by Grace

The apostle Peter makes the same connection between faith and grace and rewards. He says:

For a little while, if necessary, you have been grieved by various trials, so that the tested genuineness of your faith—more precious than gold that perishes though it is tested by fire—may be found to result in praise and glory and honor at the revelation of Jesus Christ. (1 Pet. 1:6–7)

This reference to *praise* (ἔπαινον) that faith results in is the praise believers will receive from the Lord, as in Romans 2:29 ("His praise [ἔπαινος] is not from man but from God") and 1 Corinthians 4:5 ("Then each one will receive his commendation [ἔπαινος] from God"). Similarly, the *glory* we receive on that day is the same as the glory Peter himself expects to partake in at the revelation of Christ: "I exhort the elders among you, as a fellow elder and a witness of the sufferings of Christ, as well as *a partaker in the glory* that is going to be revealed . . ." (1 Pet. 5:1). And the *honor* we receive at the revelation of Christ is the honor promised to those whose *belief* survives the fire ("The honor is for you who *believe*," 1 Pet. 2:7). It is the honor received by those who "by patience in well-doing seek for glory and *honor* and immortality" (Rom. 2:7).

This is a breathtaking expectation—that we poor, imperfect followers of Christ will be praised and glorified and honored at the revelation of Christ. And the point here is that this praise comes not to our meritorious works, but to our proven *faith*. Just as faith trusted God's grace in this life to enable us to walk worthily of the Lord, so now grace comes to a climax in rewarding this very reliance on grace. This is why Peter says six verses later, "Set your hope fully on the *grace* that will be brought to you at the revelation of Jesus Christ" (1 Pet. 1:13). As we long for the coming of Christ, our hope for the "praise and glory and honor" is a hope completely rooted in grace. Grace is coming to us. When God or angels or saints speak words of praise and glory and honor over us, it will be all grace. For what is being praised is our fire-proven faith, and that faith is the embrace of Jesus as the all-gracious treasure of our lives. Therefore, the giving of rewards (including praise and glory and honor) will in fact magnify the beauty and worth and grace of God in Christ.

Rewards Will Vary

Jesus makes clear that these rewards will be different for different disciples. For example, in the parable of the ten minas in Luke 19:11–27, Jesus makes the connection with his second coming by beginning the parable with these words: "A nobleman went into a far country to receive for himself a kingdom and then return" (19:12). He calls ten servants and gives each a mina.[2] After some time, he returns, "having received the kingdom," and he calls the servants to account in order to "know what they had gained by doing business" (Luke 19:15):

> The first came before him, saying, "Lord, your mina has made ten minas more." And he said to him, "Well done, good servant! Because you have been faithful in a very little, you shall have authority over ten cities." And the second came, saying, "Lord, your mina has made five minas." And he said to him, "And you are to be over five cities." (Luke 19:16–19)

I think this parable shows what Jesus is referring to when he says, "The Son of Man is going to come with his angels in the glory of his Father, and then he will *repay each person according to what he has done*" (Matt. 16:27). The "repayment"—or better, the awarding—of rewards differs from disciple to disciple. And there is no chastising of the servant who produced half as much as the other. Only the servant who was completely fruitless is left bereft: "Even what he has will be taken away" (Luke 19:26).

Paul and Apollos Will Receive Different Rewards

Paul taught this same diversity of rewards that accord with a disciple's "labor."

---

2   "Monetary units, each one worth three or four months' wages for a manual laborer working six days per week." Robert H. Gundry, *Commentary on the New Testament: Verse-by-Verse Explanations with a Literal Translation* (Peabody, MA: Hendrickson, 2010), 317.

I planted, Apollos watered, but God gave the growth. So neither he who plants nor he who waters is anything, but only God who gives the growth. He who plants and he who waters are one, and *each will receive his wages according to his labor.* For we are God's fellow workers. You are God's field, God's building. (1 Cor. 3:6–9)

"Each will receive his wages according to his labor." Again, the word for *wages* (μισθὸν), like the word *repay* above, has a broad range of meanings and does not demand the sense that the workers *earned* their reward by putting God in their debt. It can simply mean "reward" (Matt. 5:12; 1 Cor. 9:8). The picture of a farm laborer collecting wages is simply meant to communicate that there is a real correspondence between a disciple's faithful labors and his rewards from the Lord Jesus.

That correspondence is not merit. It is the fitness of God's recognition of the beauty and worth of *our* work done in reliance on *his* grace. Beautiful, rewardable labor is done "by the strength that God supplies—in order that in everything God may be glorified" (1 Pet. 4:11). What God rewards is the moral beauty of obedience done in reliance on his unmerited grace.

How This Is Good News

I conclude this chapter, therefore, in answer to our questions in the first paragraph, that there is a twofold function of our works—our obedience of faith—in the judgment at the second coming of the Lord Jesus. One is that our obedience will confirm our saving faith. This is why our obedience (or holiness or love) is spoken of as necessary for our final salvation (Gal. 5:21; Eph. 5:5; Heb. 12:14; 1 John 3:10). It is not necessary as foundation, but as confirmation. The other function of our works on the day of Christ is that Christ will assess them and reward them as he sees fit. Now the question is, How does this expectation help us love the Lord's appearing? That is what we turn to in chapter 11.

11

Rejoicing in the Hope of
Receiving Different Rewards

I RETURN TO THE QUESTION we posed at the beginning of chapter 10: When Christians learn that at Jesus's coming "he will repay each person according to what he has done" (Matt. 16:27), and that not every Christian will get the same commendation, such as, "Well done, good and faithful servant," how does this news help us love the Lord's appearing? I have six answers to this question—six observations about the Christian experience of diverse rewards at the appearing of Christ.

1. No Condemnation

Every true Christian—no matter how imperfect—will experience the day of rewards, and loss of rewards, with the joyful confidence that "there is . . . no condemnation for those who are in Christ Jesus" (Rom. 8:1). This is the massive Rock of Gibraltar on which the rewards ceremony will take place. No condemnation. "Whoever believes in [Jesus] is not condemned" (John 3:18).

Whatever it will be like for fire to burn up our defective ideas and works (1 Cor. 3:15), we will be confident with a deeper, God-given confidence on that day—namely, that we are walking through this fire in the asbestos covering of Christ's righteousness. In the fire, we will be singing a song from the "Great Eight": "Who shall bring any charge against God's elect? It is God who justifies. Who is to condemn? Christ Jesus is the one who died—more than that, who was raised—who is at the right hand of God, who indeed is interceding for us" (Rom. 8:33–34).

We will not be thrown off balance as we remember the words of Jesus, "Truly, truly, I say to you, whoever hears my word and believes him who sent me has eternal life. *He does not come into judgment*, but has passed from death to life" (John 5:24). We will not say, "Oh, no, look: we are coming into judgment. Jesus misled us." We will know the true meaning of Jesus's words. To "not come into judgment" means to "not come into judgment as guilty, to not come into judgment as condemnation." We will know that the judgment for the sake of rewards is taking place on the rock of the prior judgment of justification: we have already "passed from death to life" (John 5:24; cf. 1 John 3:14).

2. Every Good Rewarded

We will be stunned on that day with the overwhelming grace of God in rewarding us for every good thing we have ever done in our life of faith. Paul encourages slaves to "[render] service with a good will as to the Lord and not to man, knowing that *whatever good anyone does* [ἐάν τι ποιήσῃ ἀγαθόν], *this he will receive back from the Lord*" (Eph. 6:7–8). I include the Greek in brackets just to celebrate the unmistakable clarity of this astonishing promise. Let this sink in. *Every* good thing you have ever done—absolutely every good—is written down in heaven so that it can be duly rewarded at the day of Christ.

Depending on when you were converted to Christ and how old you are when you die, that will mean thousands and thousands of good deeds in your life to be rewarded. And lest you think I am overestimating the extent of this promise, consider these words of

Jesus: "Whoever gives one of these little ones even a cup of cold water because he is a disciple, truly, I say to you, he will by no means lose his reward" (Matt. 10:42). Is not the point of this promise the seeming insignificance of a cup of water? I realize that the cup is given "because he is a disciple." But the wider implication of these words is that God rewards the smallest acts that come from a Christ-honoring heart.

Let me linger over this for a moment, since its implications are deep and pervasive. One of the reasons many people abandon their commitments (in marriage, parenting, friendships, jobs, etc.) is because we are called upon to return good for evil so often, when nobody knows. We try to love people well—say, our spouse—and he or she responds indifferently or negatively, maybe thousands of times, for decades. I'm not talking about horrific cases of abuse here. I am talking about the kinds of disappointments, discouragements, frustrations, irritations, and regrets that 95 percent of us deal with in our relationships. And my point is this: those hundreds or thousands of efforts to do right in the face of continual thanklessness (to child, or spouse, or friend, or colleague) are most often unnoticed by anyone on earth, but are seen and recorded by God in heaven. In ways that we can't imagine, these small or large acts of grace will come back to us with such rewards that we will say, with overflowing joy, "It was worth it." "Whatever good anyone does, this he will receive back from the Lord" (Eph. 6:8). This is true no matter how many shortcomings will be burned up. Absolutely amazing!

3. No Faithful Suffering Unrewarded

Included in the varied rewards on the day of Christ will be varying measures of glorious recompense for suffering. I have in mind here three kinds of suffering: suffering for physical debilitation and illness, suffering for persecution, and suffering embraced in the service of others.

Rewards for Suffering Physical Debilitation and Illness

> We do not lose heart. Though our outer self is wasting away, our inner self is being renewed day by day. *For this light momentary affliction is preparing for us an eternal weight of glory beyond all comparison,* as we look not to the things that are seen but to the things that are unseen. For the things that are seen are transient, but the things that are unseen are eternal. (2 Cor. 4:16–18)

This is not persecution. This is aging, or the debilitation of illness, or the weakness of disability. Not all Christians are called to endure the same measure of suffering in this way. What comfort is there for one who suffers right up to the very end—when there is no life left on earth where one could profit from the sanctifying effects of suffering? Paul's answer: No Christian suffering is pointless. It is "preparing an eternal weight of glory." In other words, there is a real correlation between our suffering here and the measures of glory we know there. God will award the Christian sufferer in accord with his or her suffering. These rewards will differ greatly, and those of us who suffered less will leap for joy that the rewards of those who suffered more exceed ours.

Rewards for Suffering Persecution

> Blessed are you when others revile you and persecute you and utter all kinds of evil against you falsely on my account. Rejoice and be glad, for your reward is great in heaven, for so they persecuted the prophets who were before you. (Matt. 5:11–12)

It is possible to construe this to mean only that *all* Christians have a great reward coming—namely, eternal life—and so those who are persecuted should take heart. But I don't think that is what Jesus means. When he calls us to rejoice in specific persecutions, and when he points to the peculiar experience of the prophets, I think Jesus intends to say, "There are peculiar rewards for peculiar persecutions."

Rewards for Suffering Embraced in the Service of Others

> When you give a feast, invite the poor, the crippled, the lame, the blind, and you will be blessed, because they cannot repay you. For you will be repaid at the resurrection of the just. (Luke 14:13–14)

Jesus promises that at the resurrection—at his coming in glory—one of the factors he will take into account in giving his rewards is the self-denial, discomfort, or suffering we embraced in trying to serve people who could not reward us in this life. The point is not only that all Christians will gain eternal life, which will be ample recompense for every sacrifice. The point is more: you saw that your good deed could not be rewarded in this life, and you trusted the promise of Jesus that the reward you lost here would be repaid at the resurrection. It will be.

4. Experiencing Loss Sinlessly

All of us will experience significant measures of lost rewards when the fires of judgment consume our defective ideas and teachings and words and deeds (1 Cor. 3:14–15), but this will be good for us. It will be what we need. And we will experience this chastisement as sinless persons who have been perfected either at death (Heb. 12:23) or at the sight of Christ at his coming (1 John 3:2). And without sin filling us with self-pity, we will profit from this discipline as we ought.

Paul pointed to what I mean when he said, "Godly grief produces a repentance that leads to salvation without regret" (2 Cor. 7:10). He was referring to an experience in this life, while our hearts are imperfect. What then will it be like to experience loss as Christians who are perfectly sinless in the presence of Christ? Every one of us will look back over our lives and realize that at almost every point, we could have been more faithful managers of what Christ entrusted to us. It will not be a small fire when the shortcomings of our lives are burned up.

But as we ponder with purified minds and hearts what this means, there will be a sinless regret—no self-pity, no complaining, no neglect of grace, no joylessness. Our regret will be without destructive pain. It will be a constructive regret. It will serve the intensity of our amazed thankfulness that "the righteous is scarcely saved" (1 Pet. 4:18). We cannot conceive of, but will experience, the limitation of our joy from lost reward—a limitation without sin or condemnation. Our capacity for joy will be smaller, but we will be eternally content in God's wise and gracious ways.

5. Your Greater Reward Will Be Part of My Joy

The good that happens to others on the day of Christ, when rewards are given out, will be part of my joy. There is no mistaking that the judgment of that day will be intensely individual. (Notice the word *each* in Matthew 16:27 and 1 Corinthians 3:8 and Revelation 22:12.) But it is a great mistake if we think the saints on that day will be consumed with self-focus. We will not. And the rewards of others will be a great part of our joy on that day.

Paul alludes to this experience several times. For example, "For what is our hope or joy or crown of boasting before our Lord Jesus at his coming? Is it not you? For you are our glory and joy" (1 Thess. 2:19–20). Notice, Paul is referring explicitly to his experience at the coming of Christ. Whatever rewards Paul may lose in the fires of that judgment, he is not focused on that. He is focused on the fact that the Thessalonian believers will be there with him. And as they are perfected and rewarded, their joy will be his.

Similarly, he urges the Philippian believers to "hold fast to the word of life, so that in the day of Christ I may be proud that I did not run in vain or labor in vain" (Phil. 2:16). Again, the direction of his gaze is the second coming—"the day of Christ." And his hope is that on that day, the believers in Philippi will be his boast. That is, they will be the fruit of his faithfulness, and what happens to them on that day will compound his reward from Christ.

So it will be for all of us, to one degree or another. If you have lived a life of faith in Jesus and sought to shape your life around his word, there will be more people than you realize who were affected by your life. I mean in very small and simple ways that you do not now know. Some word you spoke caused them to act better than they would have. Some deed you did prompted a decision for good in their life. All of these hundreds of influences for good in others' lives will be revealed at the last day. And they will be your boast and your joy.

6. Increased Capacity for Joy in God

Finally, whatever outward form they take, the essence of every reward will be an increased capacity for joy in God. And the corporate experience of this vast diversity of complete happiness will be without pride or envy, but will be luminous with everlasting harmony, where it will be gloriously true that "if one member is honored, all rejoice together" (1 Cor. 12:26).

What inclines me and many others in the history of the church to see the essence of rewards as differing *capacities* for happiness is that our diversity in eternity will not come from some saints having mixed happiness and others having complete happiness, because *all* Christians are promised pain-free, sinless joy in God forever:[1]

---

1   "After the resurrection, however, when the final, universal judgment has been completed, there shall be two kingdoms, each with its own distinct boundaries, the one Christ's, the other the devil's. . . . But among the former *there shall be degrees of happiness*, one being more pre-eminently happy than another; and among the latter there shall be degrees of misery, one being more endurably miserable than another." Augustine, *The Enchiridion*, in *St. Augustin: The Holy Trinity, Doctrinal Treatises, Moral Treatises*, ed. P. Schaff, trans. J. F. Shaw (Buffalo, NY: Christian Literature Co., 1887), 3:273.

"There are diverse degrees of Happiness, and Happiness is not equally in all." Thomas Aquinas, *Summa theologica*, trans. Fathers of the English Dominican Province (London: Burns Oates & Washbourne, n.d.).

156 REASONS TO LOVE CHRIST'S APPEARING

> Behold, the dwelling place of God is with man. He will dwell with
> them, and they will be his people, and God himself will be with
> them as their God. He will wipe away every tear from their eyes, and
> death shall be no more, neither shall there be mourning, nor crying,
> nor pain anymore, for the former things have passed away. . . . No
> longer will there be anything accursed, but the throne of God and
> of the Lamb will be in it, and his servants will worship him. (Rev.
> 21:3–4; 22:3)

But it seems that differing roles or functions of the saints in
the age to come would not be experienced as *rewards* if they had
no bearing on the happiness of our experience of God. Moreover,
Paul's description of the resurrection points to diversities of glory
that would seem to suggest greater or lesser reflections of God's
glory, which we would experience as greater or lesser joy. "There is
one glory of the sun, and another glory of the moon, and another
glory of the stars; for star differs from star in glory. So is it with the
resurrection of the dead" (1 Cor. 15:41–42). Therefore, I conclude
that the essence of rewards at the day of Christ is that, while every
glorified Christian will be completely happy, our capacities for happiness will be diverse.

If we are on the right track, then the question becomes, How is such
vast diversity a beautiful future? How does it help us love the appearing

---

The Orthodox Confession of the Eastern Church, Question 382: "Will all be equally happy? No.
There will be different degrees of happiness, in proportion as every one shall have here endured
the fight of faith, love, and good works. *There is one glory of the sun, and another glory of the moon,
and another glory of the stars; for one star differeth from another star in glory. So also is the resurrection
of the dead.* 1 Cor. 15:41, 42." *The Creeds of Christendom, with a History and Critical Notes: The
Greek and Latin Creeds, with Translations*, ed. P. Schaff (New York: Harper & Brothers, 1890),
2:505; emphasis added.

Robert Gundry on 2 Cor. 5:10: "On the one hand, salvation won't necessarily be lost (see in
particular 1 Corinthians 3:15), but the enjoyment of it will be diminished just as a reward will
consist in enhanced enjoyment of salvation." Robert H. Gundry, *Commentary on the New Testament:
Verse-by-Verse Explanations with a Literal Translation* (Peabody, MA: Hendrickson, 2010), 703.

of the Lord, when he will put all this amazing diversity of complete happiness in motion? I know of no better description of the beauty of this future than that of Jonathan Edwards from his sermon on Romans 2:10. First, he expresses for us the biblical reality that the happiness of the saints in eternity will be complete, uninterrupted, and eternal in every glorified person:

> This happiness of the saints shall never have any interruption. There will never be any alloy to it; there never will come any cloud to obscure their light; there never will be anything to cool their love. The rivers of pleasure will not fail, the glory and love of God and of Christ will forever be the same, and the manifestation of it will have no interruption. No sin or corruption shall ever enter there, no temptation to disturb their blessedness: the divine love in the saints shall never cool, there shall be no inconsistency in any of them, the faculties of the saints shall never flag from exercise; and they will never be cloyed, their relish for those delights will forever be kept up to its height, that glorious society shall not grow weary of their hallelujahs. Their exercises, though they are so active and vigorous, will be performed with perfect ease; the saints shall not be weary of loving, and praising, and fearing, as the sun is never weary of shining.[2]

Then comes the glorious picture of how this diverse, but unalloyed and complete, happiness among millions of saints will be a perfect corporate experience of the body of Christ:

> The glory of the saints above will be in some proportion to their eminency in holiness and good works here. Christ will reward all according to their works. . . . It will be no damp to the happiness of

2 Jonathan Edwards, *The Works of Jonathan Edwards*, 2 vols. (Edinburgh, UK: Banner of Truth, 1974), 2:902.

those who have lower degrees of happiness and glory, that there are others advanced in glory above them: *for all shall be perfectly happy, every one shall be perfectly satisfied.* Every vessel that is cast into this ocean of happiness is full, though there are some vessels far larger than others; and *there shall be no such thing as envy* in heaven, but *perfect love shall reign through the whole society.*

Those who are not so high in glory as others, will not envy those that are higher, but they will have so great, and strong, and pure love to them, that they will rejoice in their superior happiness; their love to them will be such that they will rejoice that they are happier than themselves; so that instead of having a damp to their own happiness, it will add to it. They will see it to be fit that they that have been most eminent in works of righteousness should be most highly exalted in glory; and they will rejoice in having that done, that is fittest to be done. . . .

Those that are highest in glory, as they will be the most lovely, so they will be fullest of love: as they will excel in happiness, they will proportionally excel in divine benevolence and love to others. . . . And besides, those that will excel in glory will also excel in humility. Here in this world, those that are above others are the objects of envy, because . . . others conceive of them as being lifted up with it; but in heaven it will not be so, but those saints in heaven who excel in happiness will also . . . in humility. The saints in heaven are more humble than the saints on earth, and still the higher we go among them the greater humility there is; the highest orders of saints, who know most of God, see most of the distinction between God and them, and consequently are comparatively least in their own eyes, and so are most humble. The exaltation of some in heaven above the rest will be so far from diminishing the perfect happiness and joy of the rest who are inferior, that they will be the happier for it; such will be the union in their society that they will be partakers of each other's happiness. Then will be fulfilled in its perfection that which is declared in 1 Corinthians 12:[26], "If one of the members be honoured all the members rejoice with it."[3]

As with many other mysteries, we may need to leave totally in the hands of God how we are to conceive of the way the differences of happiness are sustained for millions and millions of years as we together discover more and more of the excellencies of Christ. I am happy to leave the mystery there. Enough has been revealed for us that we may be well occupied meditating and rejoicing on what we know, rather than fretting over what God keeps for himself (Deut. 29:29).

Let Us Love His Appearing

In view of these six observations, I repeat the question: Can we joyfully and fearlessly look forward to this time of judgment at the appearing of Christ? The answer is yes. Jesus will do all things well. His people have nothing to shrink back from. Even our "losses" will be sanctified and take us into new experiences of God's grace. And so it will be that "the name of our Lord Jesus [will] be glorified in you, and you in him, according to the grace of our God and the Lord Jesus Christ" (2 Thess. 1:12).

3 Edwards, *Works*, 2:902.

12

The Joy of Personal Fellowship
with the Sovereign Servant

THE JOY OF PERSONAL FELLOWSHIP with Jesus in our new resurrection bodies will be a surpassing joy beyond anything we have been capable of in this life. Already in his earthly ministry, Jesus had offered his own joy to his followers. "These things I have spoken to you, *that my joy may be in you, and that your joy may be full*" (John 15:11). "These things I speak in the world, that they may have *my joy fulfilled in themselves*" (John 17:13). Jesus's joy was supremely an eternal joy of love toward his Father: "I love the Father" (John 14:31). To share the joy of Jesus is to share the joy of the Son in the Father. It is also to share the joy of the Father in the Son (as we will see). This is why the joy would be full. But Jesus knew that this *fullness* of joy would not reach its climax in the limits of this earthly life.

Therefore, he prayed for us (John 17:20) that in the future we would be given supernatural capacities to enjoy fellowship with him as much as a created being can. He prayed, "O righteous Father . . . I made known to them your name, and I will continue to make it known, *that the love with which you have loved me may be in them, and I in them*" (John 17:25–26). This is a promise that we will not be left to ourselves in our capacities to love and enjoy the Son of God. We will be given the Father's love for the Son. "The love with which you have loved me [will] be in them." We will be able to share in the Father's delight in his Son. "This is my beloved Son, *with whom I am well pleased*" (Matt. 3:17). "Well pleased" the way an infinite God is pleased with an infinitely glorious and precious Son.

Our Hope to Enjoy Christ with the Enjoyment of God

This hope is wonderful, especially when we realize how broken and deficient we are in our emotions now. We all know that our love for Jesus, and its attendant joy, is pathetically weak compared to what he is worth. Our affections in the relationship we have with him fall far short of what we know they should be. What then is our hope for appropriate joy when we see him face-to-face in our glorified bodies at his coming?

Our hope is that the joy we have tasted in this life (1 Pet. 2:3) will be given an injection of supernatural capacity beyond imagination. This is what Jesus prayed for. This is what will happen. God will pour his own love for Christ into us. We will enjoy Christ with the very enjoyment of God. It is true that our joy in Jesus even now is a work of God—God the Holy Spirit. Our joy in God and his Son is owing to the presence of the Holy Spirit in our lives, creating the capacity to delight in God and Christ (Rom. 14:17; 15:13; 1 Thess. 1:6).

But when Jesus prays in John 17:26, he is asking for something more. We have known God now in some measure. And our love and joy have been awakened. This is the new birth. But now Jesus promises that he will go further: he will make God known in new and unimagined ways, with the result that God's own love for the Son will become more fully our own love for the Son, so that we will be able to enjoy Christ with the purity and intensity we ought. We will not be lamed by our present worldliness and remaining corruptions, and by the constraints of a fallen body.

Increase of Joy after Death

This new level of joy in God, which we will have in fellowship with Christ, will be partially experienced when we die (if Christ has not yet returned), and then most fully at the second coming. Paul says in Philippians 1:23, "My desire is to depart and be with Christ, for that is far better." Immediately when we die, our souls will be perfected in the presence of Christ (Heb. 12:23). Worldliness and corruption will no longer hinder our heart's affections for Jesus. And our fellowship with him will be more immediate in heaven than it was here. That's why Paul says that death will be "far better." The joy of that fellowship will surpass anything we have known here on earth.

But a bodiless fellowship with Jesus is not the final or highest hope of a Christian believer. Paul gives us a glimpse of our final hope in 2 Corinthians 5. On the one hand, he repeats the essence of Philippians 1:23: "We would rather be away from the body and at home with the Lord" (2 Cor. 5:8). That's "far better." But on the other hand, he bemoans being stripped of his body and being "unclothed," when he would much rather be "further clothed" with his resurrection body: "While we are still in this tent [our mortal body], we groan, being burdened—not that we would be unclothed [bodiless], but that we would be further clothed [with our resurrection body], so that what is mortal may be swallowed up by life" (2 Cor. 5:4). This must mean that the "*far* better" of dying and being with Christ (Phil. 1:23) is exceeded by a *far far* better of being clothed with a new body at the coming of Christ.

I infer from this that our enjoyment of Jesus's fellowship when he comes will be greater than our enjoyment of his fellowship between our death and the second coming. And this greater joy will be owing in part to the fact that we will relate to him in our resurrection bodies. Part of the reason for attributing our greater joy to having new bodies is that our new, glorified physical senses will be powerful beyond our present conceiving, so that by them we will both perceive and express dimensions of Christ's person and work in ways formerly impossible. Another reason our joy in Jesus will be greater when we have glorified bodies is that the interrelationship between our glorified spiritual bodies (1 Cor. 15:44) and our glorified spirits will be unimaginably closer and more perfectly interwoven than our spirits and bodies are now.

"Enter into the Joy of Your Master"

Regardless of how we try to explain it, Jesus makes clear that at his coming we enter into a new experience of joy that he calls *entering his own joy.* In the parable of the talents, Jesus pictures himself returning to earth like a man who had gone on a journey and entrusted his property to servants. As he calls them to account and gives rewards according to their faithful work, he says to the faithful servants, "Well done, good and faithful servant. You have been faithful over a little; I will set you over much. *Enter into the joy of your master"* (Matt. 25:21, 23). This is the consummation of the purpose expressed in John 15:11: "These things I have spoken to you, *that my joy may be in you, and your joy may be full."* At the second coming, Jesus continues and completes the purpose he began in our lives in this age: "Enter that very joy—my joy, the joy of your Master. At last it will be full."

Personal Fellowship Delights in the Person and His Delights

If we ask, "Will our joy in that day be joy in Jesus himself, or in Jesus's joy in his Father?" the answer is *both.* We will experience the Father's joy in the Son as our own (John 17:26). That is, we will enjoy Jesus himself with something of the intensity his Father does. And we will experience the Son's joy in the Father as our own (Matt. 25:21).

But the question is also misleading: Will our joy in that day be joy in Jesus, or Jesus's joy in his Father? It's misleading because when we speak of enjoying Jesus himself, we mean real, personal fellowship with him.

And what is personal fellowship but the sharing of what each one loves? Therefore, the question assumes a false dichotomy. When we delight in personal fellowship with Jesus himself, we delight in his delights.

Too Spectacular to Be Personal?

We have good reason to think of the joy of the second coming as including the joy of *personal fellowship*. We need to be reminded of this, because in the previous chapters, significant emphasis has fallen on the majesty of the Lord and the grandeur of the event of the second coming, with its trumpet of God, and cry of command, and archangel's voice, and millions of angels, and great power, and flashes of lightning, and vast glory, and resurrection of millions of Christians, and transformation of bodies, and giving of rewards. All this can sound like such a massive event that there might be no place for a *personal relationship*, or personal fellowship.

But the New Testament prevents us from making that mistake. Consider, for example, one familiar text from the Gospel of John that refers to the second coming of Christ. The focus of this text on personal relationship with Jesus is sometimes overlooked because of a mistaken focus on going to heaven:

> Let not your hearts be troubled. Believe in God; believe also in me. In my Father's house are many rooms. If it were not so, would I have told you that I go to prepare a place for you? And if I go and prepare a place for you, I will come again and will take you to myself, that where I am you may be also. (John 14:1–3)

Jesus has just told the disciples that he is going away (John 13:36). They are troubled at this. Now he tells them not to be: "Let not your hearts be troubled." He urges them to replace troubled hearts with hearts of faith: "Believe in God; believe also in me" (John 14:1). Trust me. Trust my Father. Then he supports their faith with at least three arguments, which all point to a personal relationship at the second coming.

1. *Don't be troubled, but trust me, because my Father has many rooms in his house, and each of you will have one.*

> In my Father's house are many rooms. If it were not so, would I have told you that I go to prepare a place for you? (John 14:2)

The emphasis here does not fall on isolation—each to his own room. The emphasis falls on no one being excluded because of limited accommodations. And so the emphasis includes personal attention to each disciple. There are "many" rooms. And that means a place for you. There's no point in stressing *many* rooms if everyone will be in the same room. The point is personal space, personal attention. The focus is not individual isolation but personal consideration.

2. *Don't be troubled, but trust me, because I myself am going to make ready your dwelling place with God.*

> In my Father's house are many rooms. If it were not so, would I have told you that *I go to prepare a place for you*? And if *I go and prepare a place for you* . . . (John 14:2–3a)

Two times Jesus says, "I go to prepare a place for you." What does that mean? I don't think it means that heaven is a mess that must be cleaned up. Nor does it mean that God's abode is under construction. Preparing a place where each disciple can enjoy nearness to God means preparing the possibility for sinners to be near God. Preparing a place means making a place available. It's as if a generous man finds you sleeping on the street and says, "Come, I'll prepare a place for you," and then he pays for your hotel room.

When Jesus says, "I go to prepare," he means, "I go to the cross tomorrow morning, and then out of the tomb three days later. This is the great work of preparation. This is how you will be able to dwell with God. I bear your sins tomorrow morning (1 Pet. 2:24). I become a curse for you tomorrow morning (Gal. 3:13). I secure your justification tomorrow morning (Rom. 5:9)." This is why in verse 6 the emphasis falls on, "I am the way, and the truth, and the life." "I go to prepare a place" means I make a way for sinful disciples to have personal accommodations in the house of God.

3. *Don't be troubled, but trust me, because I myself will be your dwelling, and I will do everything it takes to make sure you enjoy it.*

And if I go and prepare a place for you, I will come again and will take you to *myself,* that where *I am* you may be also. (John 14:3)

This verse is a lightning bolt of clarification. Until now, he has spoken of a house, a room, and a place. Now all those images fall away and he says, "Actually, the aim of my preparation is to 'take you to *myself.*' My aim in all my preparation is that 'where *I am* you may be also.'" Suddenly, Jesus is not only the *way preparer* but also the *destination.* This verse changes everything. Everything has become personal. The aim of his coming is now personal fellowship: "I will *come again* and will take you *to myself.*" This is how their joy would become full (John 15:11).

Father's House and the Rooms

Two clues should have alerted us that this was coming, that Jesus would be our dwelling.

First, the reference to "my Father's house" in John 14:2 should have recalled the one other place in this Gospel where Jesus speaks of "my Father's house." When he drives the money-changers out of the temple, he says, "Take these things away; do not make *my Father's house* a house of trade" (John 2:16). Then Jesus immediately connects the temple as God's dwelling to himself. He says, "Destroy this temple, and in three days I will raise it up. . . . But he was speaking about *the temple of his*

168 REASONS TO LOVE CHRIST'S APPEARING

body" (John 2:19, 21). So when we read in John 14:1 that in *the Father's house* are many personal accommodations for Jesus's disciples, we might wonder, "Does he mean that *Jesus* is that house—that *Jesus* is the place where God dwells, and where each disciple may dwell with him?"

Second, the word translated *rooms* (μοναὶ) in John 14:2 means "place of abode." It might be a room, or it might be some other way of abiding. It is the noun form of the verb *abide* (μένω). It is not a common word. It is only used one other time in the New Testament, namely, in this same chapter of John where Jesus says, "If anyone loves me, he will keep my word, and my Father will love him, and we will come to him and make our *home* [μονὴν, our abode] with him" (John 14:23). But frequently in this Gospel, the verb *abide* describes Jesus as our dwelling place: "Abide [μείνατε] in me, and I in you. As the branch cannot bear fruit by itself, unless it abides [μένῃ] in the vine, neither can you, unless you abide [μένητε] in me" (John 15:4).

These two clues were preparing us for the lightning bolt of clarification in John 14:3. The *house*, the *rooms*, and the *place* were all about Jesus himself. "If I go and prepare a place for you, I will come again and will take you to *myself*, that where *I am* you may be also." In other words, "I am your room in the Father's house. Preparing this room for you meant dying for you and rising again so that you would have access, and I would be a glorious accommodation."

Not to Take Us to Heaven, but to Himself

We need to correct a misunderstanding of John 14:1–4. Sometimes the text is used to show that when Jesus returns, he will take his people home to heaven.[1] But it does not say that. It says, "I will come again

---

1   Some commentators argue that Jesus's words, "I will come again," refer to his return three days later from the grave. For example, Robert H. Gundry, *Commentary on the New Testament: Verse-by-Verse Explanations with a Literal Translation* (Peabody, MA: Hendrickson, 2010), 429. But because of the words Jesus uses, I find it hard to exclude a reference to the second coming. Given the multilayered meanings that John regularly intends, Alford may be close to the truth to try to have it both ways: "In order to understand this, we must bear in mind what Stier well calls the

and will take you to *myself*, that where *I am* you may be also." And where will he be when he comes? We will meet him in the air and welcome him to earth for the establishing of his kingdom.[2] And so we will forever be *with the Lord* (1 Thess. 4:16–17).

What this text in John 14 focuses on in the second coming is not a new access to heaven but a new access to Christ. "I will . . . take you to *myself*." "Therefore, trust me," Jesus is saying. "I am coming for you. You will be *with me* forever." The coming of Christ is not only a magnificent spectacle; it is a personal welcome. And the welcome is supremely to himself. Along with many other mysteries about an unimaginable future, we do not need to explain how Jesus relates personally to millions of people. Those will be days of discovery, not disappointment. All the treasures of wisdom and knowledge are in Jesus Christ (Col. 2:3). Nothing that accords with his word will be impossible for him. Nothing will ruin the joy of personal fellowship with Jesus.

The Joy of His Coming Is Like the Joy of a Wedding Feast

The joy of this fellowship will have in it an almost inconceivable surprise dimension, a dimension that turns ordinary rational, even biblical, expectations on their head. Let me come at it indirectly. One aspect of unexpectedness has to do with the way Jesus's coming is related to a marriage feast. Typically we think of the portrayal in Matthew 25:1–12, where the second coming is compared to the coming of a bridegroom to his marriage feast. At the very least, this is meant to communicate

---

'perspective' of prophecy. The *coming again of the Lord* is not one single act—as His resurrection, or the descent of the Spirit, or His second personal advent, or the final coming to judgment; but the *great complex* of all these, the result of which shall be, His taking His people to Himself to be where He is. This ἔρχομαι, is *begun* (ver. 18) in His Resurrection—*carried on* (ver. 23) in the *spiritual life* (see also ch. 16:22 f.), the making *them* ready for the place prepared;—*further advanced* when each by death is fetched away to be with Him (Phil. 1:23); *fully completed* at His coming in glory, when they shall forever be with Him (1 Thess. 4:17) in the perfected resurrection state." Henry Alford, *Alford's Greek Testament: An Exegetical and Critical Commentary* (Grand Rapids, MI: Guardian Press, 1976), 1:849–50.

2 See especially chapters 8 and 9.

that it will be an event of great joy. But we must be careful not to press the details to mean that, in this portrayal, Christ is coming to marry his bride the church. There is a "marriage supper of the Lamb" where the bride is the people of God clothed with righteous deeds (Rev. 19:7–19; 21:2, 9). But the feasts that Jesus pictures at his second coming are not meant to portray that supper.[3]

For example, when the bridegroom comes in Matthew 25:1, the obedient church is pictured not as the bride but as five wise virgins who are the bridegroom's servants, waiting to welcome him to the feast. The point of the parable appears in verse 13: "Watch therefore, for you know neither the day nor the hour." The story comes to a climax not with a wedding, or even the introduction of a bride, but with the words, "Those who were ready went in with him to the marriage feast, and the door was shut" (Matt. 25:10). The point is eager readiness for the Lord's coming, in a context of festive joy.

That is the typical, expected picture that many of us are familiar with: Jesus's coming is like the coming of a bridegroom to a wedding. The point of this picture is joy. For in most cultures, weddings and their feasts are among the happiest celebrations we experience. That's how we should think about the second coming of Christ.

Unthinkable Dimension of Joy at His Coming

But then comes the surprise in Luke 12:35–38:

> Stay dressed for action and keep your lamps burning, and be like men who are waiting for their master to come home from the wedding feast, so that they may open the door to him at once when he comes and knocks. Blessed are those servants whom the master finds awake

---

3 The parable of the wedding feast in Matt. 22:1–14 is not presented as portraying the second coming. And the picture does not fit a marriage feast with Jesus as the bridegroom and the disciples as the bride, because the disciples who are converted and come to the feast are *guests* at the feast. They are not the bride. It is a parable about the kinds of worldly reasons people use to turn away from the lavish generosity of the kingdom invitations.

when he comes. *Truly, I say to you, he will dress himself for service and have them recline at table, and he will come and serve them.* If he comes in the second watch, or in the third, and finds them awake, blessed are those servants!

Here the second coming is pictured not as a bridegroom coming to a wedding feast, but as a master coming *from* a wedding feast. Suddenly things are turned upside down. No explanation is given, but Jesus is portrayed as coming *from* a wedding feast. So I assume the point is that he is full of joy and celebration already when he comes. He is not coming from sadness to joy, but from joy to joy.

We wonder what else is going to be turned upside down in this picture. The people waiting for their "master" (τὸν κύριον) are called "servants" or "slaves" (δοῦλοι). The first point of the story is to be like them. "Stay dressed for action and keep your lamps burning, and be like men who are [eagerly] waiting for their master to come" (Luke 12:35–36). In other words, do with a hearty obedience what the master assigned for you to do. In this case, stay "awake" so that you can open for him when he comes. The command to be "dressed for action" means eager alertness to always be about the master's business. The fact that "slaves" are in view is going to intensify the surprise dimension of our joy.

Then Jesus tells us why we should be so vigilant to be found doing the master's will—because it will result in *blessedness*. "Blessed [μακάριοι] are those servants whom the master finds awake when he comes" (Luke 12:37). "Happy!" Then Jesus drops the bomb. We thought we had some idea what the joy would be like at the second coming when we get to be part of Jesus's intimate household. Even if we are called "slaves," we know we will not be slaves in any ordinary sense, because he has called us children (Rom. 8:16) and friends (John 15:15). But now Jesus tells us something about the joy of that household that defies all expectation.

Sovereign Son as the Table Waiter

The owner, the master, is going to tell us—the "slaves" (he uses the word to intensify the paradox)—to sit down at the dinner table as his guests because he is going to "dress for action" and serve us! The word "dress himself for service" (περιζώσεται) is the same as the word in Luke 12:35, where the slaves were told to "stay dressed for action" (περιεζωσμέναι). Which means that Jesus is intentionally reversing the roles. We are made to sit as household members, while he takes the role of slave to serve us.

Jesus will give an illustration of discipleship five chapters later (Luke 17:7–10) in which he says in essence, "This is not what masters do. Nor should any slave ever expect it":

> Will any one of you who has a servant plowing or keeping sheep say to him when he has come in from the field, "Come at once and recline at table"? Will he not rather say to him, "Prepare supper for me, and dress properly [περιζωσάμενος], and serve me while I eat and drink, and afterward you will eat and drink"? Does he thank the servant because he did what was commanded? So you also, when you have done all that you were commanded, say, "We are unworthy servants; we have only done what was our duty."

Masters do not serve their slaves. They don't even thank their slaves. What more could Jesus have said to make his behavior at the coming of the Son of Man more mind-blowing? And make no mistake, Luke 12:37 *is* a description of the glorious coming of the Son of Man. Three verses later, Jesus concludes, "You also must be ready, for the Son of Man is coming at an hour you do not expect" (Luke 12:40). Jesus had already pictured the majesty of the spectacular second coming. He had said, "The Son of Man . . . comes in his glory and the glory of the Father and of the holy angels" (Luke 9:26). This glorious, sovereign victor over all adversaries will come seat his "slaves" (who are treated as masters) at table and will bind himself with the garments of a slave and serve them.

First Suffering Servanthood, Then Glorious Servanthood

Then add this teaching of Jesus from Luke 22:25–27:

> The kings of the Gentiles exercise lordship over them, and those in authority over them are called benefactors. But not so with you. Rather, let the greatest among you become as the youngest, and the leader as one who serves. For who is the greater, one who reclines at table or one who serves? Is it not the one who reclines at table? But I am among you as the one who serves.

Perhaps we thought that the pattern of Jesus as servant would end with this earthly ministry. Isn't that what Philippians 2:6–9 seems to suggest?

> Though he was in the form of God, [he] did not count equality with God a thing to be grasped, but emptied himself, by taking the form of a servant, being born in the likeness of men. And being found in human form, he humbled himself by becoming obedient to the point of death, even death on a cross. *Therefore* God has highly exalted him and bestowed on him the name that is above every name.

First comes humility and servanthood during the incarnation; then comes the reward of exaltation after the resurrection. Right? Yes. But it's not that simple. Luke 12:37 prevents that oversimplification. The King of kings, the Creator of the world, the radiance of the glory of God, the upholder of the universe (1 Tim. 6:15; Heb. 1:2–3) is going to take the "form of a servant" at his second coming and make our joy in his banquet tearfully, mouth-stoppingly happy with head-shaking wonder. The pattern is this: suffering then glory (1 Pet. 1:11; 5:1). Or more accurately, the pattern is this: first suffering servanthood, then glorious servanthood.

Everlasting Paradox

Don't dampen your wonder with perplexity about how this is going to fit together with the flaming fire that brings vengeance on enemies (2 Thess. 1:8), or the giving out of rewards (Matt. 16:27). The prophetic perspective of Scripture allows for the day of the Lord to include as much time as it takes for all God intends to do.[4]

In fact, I think it would be a mistake to think of Luke 12:37 as only an event. "He will dress himself for service and have them recline at table, and he will come and serve them." These words are valid not for one brief banquet, after which Christ puts his armor back on, to be only the warrior king for all eternity.

No. The point is that the glory of Christ has always been, and always will be, the kind of glory that combines diverse, and even paradoxical, excellencies. His glory is not monochromatic. It is dazzlingly diverse. The music of his greatness is not mere unison but vast, deep harmony. He mingles, and always will mingle, majesty and meekness, reverence for God and equality with God, obedience and dominion, lordship and servanthood, transcendence and intimacy, justice and mercy. He will always be at home in the robes of a king and the towel of a slave.

There is a reason for this. And it lies at the root of our happiness when Christ comes. The giver gets the glory. He will always be the grace giver, and we will always be the grace dependent. We will always be beneficiaries of grace. We will never be benefactors of God. He will always have the glory of being self-sufficient and all-supplying. He will always be the inexhaustible spring, and we the thirsty. He will be the living bread, and we the hungry. He the shepherd, and we the sheep.

---

4 See chapter 8, note 1.

He the sun, and we the moon. He the health-sustaining doctor, and we the ever-dependent patients.

Which is another way of saying that our destiny, from eternity to eternity, is not just that we praise God's glory, but that we "praise the glory of his *grace*" (Eph. 1:6, my translation). The apex of his glory is the overflow of grace. God will never surrender the glory of being free from need. He will never be in our debt. And if you lose your senses for a moment and wonder if this is good news, let this word from Ephesians 2:6–7 bring you back to sanity: "[God] raised us up with [Christ] and seated us with him in the heavenly places in Christ Jesus, so that in the coming ages he might show the immeasurable riches of his grace in kindness toward us in Christ Jesus."

When Jesus said that at the second coming the Son of Man "will dress himself for service and have [his disciples] recline at table, and he will come and serve them," he was not describing an exception for a day, but a pattern for eternity. It will require all the "coming ages" for Christ to exhaust on us the "immeasurable riches [ὑπερβάλλον πλοῦτος] of his grace in kindness." That is what *immeasurable* means.

Personal Fellowship with the Sovereign Servant

So I conclude that the glory of the second coming will include the preciousness of personal fellowship with Christ. And this personal fellowship will have a dimension to it that is inexpressibly great: it will be intimate and transcendent. He will *take us to himself* (John 14:3). And in that fellowship, he will take us into experiences of servant-grandeur that will require an eternity to fully enjoy.

PART 2

———

THE TIME OF HIS APPEARING

THE TIME AND THE LOVE
OF CHRIST'S APPEARING

THE QUESTION I AM TRYING to answer in part 2 is, How are we to think about the time of Jesus's appearing? Guiding what I include and omit is a specific question: How important would this be in helping us love the Lord's appearing? Of course, my judgments about that question may not be the same as yours. I hope they are helpful, as far as they go.

Love for Christ's appearing is deepened not only by seeing reasons for what makes it wonderful, but also by overcoming obstacles and misunderstandings. By way of analogy, my love for my wife is deepened by being reminded of her precious personal qualities, but also by coming to understand better the note she might write if she were (like Jesus) to go away for a long time.

I will try to say enough so that our love for Christ's coming is not undermined by excessive perplexity about when he is coming. I say *excessive* perplexity because I think *some* perplexity about the biblical teaching on the time of the Lord's coming is inevitable. I say this as an observation from my experience and from my reading of the history of interpretation.

To the best of my knowledge, I've never spoken to any Christian—scholar or layman—who is not perplexed about some biblical text on the second coming. Nor do I see any time in the history of the church when there has been a consensus on the identity of the signs leading up to the second coming or on the timeframe of the proposed events connected with the second coming itself. Practically, then, it seems to me that I should try to say what would help us love the Lord's return, and help us live our lives with the kind of vigilance and expectancy commended by Scripture.

So the three questions I will try to answer in part 2 are:

1. Did Jesus teach that he would return within *one generation*?
2. What does the New Testament mean that Jesus would come *soon*?
3. Does the New Testament teach that Jesus may come *at any moment*?

13

Did Jesus Teach That He Would Return within One Generation?

IT WOULD BE DIFFICULT TO LOVE the appearing of Christ if he were morally compromised by promising his coming within a timeframe of which he was ignorant. Note carefully how I am stating the problem. I am not primarily asking if Jesus made a mistake. That would be bad enough. I am asking if his mistake was morally culpable. In other words, the question is not just, "Did he get the timing of his return wrong?" but, "Did he venture to predict what he was in no position to predict?"

I state the problem like this because of what Jesus says in Matthew 24:36, one of the most important sentences in the Bible about the time of the second coming: "Concerning that day and hour no one knows, not even the angels of heaven, nor the Son, but the Father only." To be sure, it is mysterious that Jesus, the God-man, can be ignorant of something God the Father knows. But that is what he said. Which means that if he predicts the time of his own coming when he does not know its time, he is morally compromised. It would be hard to love his appearing.

Three passages of Scripture (with their parallels) raise this question. I will deal with them one at a time.

Some Will Not Taste Death before They See His Coming

First is the prediction of Christ's coming before some of his contemporaries taste death. It occurs in each of the first three Gospels:

> "Truly, I say to you, there are some standing here who will not taste death until they see the Son of Man coming in his kingdom." And after six days Jesus took with him Peter and James, and John his brother, and led them up a high mountain by themselves. (Matt. 16:28–17:1)

> He said to them, "Truly, I say to you, there are some standing here who will not taste death until they see the kingdom of God after it has come with power." And after six days Jesus took with him Peter and James and John, and led them up a high mountain by themselves. And he was transfigured before them. (Mark 9:1–2)

> I tell you truly, there are some standing here who will not taste death until they see the kingdom of God. Now about eight days after these sayings he took with him Peter and John and James and went up on the mountain to pray. (Luke 9:27–28)

In these three texts, only Matthew 16:28 explicitly mentions the second coming ("until they see the Son of Man coming"). Mark and Luke refer only to the coming of the kingdom. But they are all probably speaking of the same event. All three Gospels say that the coming of the kingdom will be seen by "some" of those who are "standing here" before they taste death. Then, in all three Gospels, this saying is followed by the transfiguration of Jesus on the mountain.

The Mountain Where They Saw

That fact—the juxtaposition of Jesus's words and the transfiguration— is critical for understanding what Jesus meant. I think he meant that

Peter, James, and John would not taste death before they see a preview on the mountain of the second coming of Christ. These were the three who went up on the mountain with him. Jesus considered the revelation of his majesty and glory on the mountain to be a prefiguring of his coming at the end of this age:

> He was transfigured before them, and his face shone like the sun, and his clothes became white as light. And behold, there appeared to ["was *seen* by"!] them Moses and Elijah, talking with him. And Peter said to Jesus, "Lord, it is good that we are here. If you wish, I will make three tents here, one for you and one for Moses and one for Elijah." He was still speaking when, behold, a bright cloud overshadowed them, and a voice from the cloud said, "This is my beloved Son, with whom I am well pleased; listen to him." When the disciples heard this, they fell on their faces and were terrified. But Jesus came and touched them, saying, "Rise, and have no fear." And when they lifted up their eyes, they saw no one but Jesus only. (Matt. 17:2–8)

Besides the immediate juxtaposition of the transfiguration with Jesus's saying about his (or the kingdom's) coming, there is another reason for interpreting the transfiguration as the foreshadowing of the second coming. Peter, who was on the mountain with Jesus during the transfiguration, treats this experience in his second epistle as a preview or preliminary validation of the second coming:

> We did not follow cleverly devised myths when we made known to you the power and coming [παρουσίαν] of our Lord Jesus Christ, but we were eyewitnesses of his majesty. For when he received honor and glory from God the Father, and the voice was borne to him by the Majestic Glory, "This is my beloved Son, with whom I am well

pleased," we ourselves heard this very voice borne from heaven, for we were with him on the holy mountain. (2 Pet. 1:16–18)

Peter considers his eyewitness testimony of the transfiguration as a proof that his prophecy of "the power and coming of our Lord Jesus Christ" is not a myth. This term "power and coming" of the Lord in verse 16 is a reference to the second coming, which Peter will take up again in chapter 3. The word *coming* is the usual word for second coming in the New Testament (*parousia*). And the word *power* is used to describe Jesus's second coming in Matthew 24:30: "They will see the Son of Man coming on the clouds of heaven with *power* and great glory."

I conclude, therefore, that in Peter's understanding, what he saw on the Mount of Transfiguration was a foretaste or prefiguration of Jesus's second coming. This means, then, that those who would "not taste death" before they saw "the Son of Man coming in his kingdom" (Matt. 16:28) were Peter, James, and John. They saw Jesus's coming and his kingly reign prefigured and confirmed in the transfiguration.

Stepping back and asking why Jesus would choose to give such a preview of his coming, one answer is that he wanted there to be an extraordinary apostolic witness to the nonmythical, glorious reality of his future coming. He wanted their testimony to have the taste of reality so that our savoring of the hope of Christ's appearing would be sweet. In other words, he did it so that we would love the Lord's appearing.

Before This Generation Passes Away

Second is Jesus's prediction that "this generation will not pass away until all these things take place." Following are the parallel texts that have caused some to think Jesus predicted his own return within a generation:

So also, when you see these things taking place, you know that he is near, at the very gates. Truly, I say to you, this generation will not pass away until all these things take place. (Mark 13:29–30)

So also, when you see all these things, you know that he is near, at the very gates. Truly, I say to you, this generation will not pass away until all these things take place. (Matt. 24:33–34)

So also, when you see these things taking place, you know that the kingdom of God is near. Truly, I say to you, this generation will not pass away until all has taken place. (Luke 21:31–32)

Both Mark and Matthew say that when we see "[all] these things" taking place, we can know "that he is near." This means that "these things" cannot include the actual coming of the Lord, because when "these things" happen, the Lord is only *near*, not present. So none of these texts teaches that Jesus will return within a generation. What, then, do they teach?

Birth Pains of the Age to Come

They confirm the whole New Testament perspective that, beginning with the coming of Jesus, we have been living in the "last days." "In these last days [God] has spoken to us by his Son" (Heb. 1:2; cf. Acts 2:17; 2 Tim. 3:1–5; James 5:3; 2 Pet. 3:3). From the first generation of the church until the end of the age at Jesus's coming, the "last days" will be marked by the "birth pains" (Matt. 24:8; Mark 13:8) of the final consummation. In other words, "these things" that take place within one generation are the kinds of upheavals that mark all the last days from the incarnation to the second coming.

For example, after mentioning false christs, wars, rumors of wars, nation rising against nation, famines, and earthquakes (Matt. 24:5–7), Jesus says, "*All these* are but the beginning of the birth pains" (24:8). "The end is not yet" (Matt. 24:6). The phrase "all these" (πάντα ταῦτα) in verse 8 is the very phrase used in verse 34: "This generation will not pass away until all these things [πάντα ταῦτα] take place." In other words, "these things" do happen within one generation, but they are only the beginning of the birth pains, which will mark all of history, and then reach a crescendo at the very end. One can hear the crescendo in Matthew 24:12–13: "And because lawlessness will be *increased*, the love of many will grow cold. But the one who *endures to the end* will be saved."

For this and other reasons that we will see,[1] I understand Matthew 24:1–44 (and parallels) as predicting events that will take place within a generation, including the destruction of Jerusalem in AD 70, *and* events that will take place throughout church history, *and*, coming to a crescendo, events that will occur at the end of the age just before Jesus returns. For example, Luke's version of this teaching makes the destruction of Jerusalem explicit: "When you see Jerusalem surrounded by armies, then know that its desolation has come near" (Luke 21:20). But I think it is a mistake to interpret Jesus's prophecies about the future in Matthew 24 (and parallels) as referring *only* to the devastation of Jerusalem in AD 70 and the events leading up to it. Instead, Jesus's intention is that we see the events surrounding AD 70 as harbingers of end-time horrors. They are part of the beginning of the birth pains.

Near and Far in "Prophetic Perspective"

We already have described this way of viewing biblical prophecy,[2] calling it with George Ladd the "prophetic perspective." Which means that distant events are seen foreshadowed in the near, and near events are seen as previews of the distant. This perspective runs throughout the prophetic parts of Scripture. Here again is Ladd's summary of Matthew 24 and Mark 13 and Luke 21 in view of this prophetic perspective, as we saw in chapter 9:

From the totality of his teaching one thing is clear: Jesus spoke both of the fall of Jerusalem and of his own eschatological parousia.

1   See chapter 16.
2   See chapter 8, note 1.

Cranfield has suggested that in Jesus' own view the historical and the eschatological are mingled, and that the final eschatological event is seen through the "transparency" of the immediate historical. The present author has applied this thesis to the Old Testament prophets and found this foreshortened view of the future to be one of the essential elements in the *prophetic perspective*. In Amos, the Day of the Lord is both an historical (Amos 5:18–20) and an eschatological event (Amos 7:4; 8:8–9; 9:5). Isaiah describes the historical day of visitation on Babylon as though it was the eschatological Day of the Lord (Isa. 13). Zephaniah describes the Day of the Lord (Zeph. 1:7, 14) as an historical disaster at the hands of an unnamed foe (Zeph. 1:10–12, 16–17; 2:5–15); but he also describes it in terms of a world-wide catastrophe in which all creatures are swept off the face of the earth (Zeph. 1:2–3) so that nothing remains (Zeph. 1:18). This way of viewing the future expresses the view that "in the crises of history the eschatological is foreshadowed. The divine judgments in history are, so to speak, rehearsals of the last judgment and the successive incarnations of antichrist are foreshadowings of the last supreme concentration of the rebelliousness of the devil before the End."[3]

I think this view is correct. One implication is that we are not compelled to choose between first-century fulfillments and final, end-time fulfillments.[4] And we are certainly not compelled to say that Jesus mistakenly predicted his final coming within one generation.

---

3 George Eldon Ladd, *A Theology of the New Testament* (Grand Rapids, MI: Eerdmans, 1974), 198–99; emphasis added. The sentence in quotation marks is from C. E. B. Cranfield, *The Gospel according to St Mark: An Introduction and Commentary* (Cambridge, UK: Cambridge University Press, 1959), 404.

4 Sam Storms makes a case that Matt. 24:4–31 refers "immediately and primarily" to the events leading up to AD 70. But then he concludes like this:

> In conclusion, my argument that Matthew 24:4–31 refers immediately and primarily to the events leading up to and including the destruction of Jerusalem in 70 does not necessarily exclude the possibility that the end of the age is, at least indirectly, also in view. It may well be that future events associated with the second advent of Christ at the end of

Going through All the Towns of Israel

Third, Jesus predicts in Matthew 10:23, "When they persecute you in one town, flee to the next, for truly, I say to you, you will not have gone through all the towns of Israel before the Son of Man comes."

Matthew 10:23 is the most perplexing text about the coming of the Son of Man. Do these words mean Jesus predicted that he would return before the disciples had finished evangelizing the geographic region inhabited mainly by the people of Israel? One might, at first, reasonably think so.

---

the age are *prefigured* by the destruction of the temple and the city in 70. James Edwards argues "that events surrounding the destruction of the temple and fall of Jerusalem are a type and foreshadowing of a final sacrilege before the eschaton" [James R. Edwards, *The Gospel according to Mark* (Grand Rapids, MI: Eerdmans, 2002), 384].

In other words, the events of 70 *may* well portray in a localized way what will happen *globally* at or in some way associated with the second advent. . . . Therefore, my opinion is that the pattern of events that transpired in the period 33–70, leading up to and including the destruction of Jerusalem and its temple, *may* function as a *local, microcosmic foreshadowing* of the *global, macrocosmic* events associated with the parousia and the end of history. The period 33–70 conceivably, then, provides in its *principles* (though not necessarily in all particularities), a template against which we are to interpret the period 70–parousia. (Sam Storms, *Kingdom Come: The Amillennial Alternative* [Fearn, Ross-shire, UK: Mentor, 2013], 279; emphasis original).

You can hear in the words "not necessarily exclude the possibility" and "it may well be" and "may well portray" and "may function" and "conceivably" an uncertainty that does provide much guidance for how to see in Jesus's words what may yet be future. Practically, how are we to apply Storms's words, "[These first-century events] *may* function as a *local, micro-cosmic foreshadowing* of the *global, macrocosmic* events"? If we are left only with the *possibility* that Jesus intended his words to illuminate the end time, are we to think that they do or don't? The difference between my view and Storms's view is twofold. One, he only sees a *possibility* that Matt. 24:4–31 foreshadows events at the very end of the age, whereas I think there is good evidence that both Matthew and Paul understood Jesus's teaching as definitely having the final end in view. And while Storms might allow that first-century events are the main earthquake, so to speak, in Matt. 24:4–31, with possible aftershocks at the very end of history, I think the events surrounding the second coming are the earthquake in Matt. 24:4–31, and the events of the first century are warning tremors. The basis for this is mainly the observation that Paul and Jesus conceptualize the second coming in the same way, as shown from their shared language; and Paul makes clear that this language and conceptualization, drawn largely from Matt. 24:4–35, refers to the very end, not only to AD 70. See chapter 16.

But it is not so simple. For one thing, the word *Israel* in Matthew does not by itself refer to a geographic region. The word is used twelve times in Matthew in phrases like, "people [of] Israel" (2:6), "land of Israel" (2:20), "house of Israel" (10:6), "God of Israel" (15:31), "tribes of Israel" (19:28), "sons of Israel" (27:9), and "King of Israel" (27:42). Does the term "towns [or cities] of Israel" (πόλεις τοῦ Ἰσραὴλ) clearly mean towns or cities of a certain geographic area defined by the people of Israel? Or could it have a wider meaning? Could it mean, "cities of the *people* of Israel" or "cities where Israel dwells"? Could Jesus be speaking loosely, or even figuratively, about the people of Israel scattered abroad who will be in need of the gospel until the Son of Man comes?

For another thing, does the logic of the verse point primarily to towns for evangelism or towns for refuge? Notice that the clause that begins with *for* argues that there will always be another town for refuge until the Son of Man comes: "When they persecute you in one town, flee to the next, *for* truly, I say to you, you will not have gone through all the towns of Israel before the Son of Man comes." This is Herman Ridderbos's interpretation—namely, that even though the disciples will continue to be persecuted until the very end, there will always be a place to which they can flee.[5]

For yet another thing, Ladd points out that the paragraph that Matthew 10:23 concludes "clearly looks beyond the immediate mission of the twelve to their future mission in the world." For example, the immediately preceding verse says, "You will be hated by all for my name's sake. But the one who endures to the end will be saved" (Matt. 10:22). Ladd concludes, "The present verse says no more than that the mission of Jesus's disciples to Israel will last until the coming of the Son of Man. It indicates that in spite of its

---

5 Herman Ridderbos, *The Coming of the Kingdom*, ed. Raymond O. Zorn, trans. H. de Jongste (1950; repr., Philadelphia: Presbyterian & Reformed, 1962), 507–10.

blindness, God has not given up Israel. The new people of God are to have a concern for Israel until the end comes."[6]

There are other interpretations of Matthew 10:23.[7] I do not have a clear or strong conviction about which of these interpretations is correct. What guides me in situations like this is (1) my confidence in Jesus as he is presented in the Gospels, namely, that he is trustworthy and would not predict a timeframe for his coming that he said he did not know (Matt. 24:36); (2) the fact that prophetic language is often temporally flexible and figurative; and (3) that other biblical passages that are clearer provide guidance when obscure passages perplex us. In this case, for example, I believe there is indeed a future for ethnic Israel, and a hope for her conversion in this age (Rom. 11:15–32), and a call for ongoing Jewish evangelism in all "her cities."[8] And there is Jesus's statement, "Heaven and earth will pass away, but my words will not pass away" (Matt. 24:35). In other words, I think we are the ones who would be mistaken if we thought Jesus was mistaken about such a crucial point about the future of his mission.

6   Ladd, *Theology of the New Testament*, 200. Similarly, Hoekema concludes, "We may understand Matthew 10:23 as teaching us, first, that the church of Jesus Christ must not only continue to have a concern for Israel but must keep on bringing the gospel to Israel until Jesus comes again. In other words, Israel will continue to exist until the time of the Parousia, and will continue to be an object of evangelism." Anthony A. Hoekema, *The Bible and the Future* (Grand Rapids, MI: Eerdmans, 1994), 119.

7   For example, Don Carson argues that "the 'coming of the Son of Man' here refers to his coming in judgment against the Jews, culminating in the sack of Jerusalem and the destruction of the temple. . . . Interpreted in this way the 'Son of Man' saying of v. 23 belongs to the eschatological category . . . but the eschatology is somewhat realized. The strength of this interpretation is sometimes diluted by applying it unchanged to 16:28; 24:31 (so France, *Jesus*). In fact there are important differences disallowing the view that all these texts refer to the Fall of Jerusalem in A.D. 70. Nevertheless they confirm the view that 'the coming of the Son of Man' bears in Matthew the same rich semantic field as 'the coming of the kingdom.'" D. A. Carson, "Matthew," in *The Expositor's Bible Commentary: Matthew, Mark, Luke*, ed. F. E. Gaebelein (Grand Rapids, MI: Zondervan, 1984), 8:253.

8   See John Piper, "Five Reasons I Believe Romans 11:26 Means a Future Conversion for Israel," Desiring God, February 16, 2012, https://www.desiringgod.org/.

Not within One Generation

When we step back from these three groups of texts, which some have taken to imply that Jesus predicted the second coming and the end of the age within one generation, my conclusion is that Jesus did not teach that he would return within one generation. Therefore, whatever other perplexities may trouble the waters of our love for his appearing, this need not be one of them. But, one may ask, does not the New Testament repeatedly speak of the second coming as happening soon? Yes. And to that question we turn in the next chapter.

14

What Does the New Testament Mean That Jesus Will Come Soon?

THE NEW TESTAMENT EXPRESSES the idea of a "soon" expectation of the Lord's coming in several ways:

Rejoice in the Lord always; again I will say, rejoice. Let your reasonableness be known to everyone. The Lord is *at hand* [ἐγγύς]. (Phil. 4:4–5)

You have need of endurance, so that when you have done the will of God you may receive what is promised. For, "Yet *a little while* [μικρὸν ὅσον ὅσον] and the coming one will come and will not delay." (Heb. 10:36–37)

You also, be patient. Establish your hearts, for the coming of the Lord is *at hand*. Do not grumble against one another, brothers, so that you may not be judged; behold, the Judge is *standing at the door* [θυρῶν]. (James 5:8–9; cf. Matt. 24:33, "When you see all these things, you know that he is near, at the very gates [θύραις].")

The end of all things is *at hand* [ἤγγικεν]; therefore be self-controlled and sober-minded for the sake of your prayers. (1 Pet. 4:7)

The revelation of Jesus Christ, which God gave him to show to his servants the things that must *soon* [ἐν τάχει] take place. . . . Behold, I am coming *soon* [ταχύ]. Blessed is the one who keeps the words of the prophecy of this book. . . . He who testifies to these things says, "Surely I am coming *soon* [ταχύ]." Amen. Come, Lord Jesus! (Rev. 1:1; 22:7, 20)

Here's the key question: If an infallible spokesman for Jesus Christ does not know when the Lord is going to return (as Jesus said would be the case, Matt. 24:36), what would that spokesman mean by saying it will be "soon" (Rev. 22:20), or "at hand" (1 Pet. 4:7), or "at the door" (James 5:9)? I think it misses the point of Matthew 24:36 to say Jesus didn't know "the day and hour" but that he did know the month or the year. The point of Jesus's ignorance of the time is to remove the possibility of calculating how long we dare be indifferent to his coming. Not knowing "the day or the hour" is a graphic way of saying that neither he nor we can predict the time.

So the question remains, What would it mean, then, for an infallible spokesman (an apostle!) of the Lord Jesus, who cannot predict the time, to say that Jesus is coming soon, or that Jesus is at the door, or that Jesus is at hand, or that Jesus will come after a little while? What do the New Testament writers mean by their predictions of Jesus's nearness? In what sense do they mean he is near?

In answer to those questions, I'm going to offer three phrases that I believe are rooted in biblical texts and then give a brief explanation of each: potentially near, holistically near, and divinely near.

Potentially Near

First, the apostles mean Jesus is *potentially near.*

That is, he is near in the sense that any presumption of his delay on our part would be folly. It is as if the apostles should say, "You know that we cannot predict the time of the Lord's coming, because the Lord himself did not know the time (Matt. 24:36), and he told us, 'It is not for you to know times or seasons that the Father has fixed by his own authority' (Acts 1:7). Therefore, you know that when we say 'soon' we are not doing what we cannot do. We are not predicting what we cannot predict. Rather, we are telling you that it is *potentially* soon, meaning that the replacement of *hope* for this soon-ness with *presumption* of delay will unfit you for his coming and lead to destruction."

By *presumption* I mean the unwarranted assumption that his coming is so distant that I am not in danger of his coming while I neglect my vigilance to walk uprightly. This presumption fails to reckon with the fact that lack of vigilance now may lead to utter obliviousness for the rest of your life so that the so-called distant coming finds you utterly unprepared.

I draw this meaning of "soon" from Jesus's illustration of the second coming in Matthew 24:45–51:

Who then is the faithful and wise servant, whom his master has set over his household, to give them their food at the proper time? Blessed is that servant whom his master will find so doing when he comes. Truly, I say to you, he will set him over all his possessions. But *if that wicked servant says to himself, "My master is delayed," and begins to beat his fellow servants and eats and drinks with drunkards, the master of that servant will come on a day when he does not expect him and at an hour he does not know* and will cut him in pieces and put him with the hypocrites. In that place there will be weeping and gnashing of teeth.

The warning is this: never presume upon the Master's delay. That is, never presume that neglecting spiritual wakefulness will not be met with the surprise of his appearing. Always hope for his soon arrival and act in the light of it. Saying that Jesus's coming is near when you do not know when he is coming means that he is *potentially near*, and all presumption otherwise is dangerous.

Holistically Near

Second, the apostles mean Jesus is *holistically near*.

That is, as part of a whole, unified vision of the end time, he is near because, considered as a whole, the "end," the "last days," are already present. Taken as a whole, the end has begun. When we say that Jesus and the apostles did not know when the second coming would take place, we are saying that the future God granted them to see was like successive mountain ranges that appear as a single range. This telescoped range of mountain ridges, appearing as one, is what I mean by a whole, unified vision of the end time.

My family has spent time at a home in Tennessee that has a front porch facing northeast. On a crystal-clear evening, we can see at least seven distinct mountain ranges from that porch. But on a hazy evening, they look like one mountain range. I have used George Ladd's phrase *prophetic perspective* to describe this way of seeing the future.[1] It sees the distant reality and the nearer reality as one. I'm using the phrase *holistically near*, rather than *prophetically near*, because I think it might trigger in our memory more clearly the idea of the second coming being part of a telescoped or foreshortened vision of a history of events seen as a whole.

We Live at the End of the Ages

We have already pointed out that the "last days" began with the first coming of the Messiah. "He was foreknown before the foundation of the world but was made manifest *in the last times* for the sake of you who through him are believers in God" (1 Pet. 1:20–21). "In these last days he has spoken to us by his Son" (Heb. 1:2). "He has appeared once

1   See chapter 8, note 1.

for all *at the end of the ages* to put away sin by the sacrifice of himself" (Heb. 9:26; cf. 1 Cor. 10:11).

This implies that the vision of the entire period between the incarnation and the second coming is one great mountain range with many hills and peaks that were indistinct to the apostles. They were granted to know a good many details, but very little about the overall timeframe. They saw the end largely as one reality, and they speak of it *holistically* as near because, *as a whole*, it is near. That near whole includes the *parousia*—the coming of Jesus. Therefore, it too is near—near as part of the whole that has already begun. Here's the way C. E. B. Cranfield expresses it:

> If we realize that the Incarnation-Crucifixion-Resurrection-Ascension, on the one hand, and the Parousia [second coming], on the other, belong essentially together and are in a real sense one Event, one divine Act, being held apart only by the mercy of God who desires to give men opportunity for faith and repentance, then we can see that in a very real sense the latter is always imminent now that the former has happened. It was, and still is, true to say that the Parousia is at hand—and indeed this, so far from being an embarrassing mistake on the part of Jesus or the early Church, is an essential part of the Church's faith. Ever since the Incarnation men have been living in the last days.[2]

Tarrying That Is Not a Tarrying

The roots of thinking holistically about future events are in the Old Testament. Repeatedly the prophets spoke of the day of the Lord as "near" when in fact they were seeing events separated by unknown stretches of time. They were speaking holistically. They were seeing near and distant as one:

2 C. E. B. Cranfield, *The Gospel according to St. Mark* (Cambridge, UK: Cambridge University Press, 1959), 408.

Wail, for the day of the LORD is *near*; as destruction from the Almighty it will come! (Isa. 13:6)

Multitudes, multitudes, in the valley of decision! For the day of the LORD is *near* in the valley of decision. (Joel 3:14)

For the day of the LORD is *near* upon all the nations. As you have done, it shall be done to you; your deeds shall return on your own head. (Obad. 15)

The great day of the LORD is *near*, near and hastening fast. (Zeph. 1:14)

If we are tempted to say that these promises are inaccurate because aspects of the day of the Lord were delayed, Habakkuk offers a restraint on our presumption. The Lord spoke through Habakkuk with words that caution us against speaking unwisely about the Lord's work being delayed. He said:

For still the vision awaits its appointed time;
   it hastens to the end—it will not lie.
If it seems slow, wait for it;
   it will surely come; it will not delay. (Hab. 2:3)

One of the striking things about these words is that they reckon with delay from one standpoint that is *not* delay from another standpoint. The word *seem* is not in the original Hebrew. More literally, it says:

For the vision is yet for the appointed time;
   It hastens toward the goal and it will not fail.
Though it tarries [אִם־יִתְמַהְמָהּ], wait for it;
   For it will certainly come, *it will not delay* [לֹא יְאַחֵר].
      (Hab. 2:3 NASB)

It may tarry. But it will not delay. It may tarry, but it will not tarry (which is how the KJV translates it: "Though it tarry, wait for it; / Because it will surely come, it will not tarry"). In fact, in its tarrying, it is *hastening* to the goal. What do these paradoxical statements mean? I think they mean that from man's perspective, the arrival of God's future may seem slow. But from God's perspective it is so well-timed that it may be said to be hastening (in spite of perceived slowness); indeed, there is no delay whatsoever.

When the prophets and the apostles looked holistically at God's future, they knew that every part of what they saw was "appointed," and was hastening toward the goal. It may, from a human standpoint, seem to tarry, but in fact it was not tarrying. Rather it was—and is— near. *Holistically near.*

Divinely Near

Third, the apostles mean Jesus is *divinely near.*

That is, from the *divine* perspective, the time between Jesus's first and second coming is very short. The apostle Peter introduces this meaning of *near* in his response to scoffers who already in his day mocked the fact that so much time had passed without the Lord's return. He says:

> [Know] this first of all, that scoffers will come in the last days with scoffing, following their own sinful desires. They will say, "Where is the promise of his coming? For ever since the fathers fell asleep, all things are continuing as they were from the beginning of creation." (2 Pet. 3:3–4)

After reminding the scoffers that history is not as static as they think (in view of creation and flood and final judgment, 2 Pet. 3:5–7), he then introduces the foundation of what I am calling *divinely near:*

> But do not overlook this one fact, beloved, that with the Lord one day is as a thousand years, and a thousand years as one day. The Lord is

not slow to fulfill his promise as some count slowness, but is patient
toward you, not wishing that any should perish, but that all should
reach repentance. (3:8–9)

Verse 9 is addressed to our attitude and our vocabulary: don't call God's
purposeful delay "slowness." Call it "patience." Don't scoff at God's
timing as if his promise of coming soon were a myth (2 Pet. 1:16).
Instead, give thanks that his promise of mercy and patience is being
perfectly worked out.[3]

To support his admonition about our attitude and vocabulary, Peter
introduces the concept of *divinely near*: "With the Lord one day is as a
thousand years, and a thousand years as one day." To get the full force
of the point, a scoffer might calculate: Supposing that Peter wrote this
letter thirty years after the ascension of Jesus to heaven, those thirty
years would be 3 percent of a thousand years. Since a thousand years
is "as one day," that would mean that .72 hours (.03 x 24 hours in a
day) has passed since Jesus departed. Forty-five minutes is not a long
delay. Or, from the standpoint of the twenty-first century, two days is
not a long delay.

In essence, Peter is introducing the mystery of God's relation to
time. The Bible is not a primer on Einstein's relativity theory. It does
not delve into the scientific relationship between space and time.[4]

---

3 My understanding of the statement that God "is patient toward you, not wishing that any should
   perish, but that all should reach repentance" (2 Pet. 3:9) is that the phrase "toward you" means
   toward you *believers*, and by implication, all believers—all the *elect* (1:10). Therefore, the word *any*
   in the phrase "not wishing that *any* should perish" is defined by the meaning of the words "God
   is patient toward *you*." Hence, God is "not wishing that any [*of you*] should perish"—that is, "any
   of you *elect*." The problem with construing Peter to mean that God delays the second coming
   because he wishes *all humans* to be saved is that the longer he delays, the more people are lost,
   because in every generation so many do not repent. God is not ignorant of this fact. Therefore,
   the logic of the verse would fall apart if he meant "all humans," because the logic of the verse is
   that delay is owing to the divine desire that none be lost.
4 Ben Witherington points out that the theory of relativity should at least humble us and prevent
   us from using our fragile grasp of the meaning of time to pass judgment on biblical predictions:
   "Many scientists point out that 'time is, in fact, elastic and can be stretched and shrunk by mo-

However, Paul says provocatively that "God decreed [a hidden wisdom] *before the ages* for our glory" (1 Cor. 2:7; cf. 2 Tim. 1:9; Titus 1:2). In other words, in some sense God existed before "the ages," that is, before time. Peter is suggesting to us that this mysterious relationship between God and time should make us slow to scoff at the timing of his prophecies. If Jesus and the apostles say the coming of Christ is "near" or "at hand" or "at the gates" or "soon," when they confessedly do not know when he is coming, we should reckon with the fact that the divine perspective is part of what gives meaning to their words. Jesus is *divinely near*.

His Appearing Is Near in at Least Three Senses

I conclude, therefore, that if we take into account the pointers Jesus and the apostles give us, we will not fault them for speaking of the Lord's coming as near or soon or at hand. We will take into account the agreed-upon premise that none of them knew when Jesus would return. With that pointer in view, we will take heed to Jesus's warning against every presumption of delay as a dangerous attitude (Matt. 24:48; par. Luke 12:45), and conclude that the second coming is *potentially near*. We will take heed to the prophetic perspective of the Old and New Testaments that sees the "last days" (including Christ's first and second coming) as a unified whole that has already begun, and we will conclude that Jesus is

tion.' Not only so, but 'time really does run faster in space, where the Earth's gravity is weaker.' In short, time, space and gravity are interrelated and interdependent matters. . . . Now this in itself ought to give us all pause. Our own *perception* of time lapse or the calculation of time is hardly a very firm or reliable basis to make a confident judgment about the validity of the eschatological concepts Jesus and Paul taught. . . . What we have learned about time from the theory of relativity coupled with space exploration suggests that since time, space and gravity are interdependent, whatever else one may say, eternity or heaven must be very different from Earth in regard to the whole matter of time. It may also indeed prove to be the case that the biblical author said more than he understood when he pointed out, 'With the Lord a day is like a thousand years, and a thousand years are like a day' (2 Peter 3:8)." Ben Witherington III, *Jesus, Paul and the End of the World: A Comparative Study in New Testament Eschatology* (Downers Grove, IL: InterVarsity Press, 1992), 233–34.

holistically near. And we will take seriously Peter's reminder that with God a thousand years is as a day, and we will conclude that Jesus is *divinely near*.

Which now leads to the question, What does this view of nearness imply, if anything, about whether Jesus could come at any moment? That is the focus of chapters 15–17.

15

Is There an Any-Moment Rapture
before the Second Coming?

IN CHAPTERS 15–17, I will try to answer the question, Does the New Testament teach that Jesus may come at any moment? If I answer this question by saying no, I wonder if you would infer that I am thereby denying the urgency of all the biblical warnings to be watchful. Jesus did indeed tell us to watch (βλέπετε, Mark 13:33), and be awake (ἀγρυπνεῖτε, 13:33), and be alert (γρηγορεῖτε, 13:35), and be ready (γίνεσθε ἕτοιμοι, Luke 12:40), and take heed (προσέχετε, 21:34 KJV). And one of the reasons given for all this vigilance is that "you know neither the day nor the hour" (Matt. 25:13). Any view of Jesus's coming that makes those exhortations meaningless would be doubtful.

I do think the answer to the question, Does the New Testament teach that Jesus may come at any moment? is no. The reason is that the New Testament teaches that there are events yet to happen before he comes. I will try to show what those are. And I also will try to show that this does not diminish the urgency of the commands to watch and be awake and alert and ready for his coming.

In fact, I will argue that we have no warrant to be sure that his coming is ever more than a few years away. Therefore, no one who ceases to be vigilant, and thus goes to sleep spiritually, has any reason to think he will escape the sudden, thief-like wrath of the Lord's coming.

My biblical support for this view has three steps that correspond to the next three chapters.

First, in this chapter I will show why I don't believe in a two-part second coming, with the first part snatching Christians (living and dead) out of the world and taking them back to heaven during a "great tribulation" (Matt. 24:21; Rev. 7:14), followed by the second part when Christ comes in fiery judgment.

Second, in chapter 16 I will show why most of the events prophesied in Matthew 24 are not limited to the time leading up to AD 70 but are relevant for interpreting all of history, with a special relevance for the crescendo of history just before the Lord comes. In the process, we will see that Paul's view of the second coming (1 and 2 Thessalonians) is the same as Jesus's view (especially in Matthew 24).

That will then enable us in chapter 17 to move to step three, namely, to show some of the events that are yet to happen before Christ comes.

What Is the Rapture?

We turn in this chapter to the question, Is there an any-moment rapture, when Christians are removed from the world some years before the second coming? Or is there a single second coming of Christ rather than one that is divided into two parts?

My answer is that the "rapture" happens at the single second coming, not years before. The word *rapture* comes from the Latin *rapio*, used in the Vulgate, the Latin version of the Bible, and means "to seize or snatch away." In the future tense (*rapiemur*—"we will be snatched away"), the word is used in 1 Thessalonians 4:17, describing what happens at the second coming: "Then we who are alive, who are left, will be caught up [*rapiemur*, snatched away or raptured] together with them [those who had died] in the clouds to meet the Lord in the air, and so we will always be with the Lord." Thus, one interpretation says that this snatching away "to meet the Lord in the air" refers to a departure of Christians from the earth for some years while terrible tribulation takes place on earth before the Lord returns to establish his kingdom.

This view says that before the Lord actually descends to establish his kingdom, there will be a period of "great tribulation" (Matt. 24:21) on the earth. Christians on the earth when this tribulation comes are to be spared from this period. They will be spared by being taken out of the world by the coming of the Lord Jesus on the clouds, who will take them back to heaven (the "rapture") before the tribulation. Then, after the tribulation, he will come with his saints and establish his kingdom on the earth. This view is called the "pretribulational coming of Christ" because Christ comes *before* (pre-) the tribulation and takes Christians out of it.

I will argue that this view is mistaken, and that Christ is coming back *once* in great power with his angels to establish his kingdom on the earth. His people will be caught up to meet him in the air and welcome him back to earth. Before I give my reasons, two comments will set the stage for how I would like you to think about this disagreement among Christians.

How Important Is Agreement?

First, I used to hold the view I am now disagreeing with. And I have precious friends and family today who believe in the pretribulational coming of Christ. I mention this simply as an occasion to clarify that this disagreement does not disincline me from fellowship with any Christian. When I was a pastor, I led our church in the formulation of a statement of faith that did not make this a confessional issue. Uniformity of views on this issue did not define our church.

206 THE TIME OF HIS APPEARING

My second comment is that whole books have been written to defend the view that I am now arguing for.[1] This is not another such book. Therefore, my arguments will be brief. They will leave some questions unanswered. But that's all right with me because the main aim of this book is not to change the minds of those who hold a pretribulational view of the second coming. My main aim is that both of us would love the Lord's appearing, whichever view we hold.

Eight Reasons I Am Not Pretribulational

The reason I need to address this disagreement at all is that I am trying to answer the question of whether we should believe that the New Testament teaches that Jesus may come at any moment. One of the arguments used to support the pretribulational view is that the New Testament does indeed teach that Jesus may come at any moment *and* that only by dividing the Lord's coming into two parts can an any-moment return be preserved. If the Lord comes after (after = *post*, hence, posttribulational, after the tribulation) the great tribulation, then his coming cannot be at any moment because some aspects of that tribulation are not yet upon us. Those events would have to come first. So the reason I am addressing the pretribulational view is to show that the any-moment view of Christ's coming is mistaken. And, of course, this aim is part of the larger goal to bring biblical clarity to our thinking about the Lord's coming and so remove unnecessary obstacles to loving his appearing.

1. How We Meet the Lord in the Air

The pretribulational view says that 1 Thessalonians 4:17 describes the first part of the return of Christ, after which he returns to heaven with his raptured church: "Then we who are alive, who are left, will be caught up together with them in the clouds to meet [ἀπάντησιν] the Lord in the air, and so we will always be with the Lord."

---

1 George Eldon Ladd, *The Blessed Hope: A Biblical Study of the Second Advent and Rapture* (Grand Rapids, MI: Eerdmans, 1990); Robert H. Gundry, *The Church and the Tribulation* (Grand Rapids, MI: Zondervan, 1973).

The word translated "to meet" in the ESV occurs in only two other places in the New Testament, and in both of them, the word refers to a meeting in which people go out to meet a dignitary and then accompany him in to the place from which they came out. In Acts 28, Luke describes a welcoming group of Christians who came out of Rome to meet the newly arriving Paul and welcome him in:

> And the brothers there, when they heard about us, came as far as the Forum of Appius and Three Taverns to meet [ἀπάντησιν] us. On seeing them, Paul thanked God and took courage. And when we came into Rome, Paul was allowed to stay by himself, with the soldier who guarded him. (28:15–16)

In Matthew 25:6, we have a picture of the second coming itself. It portrays the five wise virgins going out to meet the returning bridegroom and accompanying him into the marriage feast:

> At midnight there was a cry, "Here is the bridegroom! Come out to meet [ἀπάντησιν] him." . . . And while [the foolish virgins] were going to buy, the bridegroom came, and those who were ready went in with him to the marriage feast, and the door was shut. (Matt. 25:6, 10)

This suggests strongly that the picture before us in 1 Thessalonians 4:17 is one of Christian believers rising to meet the Lord in the air and accompanying him back to his rightful kingdom on earth. The word does not suggest any departure with Christ from the earth.

2. Relief and Revenge on the Same Day

The wording of 2 Thessalonians 1:5–8, when read carefully, shows that Paul, if he is alive at the coming of the Lord, expects to attain rest from suffering at the same time, and in the same event, that he expects the unbelievers to receive punishment—namely, at the revelation of Jesus with mighty angels in flaming fire:

> This is evidence of the righteous judgment of God, that you may be considered worthy of the kingdom of God, for which you are also suffering—since indeed God considers it just to repay with affliction those who afflict you, and *to grant relief to you who are afflicted as well as to us, when the Lord Jesus is revealed from heaven with his mighty angels in flaming fire,* inflicting vengeance on those who do not know God and on those who do not obey the gospel of our Lord Jesus.

This revelation of the Lord Jesus from heaven (2 Thess. 1:7) is not a pretribulational rapture, because it involves not only the relief of believers but the punishment of unbelievers in flaming fire. Which means that Paul did not expect an event at which he and the other believers would be given rest seven years *before* the glorious appearing of Christ in flaming fire. Vengeance on unbelievers and rest for the persecuted church come on the same day in the same event[2]—the one second coming.

3. Gathering to Christ Is on the Day of the Lord

Similarly, the wording of 2 Thessalonians 2:1–2 suggests that the gathering to meet the Lord in the air is the same as the "day of the Lord" when Jesus judges unbelievers and rescues believers:

> Now concerning *the coming of our Lord Jesus Christ* and our *being gathered together to him*, we ask you, brothers, not to be quickly shaken

---

2 The simultaneity of judgment and rescue is made clear by (1) Paul's saying that both occur "in the revelation of our Lord Jesus from heaven with the angels of his power" (ἐν τῇ ἀποκαλύψει τοῦ κυρίου Ἰησοῦ ἀπ᾽ οὐρανοῦ μετ᾽ ἀγγέλων δυνάμεως αὐτοῦ; see 2 Thess. 1:7), and (2) by his saying that the judgment happens "when he comes to be glorified in his saints" (ὅταν ἔλθῃ ἐνδοξασθῆναι ἐν τοῖς ἁγίοις αὐτοῦ, 2 Thess. 1:10).

in mind or alarmed, either by a spirit or a spoken word, or a letter seeming to be from us, to the effect that *the day of the Lord has come.*

It makes little sense to distinguish this "being gathered to [the Lord]" from "the day of the Lord." The flow of thought treats them as the same. The natural way to construe the gathering to the Lord is to see it in the light of 1 Thessalonians 4:17: "Then we who are alive, who are left, will be *caught up together with them* in the clouds to meet the Lord in the air, and so we will always be with the Lord." This is the same as "our being gathered together to him" in 2 Thessalonians 2:1. Which is the same as "the day of the Lord" (2 Thess. 2:2).

And the natural way to construe "the day of the Lord" is to see it in the light of the "day" Paul describes in what follows. On that "day" (2 Thess. 2:3), after the "man of lawlessness is revealed" (2:3), "the Lord Jesus will kill [him] with the breath of his mouth and bring [him] to nothing by the appearance of his coming" (2:8). Therefore, the gathering to meet the Lord and the judgment on God's enemies are the same event. The rapture does not happen seven years earlier than the "appearance of [Christ's] coming" in destructive power. They are part of the same event.

4. Paul Argues as if Posttribulational

If Paul were a pretribulationist, why did he not simply say in 2 Thessalonians 2:3 that the Christians don't need to worry that the day of the Lord has come because all the Christians are still here? They have not yet been raptured. But he does not say that. Instead, he talks just the way you would expect a posttribulational person to talk:

Now concerning the coming of our Lord Jesus Christ and our being gathered together to him, we ask you, brothers, not to be quickly shaken in mind or alarmed, either by a spirit or a spoken word, or a letter seeming to be from us, to the effect that the day of the Lord has come. Let no one deceive you in any way. *For that day will not come, unless the rebellion comes first, and the man of lawlessness is revealed, the son of destruction.* (2 Thess. 2:1–3)

Paul tells them that they should not think that the day of the Lord is here, because the apostasy and the man of lawlessness have not appeared. In other words, he describes two events that must happen before the coming of the Lord, which we have seen is the same as the gathering of believers in 1 Thessalonians 4:17, when the "rapture" takes place.

5. Jesus Pictures His Future Disciples Enduring Tribulation

When you read Matthew 24 or Mark 13 or Luke 21, which I will argue in chapter 16 are not limited to first-century events but include Jesus's descriptions of the end times leading up to Christ's second coming, there is no mention of a rapture removing believers from any of the events of the end. A normal reading gives no impression of a departure of Christians from the earth. On the contrary, Jesus talks as if the believing listeners, and then the later readers, would or could experience the events he mentions (cf. Matt. 24:4, 9, 15, 23, 26, 33).

6. Christians Experience Tribulation as Refining, Not Wrath

The pretribulational view argues that it would be contrary to God's ways to allow Christians to go through the great tribulation, which is marked by his own wrath. But the regular teaching of the New Testament is that "through many tribulations we must enter the kingdom of God" (Acts 14:22). Even when the tribulation is from God, believers are pictured as going through it, not as punishment but as purification. For example, Peter writes:

Beloved, do not be surprised at the fiery trial when it comes upon you to test you, as though something strange were happening to you. . . . For it is time for judgment to begin at the household of God;

and if it begins with us, what will be the outcome for those who do not obey the gospel of God? And "If the righteous is scarcely saved, what will become of the ungodly and the sinner?" Therefore let those who suffer according to God's will entrust their souls to a faithful Creator while doing good. (1 Pet. 4:12, 17–19)

Believers are not exempt from tribulation, even the worst kind—even when the tribulation is ordained by God.

Peter had already described in the first chapter of his letter why these fiery trials (πειρασμὸν, 1 Pet. 4:13) happen to the believers:

You rejoice, though now for a little while, if necessary, you have been grieved by various trials [πειρασμοῖς], so that the tested genuineness of your faith—more precious than gold that perishes though it is tested by fire—may be found to result in praise and glory and honor at the revelation of Jesus Christ. (1 Pet. 1:6–7)

Believers experience the fires of trial not as punishment but as gold-refining purification. To argue that Christians cannot pass through "great tribulation" (Matt. 24:21; Rev. 7:14), because it involves God's wrathful judgment, fails to distinguish how God's design in tribulation can be destructive for unbelievers and refining for believers.

7. Kept from the Hour of Trial

One of the texts used in support of the pretribulational view is Revelation 3:10: "Because you have kept my word about patient endurance, *I will keep you from the hour of trial that is coming on the whole world,* to try those who dwell on the earth." Do the words "keep . . . from the hour of trial" mean that Christians will be taken out of the world before the tribulation?

There is another natural interpretation. To "be kept from the hour of trial" is not necessarily to be taken out of the world during this hour,

212 THE TIME OF HIS APPEARING

and thus spared suffering, but to be preserved as faithful through it. Compare Galatians 1:3–5:

> Grace to you and peace from God our Father and the Lord Jesus Christ, who gave himself for our sins to *deliver us from the present evil age*, according to the will of our God and Father, to whom be the glory forever and ever. Amen.

Deliverance "from the . . . evil age" does not mean we are taken out of it, but that our faith is preserved through it. Similarly, Jesus prays in John 17:15, "I do not ask that you take them out of the world, but that you keep them from the evil one." To keep us "from the evil one" does not mean we go out of the world, or out of his range. It means we are protected from his destructive power while we are in the world.

Even in the book of Revelation (where we find this promise of 3:10), we are promised that God will require martyrdom from some of his people in the last days. "Then [the martyrs under the heavenly altar] were each given a white robe and told to rest a little longer, until the number of their fellow servants and their brothers should be complete, who were to be killed as they themselves had been" (Rev. 6:11). The promise of Revelation 3:10 means that God's people will be kept from the faith-destroying forces of that hour, not that there will be a rapture out of a troubled world.

8. Urgency of Watchfulness Will Not Be Lost

The pretribulational view puts a high premium, as it should, on the morally and spiritually purifying effects of the unexpected coming of Christ. We will see in chapter 18 that this legitimate concern is fully maintained in the view of the second coming I will commend. The urgency of watching and being alert and being ready and staying awake will not be lost. But the emphasis will fall on the purifying effects of loving the Lord's appearing, as we see it in 1 John 3:2–3: "We know that when he appears we shall be like him, because we shall see him as he is. And everyone who thus hopes in him purifies himself as he is pure."

One Future Appearing of Christ

I conclude from these eight arguments that there is a single second coming of Christ. It does not take place before a great tribulation in order to rescue Christians out of the world. Rather, it happens climactically at the resurrection of Christians and involves both deliverance for believers and judgment for unbelievers.[3]

Therefore, the pretribulational position cannot offer compelling support for the view that the New Testament teaches an any-moment return of Jesus. So, to continue our pursuit of a biblical answer to the question of what the New Testament does teach, we move now to the second of our three-step argument.

I will try to show in the next chapter that Paul's view of the second coming and Jesus's view (especially in Matthew 24) are the same. This will have significant implications for step three (chapter 17), namely, what events if any must take place before Christ comes.

3 See chapter 8.

16

Jesus and Paul

A Common Vision of Christ's Coming

MY SECOND STEP IN ARGUING that the New Testament does not teach an any-moment return of Christ is to show that most of the events prophesied in Matthew 24 are not limited to the time leading up to AD 70 but are pertinent for interpreting all of history, with a special relevance for the crescendo of history just before the Lord comes. In the process, we will see that Paul's view of the second coming (in 1 and 2 Thessalonians) is the same as Jesus's view (especially in Matthew 24). This will, in turn, enable us to move to step three (chapter 17), namely, to show some of the events that are yet to happen before Christ comes.

Single Coming in 1 and 2 Thessalonians

First, we need to see that in 1 and 2 Thessalonians, Paul is dealing with only one coming of Christ. I'm not referring here to the issue addressed in the previous chapter concerning the possible pretribulational coming of Christ, followed by another coming seven years later. Rather I am referring to the fact that all the references to the second coming of Christ in the two Thessalonian letters are references to the same event (1 Thess. 2:19; 3:13; 4:13–18; 5:1–11, 23; 2 Thess. 1:5–10; and

2:1–12). This fact will be significant as we correlate Jesus's teaching with Paul's. If I can show that Paul and Jesus picture the end times in similar ways, then both Matthew 24 and the Thessalonian letters may provide a united answer to the question, Does the New Testament teach that there are events yet to happen before the Lord will return?

Here are three pointers that Paul has in view the same event of Christ's coming throughout the Thessalonian correspondence:

1. The key Greek word for the second coming, *parousia*, is used by Paul for the second coming in 1 Thessalonians 2:19; 3:13; 4:15; 5:23; and 2 Thessalonians 2:1, 8. He does not use different vocabulary for different comings. He uses this same word in these various contexts because he is dealing with one coming.

2. Paul uses the term "day of the Lord" in 1 Thessalonians 5:2 to refer to the day that comes like a thief in the night. Believers will be on earth for this "day of the Lord," and they will be "awake" (γρηγορῶμεν, 1 Thess. 5:6) so that the day does not come to them with destruction: "You are not in darkness, brothers, for that day to surprise you like a thief. For you are all children of light, children of the day" (5:4–5). But that same term, "day of the Lord" (2 Thess. 2:2), refers to the "day" (2:3) when the man of lawlessness is revealed and killed by "the appearance of [the Lord's] coming" (2:8). Therefore, the coming of the Lord in 1 Thessalonians 5 and the coming in 2 Thessalonians 2 are the same.

3. The coming of Christ in 2 Thessalonians 1:5–10 is with "mighty angels in flaming fire, inflicting vengeance on those who do not know God" (1:7–8). So those who believe in a pretribulational coming of Christ would say that this coming in 2 Thessalonians 1:5–10 is not the same as the coming in 1 Thessalonians 4:13–18, where Jesus rescues all the living and dead believers out of the world *before* such

fiery judgment. Yet this very coming in 2 Thessalonians 1:6–7 is described as granting relief to believers who are still on the earth when he comes. "God considers it just to repay with affliction those who afflict you, and to grant relief to you who are afflicted as well as to us, when the Lord Jesus is revealed from heaven with his mighty angels." This means that the coming of Christ in 1 Thessalonians 4:13–18 and the coming in 2 Thessalonians 2:5–10 are the same coming.

So when I make the case that Paul's view of the second coming is the same as Jesus's view, I am referring to Paul's unified conception of the second coming in 1 and 2 Thessalonians.

Paul's Conception Shaped by Jesus's

The number and specificity of the parallels between Paul's descriptions of the second coming and Jesus's descriptions are astonishing. I see at least fourteen, depending on how you count them (several are clusters of parallels). I find the conclusion inescapable that the end-time events that Paul describes are the same as those that Jesus describes.

How Jesus's teachings were transmitted to Paul is uncertain. We know that soon after Paul's conversion he spent two weeks with Peter in Jerusalem: "After three years I went up to Jerusalem to visit Cephas and remained with him fifteen days" (Gal. 1:18). This wasn't the only time Paul spent time with Peter. Galatians 2:1–10 describes another visit to Jerusalem, where Peter gave Paul the right hand of fellowship (2:9; cf. Acts 15:3). And we know of at least one visit of Peter to Antioch when Paul was there (Gal. 2:11).

Which means that there was ample opportunity for Paul to learn from eyewitnesses the very language Jesus used to describe his second coming, not to mention the possibility of other oral traditions or written fragments being circulated among the churches.

Following are the fourteen parallels between Paul and Jesus in regard to the way they speak of the second coming.

1. Parousia

Both Jesus and Paul describe the coming of Christ with the typical word *parousia.*

We saw above that Paul uses *parousia* six times in 1 and 2 Thessalonians to refer to the Lord's coming (1 Thess. 2:19; 3:13; 4:15; 5:23; 2 Thess. 2:1, 8). Jesus uses the term in Matthew 24 three times (in addition to his disciples using it by posing the question, "What will be the sign of your coming?" 24:3):

- As the lightning comes from the east and shines as far as the west, so will be the coming [παρουσία] of the Son of Man. (24:27)
- As were the days of Noah, so will be the coming [παρουσία] of the Son of Man. (24:37)
- [As] they were unaware until the flood came and swept them all away, so will be the coming [παρουσία] of the Son of Man. (24:39)

2. Gathering to Meet the Lord

Paul uses the same word as Jesus does to describe the gathering of God's people at the coming of the Lord. Paul uses the noun form; Jesus uses the verb form:

Now concerning the coming of our Lord Jesus Christ and our *being gathered* [ἐπισυναγωγῆς] together to him, we ask you, brothers, not to be quickly shaken in mind or alarmed, either by a spirit or a spoken word, or a letter seeming to be from us, to the effect that the day of the Lord has come. (2 Thess. 2:1–2)

He will send out his angels with a loud trumpet call, and they will *gather* [ἐπισυνάξουσιν] his elect from the four winds, from one end of heaven to the other. (Matt. 24:31)

Second Thessalonians 2:1 is the only place Paul uses this word (in either noun or verb form) in all his writings. Thus, its only usage for him is in reference to the second coming. Matthew uses the word in one other place: Jesus's longing to gather his people as a hen gathers her chicks (Matt. 23:37).

3. Do Not Be Alarmed

Third, in all the New Testament, only Paul and Jesus use the word *alarmed* (θροεῖσθαι). And both apply it to the dangers of being disoriented by the signs of the Lord's second coming:

> Now concerning the coming of our Lord Jesus Christ and our being gathered together to him, we ask you, brothers, not to be quickly shaken in mind or *alarmed* [μηδὲ θροεῖσθαι], either by a spirit or a spoken word, or a letter seeming to be from us, to the effect that the day of the Lord has come. (2 Thess. 2:1–2)

> Many will come in my name, saying, "I am the Christ," and they will lead many astray. And you will hear of wars and rumors of wars. See that you are *not alarmed* [μὴ θροεῖσθε], for this must take place, but the end is not yet. (Matt. 24:5–6; cf. Mark 13:7)

This is remarkable. Only Jesus and Paul use the word. And both use it in exactly the same connection: being unduly alarmed at the signs of the second coming. This points to conceptual unity, if not verbal dependence.

4. Large and Definable Departure from the Faith

While not using the same vocabulary, both Paul and Jesus describe a climactic, end-time apostasy of professing Christians from their faith:

> Let no one deceive you in any way. For that day will not come, unless the *rebellion* [ἀποστασία] comes first. (2 Thess. 2:3)

See that no one *leads you astray* [πλανήσῃ]. For many will come in my name, saying, "I am the Christ," and they will *lead many astray* [πλανήσουσιν]. . . . And then *many will fall away* [σκανδαλισθή- σονται] and betray one another and hate one another. And many false prophets will arise and *lead many astray* [πλανήσουσιν]. . . . For false christs and false prophets will arise and perform great signs and wonders, so as to *lead astray* [πλανῆσαι], if possible, even the elect. (Matt. 24:4–5, 10–11, 24)

Jesus repeats this warning not to be led astray from the faith more than any warning in Matthew 24. The threat of apostasy, or being led astray, or falling away, comes to a climax with such intensity that it threatens the very elect (Matt. 24:24). But Jesus says in verse 22 that "for the sake of the elect those days will be cut short."

Only here in 2 Thessalonians 2:3 does Paul use the word *apostasia*, which the standard Greek lexicon defines as "defiance of established system or authority, *rebellion, abandonment, breach of faith.*"[1] "That day [of the Lord] will not come, unless the [abandonment, breach of faith] comes first" (2 Thess. 2:3). If we ask, "Where did Paul hit upon the idea that, at some future time, Christians will experience a great 'abandonment' of faith?" one answer would be that Paul was inspired by the Holy Spirit, who, Jesus said, "will declare to you [his apostles] the things that are to come" (John 16:13).

But given the amazing parallel with Jesus's repeated warnings of such an abandonment of faith through being led astray (Matt. 24:4, 10, 11, 24), would it not be likely that the Holy Spirit guided Paul into this truth by guiding him into a serious acquaintance with the teachings of Jesus recorded in Matthew 24? Both of them foresaw a time when there

1   W. Arndt, F. W. Danker, W. Bauer, and F. W. Gingrich, *A Greek-English Lexicon of the New Testament and Other Early Christian Literature*, 3rd ed. (Chicago: University of Chicago Press, 2000), 120.

would be something more than typical defections, but rather a large and definable departure of many professing Christians from the faith.

5. Lawlessness

Both Jesus and Paul refer to a growing lawlessness before the coming of the Lord:

> Many false prophets will arise and lead many astray. And because *lawlessness* [ἀνομίαν] will be increased, the love of many will grow cold. (Matt. 24:11–12)

> Let no one deceive you in any way. For that day will not come, unless the rebellion comes first, and the man of *lawlessness* [ἀνομίας] is revealed, the son of destruction. . . . For the mystery of *lawlessness* is already at work. Only he who now restrains it will do so until he is out of the way. And then the *lawless* one will be revealed, whom the Lord Jesus will kill with the breath of his mouth and bring to nothing by the appearance of his coming. The coming of the *lawless* one is by the activity of Satan with all power and false signs and wonders. (2 Thess. 2:3, 7–9)

In both Jesus and Paul, the departure from faith (by deceit and apostasy) is connected with the power of lawlessness. In both, there is a movement from lesser to greater lawlessness. Paul treats the "mystery of lawlessness" as something "already at work" that will become unrestrained at some time in the future (2 Thess. 2:7). Jesus speaks of its increase and its love-destroying effects.

6. Failure of Love

Both Jesus and Paul connect multiplied lawlessness with a failure of love:

> Because *lawlessness* will be increased, the *love* of many will grow cold. (Matt. 24:12)

> The coming of the *lawless* one is by the activity of Satan with all power and false signs and wonders, and with all wicked deception for those who are perishing, because they did not welcome a *love* of the truth in order to be saved. (2 Thess. 2:9–10, my translation)

This link of love's failure could be coincidental. But when seen as part of other connections like lawlessness and apostasy, it seems like another jigsaw piece fitting the picture of a shared conception of the future.

7. Signs and Wonders in the Service of a Lie

Both Paul and Jesus say that deceitful signs and wonders will be done to lead away the disciples:

> The coming of the lawless one is by the activity of Satan with all power and signs and wonders [καὶ σημείοις καὶ τέρασιν] of a *false-hood* [ψεύδους], and with all wicked deception for those who are perishing, because they did not welcome a love of the truth in order to be saved. (2 Thess. 2:9–10, my translation)

> *False* christs and *false* prophets [ψευδόχριστοι καὶ ψευδοπροφῆται] will arise and perform great *signs and wonders* [σημεῖα καὶ τέρατα], so as to lead astray, if possible, even the elect. (Matt. 24:24)

Both Paul and Jesus speak of deception in this end time and link it with the power of "signs and wonders" to deceive through their communicating a lie. Neither denies that the signs and wonders really happen. Rather, both say that they are in the service of a lie.

8. Angels, Trumpet, Clouds, Glory, Power

Both Paul and Jesus speak of angels, trumpet, clouds, glory, and power accompanying the coming of the Lord:

For the Lord himself will descend from heaven with a cry of command, with the voice of an *archangel*, and with the sound of the *trumpet* of God. And the dead in Christ will rise first. Then we who are alive, who are left, will be caught up together with them in the *clouds* to meet the Lord in the air, and so we will always be with the Lord. (1 Thess. 4:16–17)

The Lord Jesus [will be] revealed from heaven with his mighty angels in flaming fire, inflicting vengeance on those who do not know God and on those who do not obey the gospel of our Lord Jesus. They will suffer the punishment of eternal destruction, away from the presence of the Lord and from the *glory* of his *might*. (2 Thess. 1:7–9)

Then will appear in heaven the sign of the Son of Man, and then all the tribes of the earth will mourn, and they will see the Son of Man coming on the *clouds* of heaven with *power* and great *glory*.[2] And he will send out his *angels* with a loud *trumpet* call, and they will gather

---

2 Some interpreters claim that because the language here reflects the language of Dan. 7:13–14, this "coming on the clouds" is not a coming to earth but a coming of the Son of Man to the Ancient of Days in heaven. Dan. 7:13–14 says, "I saw in the night visions, and behold, with the clouds of heaven there came one like a son of man, and he came to the Ancient of Days and was presented before him. And to him was given dominion and glory and a kingdom, that all peoples, nations, and languages should serve him; his dominion is an everlasting dominion, which shall not pass away, and his kingdom one that shall not be destroyed." There are numerous problems with denying that the "coming on the clouds" (in Matt. 24:30 and 26:64) is the second coming of Christ to earth. First, the natural reading of Matthew goes against this denial. Second, the language links with 1 and 2 Thessalonians (which we are examining in this chapter) point to the meaning of the second coming. Third, it is entirely possible, indeed likely, that Jesus was drawing on the *language* of Dan. 7:13–14 rather than *reproducing* the heavenly scene itself. Fourth, even in Dan. 7 the kingdom that is received by the Son of Man coming "*to* the Ancient of Days" is, in turn, given to the saints on earth: "The saints of the Most High shall receive the kingdom and possess the kingdom forever, forever and ever" (7:18; cf. 7:22, 27). It is perfectly natural that the Son of Man would come on the clouds to God to receive the kingdom, and then return on the clouds "in his glory [with] all the angels with him" (Matt. 25:31) and say to his people, "Come, you who are blessed by my Father, inherit the kingdom prepared for you from the foundation of the world" (25:34).

his elect from the four winds, from one end of heaven to the other. (Matt. 24:30–31; cf. 25:31)

With the presence of angels, trumpet, clouds, glory, and power in the description of the appearing of Christ, it would be a stretch to think of Jesus and Paul envisioning different comings of the Lord.

9. Like a Thief

Both Jesus and Paul compare the second coming of Jesus to the coming of a thief in the night:

> But know this, that if the master of the house had known in *what part of the night the thief* [ποίᾳ φυλακῇ ὁ κλέπτης] was coming, he would have stayed awake and would not have let his house be broken into. (Matt. 24:43)

> For you yourselves are fully aware that the day of the Lord will come like a thief in the night [κλέπτης ἐν νυκτὶ]. (1 Thess. 5:2)

The comparison between the coming of Jesus and the coming of a thief is daring. It is used not only by Paul but also Peter (2 Pet. 3:10) and John (Rev. 3:3; 16:15). It is virtually certain that only Jesus would have dared to create such an image, and thus given warrant to his apostles to use it. But use it they did, giving strong evidence of their dependence on the teachings of Jesus and their sharing a common vision of Christ's second coming.

10. Meeting the Lord When He Comes

Both Jesus and Paul use the unusual word *meeting* to describe the way the reception of the Lord will take place at his coming:

But at midnight there was a cry, "Here is the bridegroom! Come out to meet [ἀπάντησιν] him." (Matt. 25:6)

Then we who are alive, who are left, will be caught up together with them in the clouds to meet [ἀπάντησιν] the Lord in the air, and so we will always be with the Lord. (1 Thess. 4:17)

We already pointed out that this word *meeting* is used only three times in the New Testament (Matt. 25:6; Acts 28:15; 1 Thess. 4:17) and always refers to a meeting in which a group goes out and accompanies someone back in.[3] So it is in the parable of the virgins who hear the cry and meet, welcome, and accompany the bridegroom to the wedding feast. And so it is in 1 Thessalonians 4:17, where the risen and living saints rise to meet and welcome and accompany the Lord Jesus to earth.

The fact that both Paul and Jesus use this word only in reference to the second coming is another remarkable linguistic connection.

11. Like a Sudden, Destructive Trap

Only Paul and Jesus use the world *sudden* (αἰφνίδιος). It occurs nowhere else in the New Testament. And again, remarkably, they both use the word in reference to the destruction that the second coming will bring to the unprepared:

While people are saying, "There is peace and security," then *sudden* [αἰφνίδιος] destruction will come upon them as labor pains come upon a pregnant woman, and they will not escape. (1 Thess. 5:3)

But watch yourselves lest your hearts be weighed down with dissipation and drunkenness and cares of this life, and that day come upon you *suddenly* [αἰφνίδιος] like a trap. (Luke 21:34)

3   See chapter 15.

12. Birth Pains

Jesus and Paul use the image of *labor pain* (ὠδίν) to describe the growing, and then climactic, sufferings of the time leading up to Jesus's return:

> Nation will rise against nation, and kingdom against kingdom, and there will be famines and earthquakes in various places. All these are but the beginning of the birth pains [ὠδίνων]. (Matt. 24:7–8; cf. Mark 13:8)

> You yourselves are fully aware that the day of the Lord will come like a thief in the night. While people are saying, "There is peace and security," then sudden destruction will come upon them as labor pains [ὠδίν] come upon a pregnant woman, and they will not escape. (1 Thess. 5:2–3)

Though Paul uses the imagery of birth pains more widely (Rom. 8:22; Gal. 4:19, 27), he and Jesus use the noun (ὠδίν, birth pain) only once each, and that is in reference to end-time events that take unbelievers totally off guard and bring destruction. "They will not escape" (1 Thess. 5:3).

13. Believers Will Escape

Jesus and Paul both refer to the necessity or impossibility of *escaping* (ἐκφεύγω) from the destructive forces coming on the unprepared at the second coming:

> Stay awake at all times, praying that you may have strength to escape [ἐκφυγεῖν] all these things that are going to take place, and to stand before the Son of Man. (Luke 21:36)

> While people are saying, "There is peace and security," then sudden destruction will come upon them as labor pains come

upon a pregnant woman, and they will not escape [ἐκφύγωσιν].
(1 Thess. 5:3)

Jesus uses this word (ἐκφεύγω) only once. Paul uses it three times, one
of which parallels Jesus's usage, namely, the hope of escape from the
suddenness of Christ's coming. Both Jesus and Paul say that believers
will not be destroyed by this suddenness. Paul says, "You are not in darkness, brothers, for that day to surprise you like a thief" (1 Thess. 5:4).
And Jesus says, "[Pray] that you have strength to escape" (Luke 21:36).

14. Stay Awake, Stay Sober

Paul and Jesus use the language of vigilant *watching* and *not sleeping*
and not *getting drunk* in relation to being ready for the second coming:

> You yourselves are fully aware that the day of the Lord will come like
> a thief in the night. . . . But you are not in darkness, brothers, for
> that day to surprise you like a thief. . . . We are not of the night or
> of the darkness. So then let us *not sleep* [μὴ καθεύδωμεν], as others
> do, but let us *keep awake* [γρηγορῶμεν] and be sober [νήφωμεν].
> For those who sleep, sleep at night, and those who get drunk, are
> drunk at night [μεθυσκόμενοι νυκτὸς μεθύουσιν]. (1 Thess. 5:2–7)

> *Stay awake* [γρηγορεῖτε], for you do not know on what day your
> Lord is coming. . . . If that wicked servant says to himself, "My master
> is delayed," and begins to beat his fellow servants and eats and drinks
> with *drunkards* [μεθυόντων], the master of that servant will come
> on a day when he does not expect him and at an hour he does not
> know and will cut him in pieces. (Matt. 24:42–51)

> Watch yourselves lest your hearts be weighed down with dissipation
> and *drunkenness* [μέθη] and cares of this life, and that day come upon
> you suddenly like a trap. (Luke 21:34)

Concerning that day or that hour, no one knows, not even the angels in heaven, nor the Son, but only the Father. Be on guard, keep
awake. . . . for you do not know when the master of the house will
come . . . lest he come suddenly and find you *asleep* [καθεύδοντας].
(Mark 13:32–36)

Both Paul and Jesus use the imagery of not sleeping (καθεύδω) but
staying awake (γρηγορέω), and not being drunk (μεθύω) but being
sober (νήφω)—both images in relation to readiness for the second
coming.

What's the Point?

What is the upshot of what we have seen in comparing Jesus's and
Paul's conception of the end time? Here are the building blocks of my
argument:

First, the Thessalonian letters contain a single, unified view of the
second coming. Throughout the two letters, Paul is talking about
one event, the *parousia* (coming), the day of the Lord.

Second, that unified view includes the final coming of the Lord on
the clouds (1 Thess. 4:17) to rescue his people (2 Thess. 1:7), deal
vengeance to unbelievers (1:6), kill the man of lawlessness (2:8), and
raise all believers from the dead (1 Thess. 4:16).

Third, the language Paul uses to describe this single future event is
so similar to the language of Jesus, especially in Matthew 24, that it
is very likely they are speaking of the same event.[4]

---

4   By way of reminder, notice how the parallels with Paul's view permeate the whole of Matt. 24:
    parousia (24:27), gathering (24:31), not alarmed (24:6), deception and loss of faith (24:4, 10, 11,
    24), lawlessness (24:12), lovelessness (24:12), signs and wonders (24:24), clouds, power, glory,
    trumpet (24:30–31), birth pains (24:8).

Fourth, therefore, in Matthew 24 Jesus has in view not just prefigurations of the second coming in the events of the first century, but
also the final events Paul describes in the Thessalonian letters. It is
a mistake to *limit* the reference of Matthew 24:4–31 to the generation immediately following Jesus, climaxing in the destruction of
Jerusalem in AD 70.[5]

The arguments could be multiplied in support of this fourth point.
For example, it seems unduly rigid to insist that when the disciples
asked Jesus in Matthew 24:3, "When will these things be, and what
will be the sign of your coming and of the end of the age?" they had
two different times in mind (near and distant), or that Jesus would
answer their question in carefully sequential order, as if they did have
two times in mind (verses 4–35 answering the question about the
destruction of Jerusalem, and verses 36–51 answering the question
about the end of the age).

Therefore, to argue from this presumed structure that Matthew
24:4–35 relates only to the first century (pre-AD 70) and the rest of the
chapter (24:36–51) describes the yet-future second coming, is, I think,
unwarranted. I suggest that both the disciples' questions (Matt. 24:3)
and Jesus's answer reflect what I have called "prophetic perspective"
(see chapter 8, note 1). The near and distant mountain ranges of the

5   See note 4 in chapter 13. Some interpreters of Matthew 24 argue that when the disciples ask in
    verse 3, "When will these things be?" they are only referring to the destruction of the temple, and
    that Jesus answers this part of their question in verses 4–35. In that view the language of those
    verses refers only to the first century. So, for example, when Jesus says in verse 14, "And this gospel
    of the kingdom will be proclaimed throughout the whole world as a testimony to all nations,
    and then the end will come," Sam Storms says, "As far as Jesus' prophecy in Matthew 24:14 is
    concerned, his point is that following his resurrection the gospel will be preached outside the
    boundaries of Judea, such that the Gentile nations in the inhabited world known as the Roman
    Empire will hear the testimony of his redemptive work. Only thereafter, says Jesus, will the 'end'
    of the city and temple occur. . . . The Great Commission in Matthew 28 leaves no loopholes. We
    simply *must* labor in the grace of God to proclaim the gospel of God and to make disciples of all
    nations. My point . . . is simply that Matthew 24:14 is not concerned with that task." Sam Storms,
    Kingdom Come: The Amillennial Alternative (Fearn, Ross-shire, UK: Mentor, 2013), 242–44.

future are seen as a whole, without making precise distinctions between them. Thus, Matthew 24 speaks in ways that throughout the chapter inform our understanding of both the ongoing history of this age and the climactic end at the second coming.

"End of the Age"

When the disciples used the phrase "end of the age" (συντελείας τοῦ αἰῶνος, Matt. 24:3), they were very likely using it the way Jesus had used it in their hearing, namely, to signify the very end of this age marked by the judgment on unbelievers. For example:

> The harvest is *the end of the age* [συντέλεια αἰῶνός], and the reapers are angels. Just as the weeds are gathered and burned with fire, so will it be at *the end of the age* [τῇ συντελείᾳ τοῦ αἰῶνος]. The Son of Man will send his angels, and they will gather out of his kingdom all causes of sin and all law-breakers, and throw them into the fiery furnace. In that place there will be weeping and gnashing of teeth. Then the righteous will shine like the sun in the kingdom of their Father. He who has ears, let him hear. (Matt. 13:39–43; cf. 13:49; 28:20)

It is unlikely that as Jesus began to speak in Matthew 24, the disciples would have understood verses 4–35 to be unrelated to this "end of the age." And all the parallels we have seen between Jesus's words and Paul's words indicate that verses 4–35 are interwoven with references to the very end of the age that is yet future.

Son of Man Coming in Universal Judgment

Let me offer one more supporting observation. The disciples had similarly heard Jesus speak of the coming of *the Son of Man* "with his angels in the glory of his Father" (Matt. 16:27). In that text, Jesus says that at this coming he will "repay each person according to what he has done." So this is a prediction of the Son of Man coming *at the very end of the age*, climaxing with a judgment for every person. Therefore, I find it unlikely that in Matthew 24 the references *to the coming of the Son of Man*—for example, in verses 27 and 30—would be limited to AD 70.

Gathering Up the Threads of the Argument

Let's gather up the threads of the last four chapters and see if we can make clear the tapestry we are weaving. Our overarching question in part 2 is how we should think about the time of Jesus's appearing. To address that question, we need to answer three others.

First, did Jesus predict that he would return to wrap up this present age within one generation? No, he did not (chapter 13).

Second, what does the New Testament mean by saying Jesus will return soon? I suggested three meanings and proposed three terms: *potentially* soon, *holistically* soon, and *divinely* soon (chapter 14).

Third, does the New Testament teach an *any-moment* return of Jesus? I suggested there are three steps in answering this question:

1. Does the New Testament teach an *any-moment rapture* that removes the church from the world, followed some years later by the second coming of Christ to establish his kingdom? I answered no (chapter 15).

2. Is the vision of the end time in 1 and 2 Thessalonians and in the teaching of Jesus (especially in Matthew 24) the same? I answered yes (chapter 16). The import of this last answer is that Matthew 24 and the Thessalonian letters may both inform our answer to the third and final question about an any-moment return of the Lord.

3. Does the New Testament teach that there are events yet to happen before the Lord will return? If there are, that would likely answer our question about the any-moment appearing of Christ. To that question we turn in the next chapter.

17

What Must Happen before the Lord's Appearing?

WE COME NOW TO OUR THIRD STEP in seeking to answer the question, Does the New Testament teach that Jesus may come at any moment? This third step is to show some of the events that are yet to happen before Christ comes.

The apostle Paul shows us quite explicitly that it is right to discern what events must precede the Lord's coming. When confronted with the apparent hysteria about the day of the Lord being already present, he responded, "Let no one deceive you in any way.[1] For that day will not come, unless the rebellion comes first, and the man of lawlessness is revealed" (2 Thess. 2:3). Paul's answer in his day to the question, What events are yet to happen before Christ comes? is twofold: (1) the rebellion must come, and (2) the man of lawlessness must be revealed.

These two events are still to come, as I write in the fall of 2021. Paul does not treat these two events as so ambiguous that they cannot be

---

[1] Just as Jesus said, "See that no one leads you astray" (Matt. 24:4). Similar to Paul's warning, the danger was that one might be caught up in the end-time frenzy and leap to the conclusion that one of the false christs was real and that the day of the Lord was at hand. "Many will come in my name, saying, 'I am the Christ,' and they will lead many astray" (Matt. 24:5).

discerned when they come. The appearance of the man of lawlessness will be globally sensational and brief:[2]

> [He] opposes and exalts himself against every so-called god or object of worship, so that he takes his seat in the temple of God, proclaiming himself to be God. . . . And then the lawless one will be revealed, whom the Lord Jesus will kill with the breath of his mouth and bring to nothing by the appearance of his coming. (2 Thess. 2:4, 8)

For any of the Thessalonians who were prone to think that this man of lawlessness was far in the future, or for any of us today who are prone to think that he is far in the future, Paul adds this remarkable warning: "The mystery of lawlessness is *already* at work" (2 Thess. 2:7). Already—in the first century, and today.

This is similar to John's way of speaking about the antichrist: "Children, it is the last hour, and as you have heard that antichrist is coming, so now many antichrists have come. Therefore we know that it is the last hour" (1 John 2:18). Paul does not say, "Many men of lawlessness have come," but he might have. What he says is, "The mystery of lawlessness is *already* at work."

The point is this: don't relax your vigilance, thinking that the man of lawlessness (or antichrist) is far off, because the very essence of his deceptive power is now at work and could so deceive you that you would be oblivious to the deadliness of his arrival. Let me say that again: just when you think the end is far in the future, the satanic mystery of lawlessness may so cloud your mind with deception that you cannot see the soon arrival of the man of lawlessness.

---

2 See chapter 9 for a description of this end-time figure.

Coming Rebellion

The "rebellion" (or apostasy) is also still in the future. This event is less definite than the appearance of a man who proclaims himself to be God, but it can't be reduced to a centuries-long process of seasons of apostasy. Paul believed that it would be discernible enough that he could use the absence of it as evidence that the day of the Lord was not yet at hand.

It would be true to say, "The mystery of *apostasy* has *already* begun," just as Paul says, "The mystery of *lawlessness* is *already* at work." In fact, Paul does speak this way about a coming defection from true faith. He says in 1 Timothy 4:1, "Now the Spirit expressly says that in later times some will depart from the faith by devoting themselves to deceitful spirits and teachings of demons," and he treats those people as already present and deals with their error (4:1–5).

Again Paul says, "Understand this, that in the last days there will come times of difficulty. For people will be lovers of self, lovers of money . . ." Then he follows this end-time prediction with, "Avoid such people" (2 Tim. 3:1–2, 5). In other words, Paul views the signs of the end as more or less always with us.[3] What will be different about the end is the degree and intensity of evil. Paul shows this by referring to the present "restraint" (2 Thess. 2:7) on evil, which will be removed, thus giving rise to greater evil at the end.

The fact that there are historically repeated prefigurations of end-time events means that most of the precursors of the second coming are not of such a nature that they allow for discerning the closeness of the end. They are real, but also imprecise. They are meant to make us vigilant, knowing that very quickly, the common evils of history might escalate into the climactic events of the end.

---

3 This understanding of the presence of the future is part of the "holistic" view of the near and distant future that I unfolded in chapter 14 under the subhead "Holistically Near."

Wars and the Jerusalem War

With that in mind, consider what Jesus says is coming, most of which has in various ways already come. I have argued that Matthew 24 should not be limited in reference to the first century but that much of verses 4–35, in concert with Paul's teaching, has reference to the end of the age. I have no disagreement that in Matthew 24 (especially verses 15–20), Jesus sees the catastrophe of Jerusalem's destruction in AD 70:

> So when you see the abomination of desolation spoken of by the prophet Daniel, standing in the holy place (let the reader understand), then let those who are in Judea flee to the mountains. Let the one who is on the housetop not go down to take what is in his house, and let the one who is in the field not turn back to take his cloak. And alas for women who are pregnant and for those who are nursing infants in those days! Pray that your flight may not be in winter or on a Sabbath. (Matt. 24:15–20)

This catastrophic event is the kind of horror that has marked history for two thousand years. Jesus weaves it into his depiction of events leading to the final coming of the Son of Man because life in this age will be marked more or less by this kind of end-time evil all the way along. The wars against Jerusalem are a concrete instance of the general prediction:

> You will hear of wars and rumors of wars. See that you are not alarmed, for this must take place, but the end is not yet. For nation will rise against nation, and kingdom against kingdom, and there will be famines and earthquakes in various places. All these are but the beginning of the birth pains. (Matt. 24:6–8)

Even the destruction of Jerusalem is the "beginning of the birth pains." "The end is not yet." Those words have been spoken over a thousand unspeakable calamities and dreadful persecutions in the last two thousand years. For those who went through the calamities, or died in them, they felt the full force of the final evils of this age. The end-time birth pains had indeed begun.

But there is no calculating how many earthquakes (Matt. 24:7), or how many famines (24:7), or how many wars (24:6), or how many false christs (24:5) or false prophets (24:10), or how much lawlessness or coldness of love (24:12), or what intensity of tribulation (24:9, 21, 29) will signal with certainty how near the second coming is. Let me say that again: most of the "signs" of the end that Jesus gives us are the kinds of events that do not lend themselves to date-setting. Quantities and intensities and frequencies of such events are not precise indicators of how close the coming of the Lord is.

Birth Pains Are Not Pointless

To be sure, we should obey Jesus when he says:

> From the fig tree learn its lesson: as soon as its branch becomes tender and puts out its leaves, you know that summer is near. So also, when you see all these things, you know that he is near, at the very gates. Truly, I say to you, this generation will not pass away until all these things take place. (Matt. 24:32–34)

Obeying these words does not involve us in doing what Jesus said that he himself could not do, namely, know the time of his coming (Matt. 24:36). Nevertheless, Jesus tells us to look at the "fig tree." He tells us to look at "all these things"—the kinds of events that were happening in the next generation and in virtually every generation since that time.

Look at them. Let whatever measure or quantity or intensity or frequency you see in your time and place remind you that these are the birth pains of the end. Birth pains are not pointless. Let the false christs and the wars and world conflicts and famines and earthquakes and hatred and betrayals and apostasy and tribulation remind you that the end is near—*potentially* near, *holistically* near, *divinely* near.[4]

Promise of Mission Triumph

What about the promise that "this gospel of the kingdom will be proclaimed throughout the whole world as a testimony to all nations, and then the end will come" (Matt. 24:14)? Does that enable us to know the time of Jesus's coming?

Those who believe that the events prophesied in Matthew 24:4–35 should be limited to the events leading up to AD 70 argue that the mission to the nations prophesied in verse 14 was fulfilled by that date.[5] And "the end" was AD 70. I argued extensively in chapter 16 that I think it is a mistake to limit these events to the first century. Besides those arguments, consider three observations relating to the promise that "the end" will come after the gospel has spread to the degree that God intends.

1. "Then the End Will Come"

It is likely that the term "the end" ("then *the end* will come") refers to the same reality the disciples asked about: "Tell us, when will these things be, and what will be the sign of your coming and of *the end* of the age?" (Matt. 24:3). Part of Jesus's answer is that the gospel will reach the nations, "and then *the end* will come." But the term the disciples used was "the end of the age."

The disciples had heard Jesus use this term. In Matthew 13:36–50, for example, it appears three times. In all three cases, it refers to the time of final judgment when good and evil are separated. "So it will be at *the end of the age*. The angels will come out and separate the evil from the righteous" (Matt. 13:49). "Just as the weeds are gathered

WHAT MUST HAPPEN . . . ? 239

and burned with fire, so will it be at *the end of the age*" (Matt. 13:40). Therefore, there is no good reason to think this is not what the disciples are asking about and what Jesus is referring to in his answer. The end that will come when the gospel has reached the nations is the universal judgment, when good and evil are separated. This *end* is not a reference merely to AD 70.

2. End Is Not Yet, nor Mission Done

In the Great Commission of Matthew 28:19–20, Jesus turns the promise of Matthew 24:14 into a command:

> Go therefore and make disciples of all nations, baptizing them in the name of the Father and of the Son and of the Holy Spirit, teaching them to observe all that I have commanded you. And behold, I am with you always, to *the end of the age* [τῆς συντελείας τοῦ αἰῶνος].

Here again is the term "the end of the age," the same term the disciples ask about in Matthew 24:3 (συντελείας τοῦ αἰῶνος) and that Jesus alludes to in Matthew 24:14: "Then the end will come." Only here, in Matthew 28:20, the mission goes on to that same "end of the age," which is marked not by the destruction of Jerusalem, but by the universal judgment (Matt. 13:40, 49).

Therefore "the end" that Jesus promises will come when the gospel reaches its final extent and depth is "the end" that has not yet come, for the mission is still underway. It is sustained by the Lord's promise to be with us to the end. And when it is complete, the end will come. That is, the Lord will come.

3. In AD 70, the End Was Not Yet

Third, in Matthew 24:6, Jesus says, "You will hear of wars and rumors of wars. See that you are not alarmed, for this must take place, but the end is not yet." I take this "end" to be the same as the "end" in verses

3 and 14 (even though the same Greek word is not used in both). But here in verse 6, Jesus says that wars will not mean the end. The natural meaning would be that this includes the war against Jerusalem in AD 70.

Thus, Jesus is saying in essence, "When you see the horrors of the war against Jerusalem, don't be alarmed. The end is not yet" (Matt. 24:6). Therefore, "the end" is not AD 70. Therefore, the words of Matthew 24:14 ("This gospel of the kingdom will be proclaimed throughout the whole world as a testimony to all nations, and then *the end* will come") refer not to AD 70 as the end but rather to the end of this age, climaxing in the second coming.

I conclude, therefore, that the promise of Matthew 24:14 means that the Great Commission will be obeyed to the end of this present age, and when it is completed, Christ will return.

Finishing the Great Commission Is Hard to Recognize

I have tried in other publications to define the nature and extent of "all nations" in Matthew 24:14 and 28:19. In other words, I have wrestled with what the completion of the Great Commission looks like.[6] But on the basis of almost fifty pages of wrestling, my conclusion is unsatisfactory to anyone hoping we could use the progress of world evangelization for predicting the time of the Lord's return. For example, I write, "The point rather is that as long as the Lord has not returned, there must be more people groups to reach, and we should keep on reaching them."[7]

The only change in that sentence I would make today is to add that that the *completion* of the Great Commission includes the extent of evangelization and obedience *within* people groups, not just reaching new ones. This is the point of 2 Peter 3:9, which teaches

6   John Piper, *Let the Nations Be Glad!: The Supremacy of God in Missions* (Grand Rapids, MI: Baker Academic, 2010), 177–24.
7   Piper, *Let the Nations Be Glad!*, 212.

that the second coming is delayed for the sake of the full ingathering of the elect.[8]

Therefore, Matthew 24:14 teaches us that every advance of the gospel is both *encouragement* that the Lord is nearing and *incentive* to "hasten" his coming (2 Pet. 3:12) by giving great energy to world evangelization.

What Will Happen before Christ Comes?

Of all the events leading up to the second coming, two are more precise than the others: the appearance of the man of lawlessness (2 Thess. 2:3) and the cosmic events described in Matthew 24:29–30.[9] Jesus describes the cosmic events like this:

> Immediately after the tribulation of those days the sun will be darkened, and the moon will not give its light, and the stars will fall from heaven, and the powers of the heavens will be shaken. Then will appear in heaven the sign of the Son of Man, and then all the tribes of the earth will mourn, and they will see the Son of Man coming on the clouds of heaven with power and great glory. (Matt. 24:29–30)

I understand these cosmic events as real cosmological events, just as the coming of Christ is a real bodily, spatial, visible, audible event. With the incarnation of Jesus Christ in literal flesh and blood, and with the resurrection in a body that ate fish and showed wounds,

8   See chapter 14, note 3.
9   I have made the case (in chapter 9 and earlier in this chapter) that the apostasy or rebellion of the last days mentioned in 2 Thess. 2:3 is treated by Paul as a discernible historical occurrence that he can cite as a reason the second coming has not happened yet: "That day will not come, unless the *rebellion* comes first, and the man of lawlessness is revealed." So I could list this event along with the coming of the man of lawlessness as another event that must happen before the Lord comes. That is true. The reason I'm not dealing with the apostasy separately is that Paul seems to view it as very closely connected with the appearing of the man of lawlessness rather than as a distinct event. In fact, it seems to me that after mentioning both the man of lawlessness and the apostasy in 2 Thess. 2:3, he then deals with the man of lawlessness in verses 4–8 and then integrally deals with the apostasy in verses 9–12. So when I focus now on the coming of the man of lawlessness, I am thinking that the apostasy is part of his coming.

and with the ascension of that body on literal clouds, and with the promise of the coming of that glorious body to a literal earth, we should be slow to treat the signs accompanying the second coming as metaphorical. Jesus and the apostles give no hint that they are not describing cosmological reality.[10]

From the way Jesus describes the events of Matthew 24:29–30, it seems that they happen in immediate conjunction with the appearing of Christ. These signs do not appear to happen far enough in advance of his coming that they could be used to calculate his near arrival. They happen *at* his coming. I do not know what a darkened sun will be like (how dark?), or a moon not shining (eclipse?), or stars falling (disappearing—or meteorites?), or the heavens shaken (with thunder?). I do not know what the "sign of the Son of Man" is, but it seems to be virtually simultaneous with Christ's appearing.

Therefore, these cosmic events do not tell us when the end *will* come. They tell us that it is now here. The cosmic displays, Jesus says, will announce his appearing like lightning: "As the lightning comes from the east and shines as far as the west, so will be the coming of the Son of Man" (Matt. 24:27).

No Warrant to Assume He Is Not Near

We do not know how much time must elapse before Jesus comes. Let that be clear. We do not know. We err to say otherwise. But we may err in the other direction as well—presuming to think that he must not be near. You may remember that I made the statement earlier that we have no warrant to be sure that Christ's coming is ever more than a few years away. To be clear, I do not know if Christ is six years or sixty years or six hundred years away. What I am saying here is that no one

---

10 The prophets' use of such language is regularly in contexts marked by what I have called "prophetic perspective" in which a near event (like the destruction of Babylon) and a distant event (like the universal judgment) are spoken of with no temporal distinction. One would need to be careful, therefore, not to assume that a reference to stars and sun being darkened (e.g., Isa. 13:10) is metaphorical in such a context, when in fact it may have a literal fulfillment at the last day.

has biblical warrant for being sure Jesus is more than a very few years away, like five to six years. And it may be closer.

Man of Lawlessness Has Not Yet Come

Why do I say that? Paul said the man of lawlessness would be identifiable enough that we would be able to know he has not yet come. Otherwise, his argument in 2 Thessalonians 2:3 breaks down: "Let no one deceive you in any way. For that day [the day of the Lord's coming] will not come, unless . . . the man of lawlessness is revealed." The argument is this: you can avoid the deception that the Lord has already come by realizing the man of lawlessness has not yet come. His coming is discernible. You can know when he has come.

The fact that church history is strewn with false identifications of the man of lawlessness does not contradict Paul's point. What is needed is not the rejection of Paul's teaching in order to avoid its misuse, but rather the improvement of our teaching about what Paul meant.

Why Five to Seven Years?

Why did I say that at no time do we have a warrant to believe that Christ's coming is ever more than a few years away, say five or six? Here's my reasoning. On almost any reckoning, the man of lawlessness does not last long before the Lord Jesus kills him by his coming. Paul says, "The lawless one will be revealed, whom the Lord Jesus will kill with the breath of his mouth and bring to nothing by the appearance of his coming" (2 Thess. 2:8). He survives long enough to do what Paul says he will do: "[He] opposes and exalts himself against every so-called god or object of worship, so that he takes his seat in the temple of God, proclaiming himself to be God" (2 Thess. 2:4). But his vaunted reign cannot be long, because his rise to prominence and his destruction by the Lord's coming are described as virtually one event: "The lawless one will be revealed, whom the Lord Jesus will . . . bring to nothing by his appearing" (2 Thess. 2:8).

Combine that fact with the fact that the man of lawlessness could emerge with global significance very quickly. We should think not only in terms of ordinary, natural processes leading to his rise, but also of extraordinary, supernatural processes—both demonic and divine. Paul says, "The coming of the lawless one is by the activity of Satan with all power and lying signs and wonders" (2 Thess. 2:9, my translation). Then he adds, "God sends them a strong delusion, so that they may believe what is false" (2 Thess. 2:11). It is easily conceivable that such divine and satanic power, with supernatural signs and wonders, would sway millions of people globally in a matter of months.

Therefore, combining how short the time may be from any given moment in history until the emergence of the man of lawlessness (possibly months, not years), with how short his dominance will be before the Lord destroys him by his coming,[11] I conclude that at no time do we ever have warrant to say with confidence that the Lord is more than a very few years away, say five or six years. And it could be much shorter. God's sovereignty over the man of lawlessness and the final apostasy in the church should guard us from thinking we know how long it will take for those events to transpire. And as Jesus said, to presume upon a certain delay is suicidal folly (Matt. 24:48–51).

Be sure you understand what I am not saying, as well as what I am saying. I am not saying that the Lord will come within five or six

11 One might reckon that the great tribulation is the seventieth week of Dan. 9:24–25, and is thus seven years long. Then one might note from Revelation that the beast or the antichrist (who is probably the same as the man of lawlessness) will hold sway in much of this time. If this line of thought is followed, then seven years is the maximum the man of lawlessness will hold sway. But even if we follow this line, numbers are often symbolic in Scripture. And add to that what Jesus says about those days of tribulation: "And if those days had not been cut short, no human being would be saved. But for the sake of the elect those days will be cut short" (Matt. 24:22). In view of this divine "shortening" of the days, and in view of the frequently symbolic character of the number seven, I do not believe we can say for sure how quickly the man of lawlessness will rise, nor how long it will be before the Lord kills him. But all things considered, five to seven years does not seem like a careless estimation for the length of time it could take from his appearance until the coming of Christ, when the man of lawlessness is destroyed (2 Thess. 2:8).

years. We do not know. I am saying, no one can legitimately say with confidence that he *cannot* or *is not* coming in such a short time, or even shorter.

Should We Expect an Any-Moment Return?

Now we have come to the end of our three-step response to the question, Does the New Testament teach that Jesus may come at any moment? My answer is no. The man of lawlessness must come first (2 Thess. 2:3). His coming will be discernible. As I write in the fall of 2021, he has not yet come. Therefore, the appearing of the Lord Jesus, as I write, is probably some months or years away. As you are reading, matters could be very different.

What about Watching and Vigilance?

Now the question is, How then shall we live? Especially pressing is the question of whether the absence of an any-moment expectation weakens or undermines Jesus's repeated commands to watch (βλέπετε, Mark 13:33), and be awake (ἀγρυπνεῖτε, 13:33), and be alert (γρη-γορεῖτε, 13:35), and be ready (γίνεσθε ἕτοιμοι, Luke 12:40), and take heed (προσέχετε, 21:34 KJV). Do these exhortations assume an any-moment coming of the Lord? One of the reasons Jesus gives for such vigilance is that "you know neither the day nor the hour" (Matt. 25:13). This issue of wakefulness and vigilance will be our first concern in part 3, after we set the stage in the prelude.

PART 3

HOW THEN
SHALL WE LIVE?

LIVING BETWEEN THE TWO APPEARINGS OF CHRIST

WE LIVE BETWEEN THE FIRST and second appearing of Jesus Christ:

> He has appeared once for all at the end of the ages to put away sin by the sacrifice of himself. . . . Having been offered once to bear the sins of many, [he] will appear a second time . . . to save those who are eagerly waiting for him. (Heb. 9:26–28)

The Old Testament prophets did not see clearly that the coming of the Messiah to establish his eternal kingdom would involve a *first coming* to inaugurate his kingdom through death and resurrection, and then, after many centuries, a *second coming* to bring the kingdom to consummation. Even the angelic announcement to Mary did not make clear that the eternal reign of Christ on the throne of David would be established not all at once but in stages:

> Behold, you will conceive in your womb and bear a son, and you shall call his name Jesus. . . . And the Lord God will give to him the throne of his father David, and he will reign over the house of Jacob forever, and of his kingdom there will be no end. (Luke 1:31–33)

It perplexed the people of his day when Jesus said, on the one hand, "The kingdom of God is in the midst of you" (Luke 17:21), and then "proceeded to tell a parable, because . . . they [mistakenly] supposed that the kingdom of God was to appear immediately" (19:11). The kingdom of God was in some sense present. And yet, in some sense, it was not present, but coming.

Uniqueness of Christian Ethics: Already and Not Yet

This perplexity is at the heart of the uniqueness of Christianity and how we are to live in this age. Something absolutely astonishing and wonderful has already happened in the incarnation of the Son of God. And yet something astonishing and wonderful is yet to happen that will complete what Christ began on earth. Salvation has come. And salvation is coming. We pursue with moral earnestness our full salvation in the future, because salvation has already been secured for us in the past. Because of Christ's work in his first coming, we are already forgiven (Col. 1:14), justified (Rom. 5:1), adopted (Gal. 4:5–6), secure (Rom. 8:30)—all of this because of our union with Christ through faith.

But that completed right standing with God does not make us passive or careless. Rather, it is the secure ground where we stand as we fight for a holiness without which we will not see the Lord (Heb. 12:14). The fight is real because final salvation is *not yet* our present experience (Rom. 13:11). But the victory is sure because we are *already* saved (Eph. 2:8–9).

This is where all Christians live: between the first and second appearing of Christ. Between what he *has done* for us, and what he *will do* for us. Between what he has become for us, and what he will fully be for us. Between the *already* and the *not yet*. For example:

- We say with Paul, "Not that I have *already* obtained [the resurrection] or am *already* perfect, but I press on to make it my own, because Christ Jesus has made me his own" (Phil. 3:12). Already grasped by Christ, but not yet finished reaching for his fullness.
- We have already been "raised with Christ." Therefore, we "seek the things that are above" (Col. 3:1), because they are not yet in our possession for the fullest enjoyment.
- Our old self has already been "crucified with [Christ]." But we must "consider ourselves dead to sin" (Rom. 6:6, 11) because we are not yet under the full sway of our death to sin and life to God.
- We "really are [already] unleavened." Therefore, we must "cleanse out the old [not-yet eradicated] leaven" (1 Cor. 5:7).
- God "has [already] delivered us from the domain of darkness and transferred us to the kingdom of his beloved Son" (Col. 1:13). And "the Lord will . . . bring [us] safely into his heavenly kingdom" (2 Tim. 4:18) because we are *not yet* in the full experience of the kingdom's treasures.

Living by Love Because of Past and Future Grace

The relevance of this *already–not yet* condition between the two appearings of Christ can be seen in this: we take into account both the *backward* look to the first appearing of Christ and the *forward* look to the second appearing. How we live is shaped and governed by the *cherished past grace* of God and the *trusted future grace* of God.

For example, "We love because [God] first loved us" (1 John 4:19). And we love "because of the hope laid up for [us] in heaven" (Col. 1:5). Our love for others is shaped and grounded by God's love for us in the past and his love for us in the future. We are willing to suffer for doing good "because Christ also suffered for [us]" (1 Pet. 2:21). And we are willing to suffer for doing good in order "that [we] may obtain a blessing" (1 Pet. 3:9). Cherished past grace and trusted future grace empower our obedience. The *already* and the *not yet* are both essential motives in Christian behavior.

Therefore, as I focus in part 3 on the practical effects of Christ's future appearing, do not think that I am unmindful of the precious and powerful and essential effects of what Christ has *already* done for us. No future motive would have any effect for Christ-exalting obedience if the massive marvel of atonement by the blood of Christ had not already happened. The *already* forgiven, justified, adopted, Spirit-inhabited Christian soul is the only soil where the *promises* of Christ can take root and bear the fruit of obedience.

It should be plain, then, that *all* attitudes and words and actions that are commended in the New Testament could be the topic of part 3 of this book. All exhortations and admonitions and warnings and commands and moral examples are to be carried out in light of the cross of Christ and in light of his second coming.

So one answer to the question, "How then shall we live?" would be, "Live the way the whole New Testament tells you to live," because the whole New Testament is written in light of the second coming. How then shall I limit what I discuss? My answer is that I will deal with attitudes and words and behaviors that are *explicitly* connected with the second coming of Christ.

18

End-Time Alertness and
Love for Christ's Appearing

AT THE CLOSE OF CHAPTER 17, I said that our first concern in part 3 would be the effect that the second coming has on our expectancy, wakefulness, and vigilance. So that is where we begin.

Stay Awake—You Do Not Know the Day or Hour

What did Jesus mean in speaking about our relationship to the second coming when he said, "Stay awake" (γρηγορεῖτε, Matt. 24:42), "be ready" (γίνεσθε ἕτοιμοι, Luke 12:40), "be vigilant" (ἀγρυπνεῖτε, 21:36), "be on guard" (βλέπετε, Mark 13:23), and "watch yourselves" (προσέχετε δὲ ἑαυτοῖς, Luke 21:34)? We can answer this by looking briefly at several key passages. I start with the parable of the ten virgins because the meaning of "stay awake" is illustrated most clearly there:

> Then the kingdom of heaven will be like ten virgins who took their lamps and went to meet the bridegroom. Five of them were foolish, and five were wise. For when the foolish took their lamps, they took no oil with them, but the wise took flasks of oil with their lamps. As the bridegroom was delayed, *they all became drowsy and slept.* But

at midnight there was a cry, "Here is the bridegroom! Come out to meet him." Then all those virgins rose and trimmed their lamps. And the foolish said to the wise, "Give us some of your oil, for our lamps are going out." But the wise answered, saying, "Since there will not be enough for us and for you, go rather to the dealers and buy for yourselves." And while they were going to buy, the bridegroom came, and those who were ready went in with him to the marriage feast, and the door was shut. Afterward the other virgins came also, saying, "Lord, lord, open to us." But he answered, "Truly, I say to you, I do not know you." Watch [γρηγορεῖτε] therefore, for you know neither the day nor the hour. (Matt. 25:1–13)

What is most illuminating about this parable is that all ten virgins—the wise and the foolish—fall asleep while they are waiting for the bridegroom. "They all became drowsy and slept" (Matt. 25:5). That would have been a flaw if they were guards or watchmen. But evidently it was not a flaw for the virgin entourage, which was charged with leading the bridegroom into the marriage feast, provided they were awake in time to fulfill their responsibility. The five wise virgins take steps to do what they were expected to do. They have sufficient oil for the welcome. They rise from sleep at the call. They trim their lamps, and meet the bridegroom. The foolish virgins fail to provide oil. They did not fulfill what they were expected to do.

It might seem strange, therefore, when the parable ends with the words, "*Watch* [γρηγορεῖτε] *therefore*, for you know neither the day nor the hour" (Matt. 25:12). "Watch" means, literally, "Stay awake," as can be seen from the way the word is used in contrast to sleep in 1 Thessalonians 5:10: ". . . whether we are awake [γρηγορῶμεν] or asleep [καθεύδωμεν]." But it is not strange, because Jesus does not mean that the way we stay ready for his coming is to stay physically awake. He means "stay awake" in the sense of being awake to reality—especially his reality—and awake to our calling and our responsibilities. He means that we should be spiritually and morally alert and clearheaded and discerning. He means not being vulnerable to worldly foolishness, like not having oil for oil-operated lamps when that's our job. He means not being oblivious, like a sleepwalker, to God's activity in the world, or to Satan's deceptions.

As we saw in part 2 (chapter 15), the ground clause in verse 13, "you know neither the day nor the hour," does not imply that Jesus is teaching an any-moment return. It teaches two things. First, there will be no time at the second coming for spiritual sleepwalkers to change their lives. There will be no time for the sleeper to fix everything he has broken while stumbling around in the darkness of spiritual slumber. Any effort at the last moment to do quick repair work of long-accustomed worldliness will be hypocritical: it will not be owing to true spiritual life, but to the mere expediency of fear. It will leave one outside the feast. "While they were going to buy [oil], the bridegroom came, and those who were ready went in with him to the marriage feast, and the door was shut" (Matt. 25:10).

The second lesson the ground clause ("you know neither the day nor the hour") teaches is that if you go to sleep spiritually, you will not be awake to discern the signs of his nearness. This is why it does not require an any-moment return to make sense of this warning. "Stay awake" means that if you go to sleep spiritually, there is no reason to think you will be spiritually awake, say, three years from now or thirty years from now, while the man of lawlessness is using supernatural, satanic power to take sleeping souls captive (2 Thess. 2:9–10). "You know neither the day nor the hour" means this: any presumption of Christ's delay as an incentive to carelessness is a deadly mistake.

Like a Sudden Trap for the Dissipated Soul

This last point is confirmed by the way Jesus speaks of the wise manager and the foolish manager in the following picture of the second coming:

> Who then is the faithful and wise manager, whom his master will set
> over his household, to give them their portion of food at the proper

time? Blessed is that servant whom his master will find so doing when he comes. Truly, I say to you, he will set him over all his possessions. But if that servant says to himself, "My master is delayed in coming," and begins to beat the male and female servants, and to eat and drink and get drunk, the master of that servant will come on a day when he does not expect him and at an hour he does not know, and will cut him in pieces and put him with the unfaithful. (Luke 12:42–46)

This is a picture of Jesus's departure to heaven after his resurrection and his leaving his disciples on earth to carry out the ministry he has given them. He probably has ministers of the word in view since he says the master "will set [them] over his household, to give them their portion of food at the proper time." But the principle here applies to all Christians.

A blessing is pronounced on the faithful manager who does what he was appointed to do. He feeds the household. Nothing is said to him about an unexpected coming of the master while the manager is faithfully carrying out his duties. He has nothing to fear, whenever the master comes, because he is doing his appointed work.

But then comes the warning. What if the manager's heart goes bad and he begins to presume on the master's delay? "My master is delayed in coming." What if this presumption leads him to "eat and drink and get drunk"? Jesus says that this drunkenness will result in his being taken off guard by the master's return. "If that servant . . . begins . . . to eat and drink and get drunk, the master of that servant will come on a day when he does not expect him" (Luke 12:45–46).

What are we to infer from this warning? The point is not that an unexpected, any-moment return of the master was overlooked by the drunken manager. The point is that the foolish manager is mentally and spiritually drunk. He has forsaken the master's will and embraced the stupefying path of worldliness. He is now blind to what is spiritually real. He will be taken off guard by the master when the master comes, because there is no reason to think he will be "sobered up" in, say, five years, or fifty years, when the trumpet sounds. "The master of that [drunken] servant will come on a day when he does not expect" (Luke 12:46). The lesson is this: stay spiritually awake and busy at the master's work, for if you give way to spiritual stupor (call it sleep or drunkenness), you will be blind to all the signs of danger, and will be taken in judgment suddenly and unexpectedly.

Jesus makes the same statement in Luke 21:34:

> Watch yourselves lest your hearts be weighed down with dissipation and drunkenness and cares of this life, and that day come upon you suddenly like a trap.

The suddenness and unexpectedness is not owing to an any-moment view of the second coming. It is owing to the spiritual sluggishness of the human heart that is weighed down and dulled by the "cares of this life." The appearing of Christ becomes a sudden trap not because it could happen any moment, but because the spiritually unseeing will be blind to Christ's coming even if it happens five years from now, with serious warnings in between. To be spiritually asleep, drunk, or blind portends unexpected destruction even if it could be tomorrow or a decade from now.

Paul's Warning to the Sleeping and Drunk

The apostle Paul combines both of the images Jesus uses to make the same point—the image of staying awake (Matt. 25:13) and staying sober (Luke 12:45; 21:34):

> You yourselves are fully aware that the day of the Lord will come like a thief in the night. While people are saying, "There is peace and security," then sudden destruction will come upon them as labor pains come upon a pregnant woman, and they will not escape. But you are not in darkness, brothers, for that day to surprise you like a thief. For you are all children of light, children of the day. We

are not of the night or of the darkness. So then let us not sleep [μὴ καθεύδωμεν], as others do, but let us keep awake [γρηγορῶμεν] and be sober [νήφωμεν]. (1 Thess. 5:2–6)

Paul says that for some, the day of Christ's coming will be like the destructive surprise of a thief. But for others, it will not be like that. "You are not in darkness, brothers, for that day to surprise you like a thief" (1 Thess. 5:4). The difference is whether we are in darkness or are "children of the day," whether we are spiritually asleep or awake, whether we are spiritually drunk or sober. He does not say that the suddenness and unexpectedness of the day is owing to an any-moment return of Christ. Rather, it is owing to an oblivious spiritual condition that says, "peace and security," because that spiritual condition is one of "darkness" and "sleep" and "drunkenness."

Presumption of Delay for the Sake of Sin Is Suicidal

My conclusion, therefore, is that Jesus's repeated command that we be awake, ready, on guard, watchful, and vigilant is not because the second coming will take obedient disciples off guard, but because spiritual stupor results in being oblivious to what is happening in the world, and thus being surprised and trapped and ruined. The uncertainty of the time of Christ's return functions to warn all of us to be spiritually alive and awake and sober because the alternative is a spiritual condition that will be blind to signs and will not be able to recover from satanic stupor when "the lightning . . . lights up the sky from one side to the other" (Luke 17:24). Any presumption of Christ's delay to justify worldliness puts a heart in a position of spiritual suicide.

Even if we are persuaded that he is three years away, or five, or six (and we never have warrant to think he must be farther away than that), that measure of nearness and the uncertainty combine to make us all the more alert and vigilant over our souls and our lives. We realize that spiritual carelessness will make all our calculations pointless, since we will be spiritually unable to fight the final battle for alertness and endurance. On the other hand, we realize that if we are spiritually awake, in fellowship with Christ, and walking in the light, we will discern "the signs of the times" (Matt. 16:3) and experience his coming not as a surprising thief (1 Thess. 5:4) but as a merciful servant-master (Luke 12:37).

Be Alert Means Love the Lord's Appearing

Another way to describe our zeal to be spiritually awake and sober and discerning is to say that we love the Lord's appearing (2 Tim. 4:8), or that we are "eagerly waiting for him" (Heb. 9:28; cf. 1 Cor. 1:7; Phil. 3:20), or that we have "set [our] hope fully on the grace that will be brought to [us] at the revelation of Jesus Christ" (1 Pet. 1:13).

You may recall from chapter 1 that immediately following Paul's summons to love the Lord's appearing in 2 Timothy 4:8, Demas is mentioned as one who loved this world more than the Lord's appearing. "Demas, in love with this present world, has deserted me" (2 Tim. 4:10). This is what Jesus is warning against. "Watch yourselves lest your hearts be weighed down with dissipation and drunkenness and cares of this life, and that day come upon you suddenly like a trap" (Luke 21:34). Demas fell out of love with the appearing of the Lord Jesus and into love with this world. It made him drunk with the illusions of better things.

So in all our discussion of Jesus's commands to stay awake and sober, we have really been talking about love for the Lord's appearing. To be spiritually awake and alert is to be in love with the Lord's coming. The alternative is to fall into the stupor of love for the world and blindness to the beauties of the coming Christ. This is the great answer to how we should live. We should live in love with the appearing of Christ. Living in love with the appearing of Christ is a great anticipatory pleasure. It is a great power to walk in freedom from sin. It is a great protection from deception in the last days.

19

Patient, Joyful, Not Deceived, Not Alarmed

ONE CRUCIAL ASPECT OF OUR WALK in the last days is that we should be especially alert to deception. This is because, as both Jesus and Paul make plain, satanic deception will intensify as the end nears. Jesus highlights this danger first when the disciples ask him, "What will be the sign of your coming and of the end of the age?" (Matt. 24:3). His first words, and his repeated words, relate to deception:

See that no one leads you astray. For many will come in my name, saying, "I am the Christ," and they will lead many astray. . . . And many false prophets will arise and lead many astray. And because lawlessness will be increased, the love of many will grow cold. But the one who endures to the end will be saved. . . . For false christs and false prophets will arise and perform great signs and wonders, so as to lead astray, if possible, even the elect. See, I have told you beforehand. (Matt. 24:4–5, 11–13, 24–25)

To be sure, deception marks the entire history from the first century until now. But Jesus's reference to an increase of lawlessness, and the love of many growing cold, and the warning to endure "to the end," and the crescendo of signs and wonders almost leading away the elect—all these point to an intensifying of deceptive evil at the very end of this age. It sounds climactic. Hence Jesus's urgent warning, "See that no one leads you astray" (Matt. 24:4). Which is another way of saying, "Stay awake." "Be alert." Love the Lord's appearing more than the deceptive allurements offered by the false prophets and false christs.

Deception and the Last Gasp of Evil

Paul ties the deceptions and the deceptive signs and wonders to the last gasp of evil as the man of lawlessness appears:

> The coming of the lawless one is by the activity of Satan with all power and *lying signs and wonders*, and with *all wicked deception* for those who are perishing, because they did not welcome a love for the truth in order to be saved. Therefore God sends them a strong delusion, so that they may *believe what is false*, in order that all may be condemned who did *not believe the truth* but had pleasure in unrighteousness. (2 Thess. 2:9–12, my translation)

The reason I call this the last gasp of evil is that, in verse 8, Paul says that this satanic, deceptive "lawless one" will be killed by the final coming of the Lord Jesus. "The lawless one will be revealed, whom the Lord Jesus will kill with the breath of his mouth and bring to nothing by the appearance of his coming." So the deception Paul alerts us to is the very last effort of Satan to destroy Christ's people.

The last phrase in verse 12 is telling: "They had pleasure in unrighteousness." This pleasure, he says, is the alternative to believing the truth. "[They] did not believe the truth but had pleasure in unrighteousness." And that "belief in the truth" includes "love for the truth" in verse 10. Which means that the great protection against satanic deception in the last days is not just *assenting* to the truth, but *loving* the truth. And the future glory at the heart of that truth is the appearing of our Lord Jesus. Therefore, Paul urges us to love the truth of his coming—to love his appearing (2 Tim. 4:8). How shall we then live in the last days? We shall live on high alert against deception. And right at the heart of that alertness is not a spirit of fear, but of love—heartfelt love for the Lord's appearing.

Alert, but Not Alarmed

Living on high alert for deception does not mean living with a spirit of alarm. Love, not alarm, is the best protection against deception. Jesus and Paul both make this clear. As we saw in chapter 16, their word for *alarm* is used in only two end-time contexts in the New Testament, one in Paul and one in the teaching of Jesus—nowhere else. Immediately after warning us not to be deceived by false christs, Jesus also cautions against alarm:

> Many will come in my name, saying, "I am the Christ," and they will lead many astray. And you will hear of wars and rumors of wars. *See that you are not alarmed* [θροεῖσθε], for this must take place, but the end is not yet. (Matt. 24:5–6; cf. Mark 13:6–7)

The words "this must take place" mean that God's invincible plans are unfolding. Things are not out of control. Be alert, but don't be alarmed. The words "the end is not yet" mean we should resist any hysteria that overstates the immediacy of the Lord's coming. God the Father, and he alone, will decide when the end comes, and he is our Lord and Savior and Friend. If he appoints more months or years or decades for us to persevere, he will give us what we need to live in alertness but not alarm—that is, to live in love with the Lord's appearing.

Paul uses the same word for *alarm* to make the same point: "We ask you, brothers, not to be quickly . . . *alarmed* [θροεῖσθαι] . . . to the effect that the day of the Lord has come" (2 Thess. 2:1–2). This is virtually the same as Jesus's warning, "See that you are not alarmed [θροεῖσθε] . . . the end is not yet." The heart of the Christian should not be vulnerable to speculations about the end times. We should not be carried away by sensational predictions without solid biblical warrant. We should not be drawn into any frenzy or mania, nor into schemes built on human theorizing about signs that are no sure evidence of the Lord's imminence.

Patience, Steadfastness, Joy

The Christian soul looks for the Lord's coming with eagerness and alertness, and without alarm. But more than that, this eager alertness not only *excludes* alarm, but it also *includes* steady, peaceful, joyful patience:

> Be *patient*, therefore, brothers, until the coming of the Lord. See how the farmer waits for the precious fruit of the earth, being *patient* about it, until it receives the early and the late rains. You also, be *patient*. Establish your hearts, for the coming of the Lord is at hand. Do not grumble against one another, brothers, so that you may not be judged; behold, the Judge is standing at the door. As an example of *suffering and patience*, brothers, take the prophets who spoke in the name of the Lord. Behold, we consider those blessed who remained *steadfast*. (James 5:7–11)

Three times James refers to "the coming of the Lord" (James 5:7), "the coming of the Lord" (5:8), and "the Judge . . . standing at the door" (5:9). And his main concern is to call us to patience, willingness to suffer, and steadfastness. Even suffering should not alarm us or knock us off balance as we patiently, steadfastly, and confidently wait for the coming of the Lord.

Not only James but also Jesus and Paul say that suffering will mark the final days. Jesus says, "Then they will deliver you up to tribulation and put you to death, and you will be hated by all nations for my name's sake" (Matt. 24:9). But even that must not cause us alarm. We must meet such suffering with patience and steadfastness, knowing that "the Judge is standing at the door" (James 5:9).

Paul explains that such sufferings are part of God's wisdom to make us "worthy of the kingdom, for which you are . . . suffering" (2 Thess. 1:5). Then he connects that divine purpose for our suffering with the justice of God at the second coming:

> We ourselves boast about you in the churches of God for your steadfastness and faith in all your persecutions and in the afflictions that you are enduring. This is evidence of the righteous judgment of God, that you may be considered worthy of the kingdom of God, for which you are also suffering—since indeed God considers it just to repay with affliction those who afflict you, and to grant relief to you who are afflicted as well as to us, when the Lord Jesus is revealed from heaven with his mighty angels in flaming fire, inflicting vengeance on those who do not know God and on those who do not obey the gospel of our Lord Jesus. (2 Thess. 1:4–8)

God's judgment is righteous, even when it includes our suffering, since he will repay the afflicter and relieve the afflicted "when [he] is revealed from heaven . . . in flaming fire." Our eager expectation and alertness, as we wait for the Lord's coming, is not alarmed even in the face of suffering.

In fact, the New Testament regularly goes beyond the mere absence of alarm and presence of patience as we wait. It calls us even to *rejoice* in suffering for Christ's sake (Matt. 5:11–12; Luke 6:23; Acts 5:41; Rom. 5:3; Phil. 2:17; Col. 1:24; James 1:2). Peter connects this rejoicing directly with our longing for the appearing of the Lord's glory:

Beloved, do not be surprised at the fiery trial when it comes upon you to test you, as though something strange were happening to you. But *rejoice* insofar as you share Christ's sufferings, that you may also rejoice and be glad *when his glory is revealed.* (1 Pet. 4:12–13)

Peter makes our joy in suffering with Christ the condition of our joy when his glory is revealed. Rejoice in his sufferings now *so that* you may rejoice in his glory when he comes. The increase of persecution at the end of the age goes hand in hand with the love of many growing cold under the icy influence of lawlessness (Matt. 24:12). But Christians are not alarmed. More than that, as we look to the glory of the Lord's appearing (1 Pet. 4:13) and to the crown of righteousness (2 Tim. 4:8), we rejoice. That is, we joyfully love the Lord's appearing more than the comforts of compromise (Mark 8:35), and more than the avoidance of shame (8:38), knowing that "the one who endures to the end will be saved" (Matt. 24:13).

Even when we must stand beside the graves of those we love, we do "not grieve as others do who have no hope" (1 Thess. 4:13). "For the Lord himself will descend from heaven with a cry of command, with the voice of an archangel, and with the sound of the trumpet of God. *And the dead in Christ will rise first*" (1 Thess. 4:16). The dead will be at no disadvantage when it comes to the firsthand experience of the Lord's glorious appearing. "We . . . will be caught up *together* with them in the clouds to meet the Lord in the air" (1 Thess. 4:17). Therefore, not even death turns our end-time alertness into alarm. We are patient, steady, full of hope. Above all allurements, and in spite of all losses, we love the Lord's appearing.

20

Coming Justice, Present Gentleness

FROM THIS LIFE OF ALERT, unalarmed, patient, steadfast, joyful love for the appearing of the Lord, there arises a passion for purity in our lives like that of the Lord Jesus whom we long to see. We see this in 1 John 3:2–3:

> Beloved, we are God's children now, and what we will be has not yet appeared; but we know that when he appears we shall be like him, because we shall see him as he is. And everyone who thus hopes in him purifies himself as he is pure.

Consider the psychological dynamics of these verses. When he says, "Everyone who *thus* hopes in him," he is referring to the hope we have to be *like* Jesus: "When he appears *we shall be like him.* . . . Everyone who *thus* hopes in him" will purify himself.

So the point is that if you really *want* to be like him by *seeing* him when he comes, you will pursue being like him *now*. It is hypocrisy to be indifferent to purity and holiness now while claiming to love the Lord's appearing. So the impulse for becoming a radically pure, holy, loving, sacrificial, Christlike person *now* comes from the intense hope and desire for that to happen when he comes. Or the apostle could say, the impulse to live a holy life comes from loving the Lord's appearing.

Moral Imperative of Global Destruction

Peter, in his second letter, refers to the second coming as an incentive to "holiness and godliness" (2 Pet. 3:11). He focuses not on the beauty of being like Christ, but on the destruction of all that is not like Christ. Then he closes his argument with a reference to the new heavens and the new earth, where only righteousness dwells (2 Pet. 3:13). Actually, he never mentions in so many words the coming or the appearing of the Lord Jesus in this connection. But he does refer to the "day of the Lord" coming "like a thief" (2 Pet. 3:10), which clearly refers to the second coming:[1]

> The day of the Lord will come like a thief, and then the heavens will pass away with a roar, and the heavenly bodies will be burned up and dissolved, and the earth and *the works that are done on it will be exposed* [for the ruin that they are]. Since all these things are thus to be dissolved, *what sort of people ought you to be in lives of holiness and godliness*, waiting for and hastening the coming of the day of God, because of which the heavens will be set on fire and dissolved, and the heavenly bodies will melt as they burn! But according to his promise we are waiting for new heavens and a new earth *in which righteousness*

1   As I explained in chapter 8, I am not attempting in this book to sort out all events that are referred to as part of the "day of the Lord." By such a "day," I do not refer to a 24-hour period. The word "day" can refer to an extended period of time. For example, "When the bridegroom is taken away from them . . . they will fast *in that day*" (Mark 2:20; cf. John 8:56; 16:23; 2 Cor. 6:2; Eph. 6:13; Heb. 8:9). In God's mind, the timeframe called a "day" has a definite duration. But from our finite standpoint, its extent is unknown. Therefore, many events can happen within that time. Thus, when I use the biblical phrases "day of the Lord," or "day of God," or "day of judgment," or "day of wrath," I leave room in those days for various events, without sorting out their order or how much time elapses between them. Thus, in the case of Peter's reference to the complete renovation of the heavens and earth, I am not specifying when that happens in relation to other acts of the "day of the Lord."

dwells. Therefore, beloved, since you are waiting for these, *be diligent to be found by him without spot or blemish, and at peace.* (3:10–14)

Probably Peter focuses on the destruction of the heavenly bodies and the earth because, earlier in the chapter, the false teachers were denying the second coming on the basis of their claim that the created universe (the heavens and the earth) is so stable that no cataclysmic change is imaginable: "[Scoffers] will say, 'Where is the promise of his coming? For ever since the fathers fell asleep, all things are continuing as they were from the beginning of creation'" (2 Pet. 3:4). So when Peter describes the effect of the "day of the Lord," he focuses on the cataclysmic effects in nature.

But his aim is to answer the question, How then shall we live? We see his logic when he says, "Since all these things"—namely, "the earth and the works that are done on it"—"are thus to be dissolved, what sort of people ought you to be in lives of holiness and godliness" (2 Pet. 3:11)? How is he thinking?

Unrighteousness Destroyed, Righteousness Endures

He seems to share Paul's understanding of the natural world that God has "subjected [creation] to futility . . . [and to] bondage to corruption" (Rom. 8:20–21). Thus, not only do sinful humans need renovation through the saving work of Christ, but nature too needs renovation. And Paul pictures that renovation happening not by God's obliterating creation and starting over with a new one, but rather by God's liberating the present creation from its "bondage to corruption." "The creation itself will be set free from its bondage to corruption and obtain the freedom of the glory of the children of God" (Rom. 8:21). Paul doesn't say how that renovation and purification happens. But Peter pictures it happening through fire.

I don't think he means that the heavenly bodies and the earth are obliterated by this fire so that the new heavens and new earth

(2 Pet. 3:13) are re-created out of nothing. Rather, since Peter seems to share Paul's understanding of creation, and since Paul says "the creation itself will be *set free from its bondage to corruption* [not obliterated] and obtain the freedom of the glory of the children of God" (Rom. 8:21), therefore, the "passing away" of the heavenly bodies, and the burning and dissolution of the earth with its works (2 Pet. 3:10), probably refers to what happens with a horrific forest fire or volcanic devastation. We say that the land, with all its trees, vegetation, and man-made structures, was "destroyed." But we don't mean the land was put out of existence.

So Peter's reasoning for how we should live goes like this: the destruction of the heavens and the earth will be so thorough that nothing will remain except what is holy and godly. Negatively, all that is contrary to holiness and godliness will be consumed. Positively, "we are waiting for new heavens and a new earth in which righteousness dwells" (2 Pet. 3:13). Unrighteousness is destroyed. Righteousness endures. Therefore, "what sort of people ought you to be in lives of holiness and godliness" (2 Pet. 3:11)? He ends by bringing both destruction and renovation to mind: "Beloved, since you are waiting for these [the destruction of the old and the establishment of the new], be diligent to be found by him without spot or blemish, and at peace" (2 Pet. 3:14).

Gentle as We Wait for Justice

The apostle Paul draws out a specific character trait in answer to Peter's question, "What sort of people ought you to be in lives of holiness and godliness" if perfect righteousness (which includes justice) will prevail? He answers that, in view of the second coming, we ought to be *gentle.* He makes this connection in Philippians 4:4–7 and Romans 12:19–21.

In Philippians 4:5, he says, "Let your gentleness be known to everyone. The Lord is at hand." I take this to mean that the certainty and potential nearness of the Lord's coming has the effect of making us gentle when we think and feel rightly about it.[2] I am aware that the ESV translates ἐπιεικὲς (*epieikes*) as *reasonableness* instead of *gentleness*: "Let your *reasonableness* be known to everyone." But in 1 Timothy 3:3, Paul explicitly contrasts this word with violence: the overseer must be "not violent but gentle" (μὴ πλήκτην, ἀλλ᾽ ἐπιεικῆ). The opposite of *violent* is more naturally *gentle* than *reasonable*.

Similarly, ἐπιεικεῖς (*epieikeis*) is parallel with ἀμάχους (*amachous*) in Titus 3:2, which literally means "without fighting," or "without a sword"; that is, *peaceable*. That makes a more fitting parallel with *gentleness* than *reasonableness*. We might render Paul's words to Titus as, "Speak evil of no one, be peaceable, gentle, showing all meekness to everyone."

Another reason I think Paul saw gentleness as an effect of the anticipated coming of the Lord is the way he argues in Romans 12:19–20:

> Beloved, never avenge yourselves, but leave it to the wrath of God, for it is written, "Vengeance is mine, I will repay, says the Lord." To the contrary, "if your enemy is hungry, feed him; if he is thirsty, give him something to drink; for by so doing you will heap burning coals on his head."

It is a manifestation of *gentleness* not to return evil for evil but to do good to your enemy. This is what Paul calls for. And the motive for it here (not the only motive) is that we should leave vengeance to the Lord. The Lord promises, "Vengeance is mine, I will repay" (Rom. 12:19). Our confidence in the Lord's exacting final justice means we do not have to exact justice from our enemy in this life. We can return good for evil. We can be gentle.

The connection with the Lord's coming is that the second coming is when the Lord's vengeance will take place. Paul makes this plain in

---

2 For the meaning of *nearness*, see chapter 14.

2 Thessalonians 1:7–8: "The Lord Jesus [will be] revealed from heaven with his mighty angels in flaming fire, *inflicting vengeance* on those who do not know God and on those who do not obey the gospel of our Lord Jesus." So Paul's way of arguing in Romans 12:19–20 shows one reason why he would connect the coming of the Lord in Philippians 4:4 with the call for Christian gentleness. "Let your [gentleness] be known to everyone. The Lord is at hand." His coming will settle all accounts justly and set right every wrong. We are free to leave vengeance with him. We are free to be gentle.

21

Go to Work, Go to Church

IF THE CALL FOR GENTLENESS in the last days (chapter 20) seemed oddly ordinary, this chapter may seem even more so. *Vigilance* we understand when the world as we know it is about to end. But *gentleness?* That seems like a virtue for a less volatile time. But the way of Jesus is not our way. His thoughts are not our thoughts. Gentleness may be so utterly countercultural in that loveless (Matt. 24:12) and hostile (24:10) time that nothing would bear clearer witness to the power of Christ. Similarly, going to work and going to church may seem so routine in the face of cultural unrest that they too testify to a deep, confident, peaceful love for the Lord's appearing.

So the New Testament teaches that another answer to the question, How then shall we live? is that those who love the Lord's appearing go to work. We do our work with trustworthiness and diligence, eager to be found faithful in our different callings when the Lord comes. Both Jesus and Paul put a clear emphasis on this.

Hysteria and Idleness at Thessalonica

Paul expresses himself so explicitly on this issue of going to work while we wait for the Lord to come because the opposite was happening at Thessalonica. Paul deals with the problem in 2 Thessalonians. First,

274 HOW THEN SHALL WE LIVE?

let's notice the failure of some to stay at their income-producing jobs. Here's Paul's description of the situation and his exhortation in response to this delinquency:

> Now we command you, brothers, in the name of our Lord Jesus Christ, that you keep away from any brother who is walking in idleness and not in accord with the tradition that you received from us. For you yourselves know how you ought to imitate us, because we were not idle when we were with you, nor did we eat anyone's bread without paying for it, but with toil and labor we worked night and day, that we might not be a burden to any of you. It was not because we do not have that right, but to give you in ourselves an example to imitate. For even when we were with you, we would give you this command: If anyone is not willing to work, let him not eat. For we hear that some among you walk in idleness, not busy at work, but busybodies. Now such persons we command and encourage in the Lord Jesus Christ to do their work quietly and to earn their own living. As for you, brothers, do not grow weary in doing good. (2 Thess. 3:6–13)

Some of the believers are "walking in idleness" (2 Thess. 3:6), "not willing to work" (3:10), proving to be "busybodies" (3:11), and apparently eating other people's hard-earned bread "without paying for it" (3:8). Why was this happening? Paul explains in 2 Thessalonians 2.

A kind of hysteria had gripped some of the members of the church because they thought "the day of the Lord has come" (2 Thess. 2:2). So they apparently thought, *What's the point in going to work? The Lord is that close.*

> Now concerning the coming of our Lord Jesus Christ and our being gathered together to him, we ask you, brothers, not to be quickly shaken in mind or alarmed, either by a spirit or a spoken word, or a letter seeming to be from us, to the effect that the day of the Lord

has come. Let no one deceive you in any way. For that day will not come, unless the rebellion comes first, and the man of lawlessness is revealed, the son of destruction. (2 Thess. 2:1–3)

I use the word *hysteria* because Paul says some of them were "shaken in mind" (2 Thess. 2:2)—literally, "shaken *from* their mind" (σαλευθῆναι ὑμᾶς ἀπὸ τοῦ νοὸς). They were acting irrationally, thinking that the day of the Lord was present. Paul exposes the error of their thinking by pointing out, "That day will not come, unless the rebellion comes first, and the man of lawlessness is revealed, the son of destruction" (2 Thess. 2:3). In other words, the day of the Lord cannot be present because the recognizable rebellion and man of lawlessness have not appeared.

I infer, therefore, from Paul's teaching that as we wait for the Lord Jesus to return from heaven, we should be faithful to our earthly callings. We should avoid end-time hysteria and "not grow weary in doing good" (2 Thess. 3:13). There will be good work to do (vocationally and socially and personally) right up to the Lord's coming. Our normal earthly duties will not end until the Lord appears. The rule then, until he comes, is, "Whatever you do, work heartily, as for the Lord and not for men" (Col. 3:23).

Blessed When Found at Work

This apostolic commitment to doing our earthly work faithfully until Jesus comes is rooted in the fact that Jesus taught the same. More than once he gave us pictures of the second coming as it relates to our work. For example, after telling his disciples to "be like men who are waiting for their master to come home from the wedding feast, so that they may open the door to him at once when he comes and knocks" (Luke 12:36), Peter asks:

"Lord, are you telling this parable for us or for all?" And the Lord said, "Who then is the faithful and wise manager, whom his master will set over his household, to give them their portion of food at the proper time? *Blessed is that servant whom his master will find so doing when he comes.* Truly, I say to you, he will set him over all his possessions." (Luke 12:41–44)

Instead of directly answering Peter's question, "Are you telling this parable for us or for all?" Jesus states the principle that applies to all, including Peter: The master has given the managers of his affairs work to do while he is gone. He expects that when he returns he will find them faithfully doing what he gave them to do (see also Matt. 24:42–51).

This is a freeing teaching. It means that we are freed from the need to focus our attention on the signs of the times, even if we see them developing. It is good to be spiritually discerning of what is happening as the end draws near. But being sharp in our end-time foresight is not the main quality the master requires of his managers. When the master says, "Well done," to his servant (Matt. 25:21, 23), this is not because the servant spotted the master on the horizon. It is because the servant has "been faithful" in the work he was given to do—right up to the end.

So by all means, we should stay spiritually awake and sober to the end. No faithful servant should drift into spiritual lethargy and blindness, lest the master "come on a day when he does not expect him and at an hour he does not know, and . . . cut him in pieces and put him with the unfaithful" (Luke 12:46). But such wakefulness and soberness is not mainly for the sake of predicting the Lord's nearness; it is for doing the Lord's work. Our watchword is to say with Jesus, "We must work the works of him who sent me while it is day; night is coming, when no one can work" (John 9:4). So as we get up in the morning and head into our day's work, let there be a love for the Lord's appearing in our heart and a happy awareness that while he delays, he has work for us to do.

As the Day Approaches, Go to Church

Even more important than going to work during the end times is going to church. And all the more as we see the day coming. The writer of the letter to the Hebrews says that as the day of Christ draws near, we should be all the more diligent to meet together as Christ's people:

> Let us consider how to stir up one another to love and good works, not neglecting to meet together, as is the habit of some, but encouraging one another, and all the more as you see the Day drawing near. (Heb. 10:24–25)

"All the more as you see the Day drawing near." The *day* he has in mind is the same event mentioned in the previous chapter: "Christ, having been offered once to bear the sins of many, will appear a second time, not to deal with sin but to save those who are eagerly waiting for him" (Heb. 9:28). It is the day of Christ's coming.

Evidently, the author of Hebrews thought that believers will be able to "see" (βλέπετε) the day drawing near. To be sure, there are in every generation signs that point to the Lord's coming. But this does not imply that as the day draws even closer, there will not be even clearer signs. I argued in chapter 17 that besides the more general pointers to Christ's coming, there will be discernible antecedents at the very end of this age, signaling the closeness of Christ's coming—like the apostasy and the man of lawlessness (2 Thess. 2:3). And for those with the most spiritually discerning eyes, "that day [will not] surprise you like a thief" (1 Thess. 5:4). They will "see the Day drawing near" (Heb. 10:25).

No Signs?

I think some scholars overstate the case that there will be "no signs" of the Lord's very near return. Sam Storms says:

> [The parousia will] transpire in the future at a time unknown even to the Lord. *No signs will point to that day*. Perhaps Jesus spoke this way to keep us from rashly concluding that every new global crisis,

war, catastrophic earthquake, or other sort of national or natural upheaval was the clear sign of his return.[1]

Storms draws the conclusion that there will be no signs pointing to that day from words like these:

> As were the days of Noah, so will be the coming of the Son of Man. For as in those days before the flood they were eating and drinking, marrying and giving in marriage, until the day when Noah entered the ark, and they were unaware until the flood came and swept them all away, so will be the coming of the Son of Man. (Matt. 24:37–39)

From this he infers the following:

> There will not be unprecedented global catastrophes or unparalleled calamities that will point people to the impending return of Jesus. Rather, humanity will be immersed in the routine affairs of life. It will be like it was in the days of Noah. The world will be caught completely off-guard by the coming of Christ. People will be engaged in normal, routine occupations of life: farming, fellowship, marriage, etc. (cf. Luke 17:28–30; 1 Thess. 5:3). Jesus will come at a time of widespread indifference, normalcy, materialistic endeavors, when everyone is thoroughly involved in the pursuit of their earthly affairs and ambitions (cf. 2 Pet. 3:3–4, 10). His coming will occur at a time so unexpected, so unannounced, that it will catch people in the middle of their everyday routines (see vv. 40–41). When will Jesus come? *Jesus will come at a time when his coming is the farthest thing from people's minds!*[2]

1   Sam Storms, *Kingdom Come: The Amillennial Alternative* (Fearn, Ross-shire, UK: Mentor, 2013), 277–78; emphasis added.
2   Storms, *Kingdom Come*, 278; emphasis added.

The problem with this conclusion is that it does not distinguish between the oblivion of the world's blindness and the expectancy of the children of light. The one will be taken unexpectedly as in a trap (Luke 21:34). The other will not be overtaken as by a thief (1 Thess. 5:4). Both Jesus and Paul make clear this distinction between those who are blind to signs and those who are not. Paul says:

> You yourselves are fully aware that the day of the Lord will come like a thief in the night. While people are saying, "There is peace and security," then sudden destruction will come upon them as labor pains come upon a pregnant woman, and they will not escape. But you are not in darkness, brothers, for that day to surprise you like a thief. (1 Thess. 5:2–4)

Jesus says:

> Watch yourselves lest your hearts be weighed down with dissipation and drunkenness and cares of this life, and that day come upon you suddenly like a trap. For it will come upon all who dwell on the face of the whole earth. But stay awake at all times, praying that you may have strength to escape all these things that are going to take place, and to stand before the Son of Man. (Luke 21:34–36)

The world is blind to Christ's coming and will experience it as a "trap." The wakeful will not be blind and trapped. They will "see the Day drawing near" (Heb. 10:25).

End-Time Reasons for Going to Church

I am sure a whole book could be written as to why we should prioritize meeting together as the day draws near. The book would include a meditation on the Lord's Supper, because Paul connected it (as Jesus did, Luke 22:16) with the second coming: "As often as you eat this bread and drink the cup, you proclaim the Lord's death until he comes" (1 Cor. 11:26). But the one reason mentioned in the Hebrews text is to *encourage one another*: ". . . not neglecting to meet together, as is the habit of some, but encouraging one another" (Heb. 10:25). That mutual encouragement, according to Hebrews 3:12–13, is focused on preventing apostasy:

> Take care, brothers, lest there be in any of you an evil, unbelieving heart, leading you to fall away [ἀποστῆναι] from the living God. But exhort one another every day, as long as it is called "today," that none of you may be hardened by the deceitfulness of sin.

Exhort each other lest you "fall away [ἀποστῆναι] from the living God." That *falling away*, Paul says, is a special mark of the "later times": "The Spirit expressly says that in later times some will depart [ἀποστήσονταί] from the faith" (1 Tim. 4:1). Jesus had highlighted this danger in the church as the end time comes:

> Then many will fall away and betray one another and hate one another. And many false prophets will arise and lead many astray. And because lawlessness will be increased, the love of many will grow cold. But the one who endures to the end will be saved. (Matt. 24:10–13)

So of all the reasons God may have in mind for why it is crucial that we continue to meet together in the last days, the one Hebrews focuses on is mutual encouragement to prevent the deceitfulness of unbelief that leads to a falling away from God. Or to put it another way: to help our love not grow cold, and to keep us burning with joyful expectation and love for the Lord's appearing.

22

End-Time Praying, for
Yourself and the Mission

CLOSELY CONNECTED TO END-TIME gatherings for the sake of encouraging each other not to grow cold in love, but to persevere in faith (chapter 21), is the summons to end-time praying. For example, Peter writes:

> The end of all things is at hand; *therefore* be self-controlled and sober *for the sake of your prayers*. Above all, keep loving one another earnestly, since love covers a multitude of sins. (1 Pet. 4:7–8, my translation)

The word *therefore* shows the connection between the second coming and prayer. "The end of all things is at hand; *therefore* pray!" Be self-controlled and sober (in spirit and body) for the sake of not growing lax in the urgency of prayer.

Why would Peter think prayer is so urgent as the end draws near? This is what he had heard Jesus say:

> Watch yourselves lest your hearts be weighed down with dissipation and drunkenness and cares of this life, and that day come upon you

suddenly like a trap. . . . But stay awake at all times, *praying that you may have strength to escape* all these things that are going to take place, and to stand before the Son of Man. (Luke 21:34, 36)

The last days will present Christians with such challenges to our faith that we will need extraordinary strength to escape their destructive effects. "The one who endures to the end will be saved" (Matt. 24:13). Both end-time church attendance and end-time prayer are designed by God to supply his people with the power to persevere through the extraordinary threats of the last days. "Understand this, that in the last days there will come times of difficulty" (2 Tim. 3:1). Peter and Jesus unite to tell us: stay sober for the sake of prayer in order to make it through these difficulties.

"Your Kingdom Come"

One of the prayers the Lord Jesus taught us to pray is, "Your kingdom come, your will be done, on earth as it is in heaven" (Matt. 6:10). There are layers of meaning in this request, just as there are layers of meaning in the coming of the kingdom.[1] The kingdom comes progressively as the saving reign of Christ is established in the hearts of more and more people (Rom. 5:21; 14:17; 1 Cor. 4:20; Col. 1:13). But the ultimate fulfillment of "Your kingdom come" is the establishment of Christ's kingdom in the new heavens and the new earth (1 Cor. 15:24; 2 Tim. 4:1).

I infer, therefore, that our prayers for the kingdom to come are prayers that God would not only establish his reign in our own hearts ever more fully, but would also advance his saving work in evangelism and world missions, and that he would bring history to a climax in the coming of Jesus. Hence our end-time prayers include the prayer for "the Lord of the harvest to send out laborers into his harvest" (Matt. 9:38),

---

1   See the prelude to part 3, "Living between the Two Appearings of Christ," for a discussion of the various senses in which the kingdom of God comes.

and that he wrap up history absolutely and come: "Our Lord, come!" (μαράνα θά, *maranatha*, 1 Cor. 16:22). "Amen. Come, Lord Jesus!" (Rev. 22:20).

Hasten the Day: Finish the Mission

Whether we are praying for the progressive advance of world evangelization or for the coming of the Lord Jesus on the clouds, we are in fact praying for God to act so as to bring history to its consummation. Jesus says in Matthew 24:14, "This gospel of the kingdom will be proclaimed throughout the whole world as a testimony to all nations, and then the end will come." I argued in chapter 17 that this verse means that the Great Commission will be obeyed to the end of this present age, and when it is completed, Christ will return. Therefore, Matthew 24:14 teaches us that every advance of the gospel is both *encouragement* that the Lord is nearing, and *incentive* to "hasten" his coming (2 Pet. 3:12) by giving great energy to world evangelization.

I find these words of George Ladd compelling as he presses home the implications of Matthew 24:14 for how we should live until Jesus comes:

Here is the motive of our mission: the final victory awaits the completion of our task. "And then the end will come." There is no other verse in the Word of God which says, "And then the end will come." When is Christ coming again? When the Church has finished its task. When will This Age end? When the world has been evangelized. "What will be the sign of your coming and of the close of the age?" (Matt. 24:3). "This gospel of the kingdom will be preached throughout the whole world as a testimony to all nations; and then, AND THEN, the end will come." When? Then; when the Church has fulfilled its divinely appointed mission.[2]

2 George Eldon Ladd, *The Gospel of the Kingdom: Scriptural Studies in the Kingdom of God* (Grand Rapids, MI: Eerdmans, 1990), loc. 2084–88, Kindle.

But what about the ambiguity of the completion of the task of world missions? Yes, we know that God's will is that Christ has "ransomed people for God from every tribe and language and people and nation" (Rev. 5:9). But what are these various groupings? Ladd responds that this ambiguity is not a hindrance to the urgency of the task:

> Someone else will say, "How are we to know when the mission is completed? How close are we to the accomplishment of the task? . . . How close are we to the end? Does this not lead to date-setting?" I answer, I do not know. God alone knows the definition of terms. I cannot precisely define who "all the nations" are. Only God knows exactly the meaning of "evangelize." He alone, who has told us that this Gospel of the Kingdom shall be preached in the whole world for a testimony unto all the nations, will know when that objective has been accomplished. But I do not need to know. I know only one thing: Christ has not yet returned; therefore the task is not yet done. When it is done, Christ will come. Our responsibility is not to insist on defining the terms of our task; our responsibility is to complete it. So long as Christ does not return, our work is undone. Let us get busy and complete our mission.[3]

If we love the Lord's appearing, we will love the advance of his mission toward completion. We will take heart from his promise that the gospel *will* be preached to all nations, that is, all the people groups ("tribe, language, people, nation"), and we will embrace his command to "make disciples of all nations" (Matt. 28:19). We will seek to share the urgency and clarity of Ladd's exhortation: "So long as Christ does not return, our work is undone. Let us get busy and complete our mission."

---

3   Ladd, *Gospel of the Kingdom*, loc. 2034–49, Kindle.

O Come, Lord Jesus, Come

A Hymn to Christ

Great crucified and risen Christ,
   Ascended, reigning, Lord of all,
Dear sovereign Lamb, once sacrificed,
   Before whom countless angels fall,
      Have mercy, Savior, on our eyes,
      So prone to count the world a prize,
      And grant that your appearing, nigh,
      Would quicken love, and wake the cry:
O come, Lord Jesus, come!

Outshining then ten-thousandfold
   The greatest spectacle on earth,
Your glory grant us to behold
   And feel its beauty, greatness, worth,
      With angel armies radiant
      In might, attending your descent,
      That we, before that final shout,
      Would see, and from the heart cry out:
O come, Lord Jesus, come!

Let not your servants shrink in fear
From that great day of flaming fire,
When those who chose not to revere
Your name will have what they desire,
But never dreamed would be a place
So dreadful, banished from your face.
Grant us, O Christ, from judgment freed,
That we might ever fearless plead:
O come, Lord Jesus, come!

O haste the day when we will hear
You say, "Well done, dear child," though we
Are bent and flawed—the day, severe,
When, all the stubble burned away, we see
Your smile, the all-transforming face,
And then the everlasting grace:
The moment we as fallen men
Will never fall or sin again.
O come, Lord Jesus, come!

Sound forth, O God, your trumpet soon.
Unleash, O Christ, your last command.
Archangel, speak, and tell the moon
And sun to veil their face, the land
And sea to yield to Christ his wife,
The church triumphant raised to life,
Yes, in the twinkling of an eye
With bodies that will never die.
O come, Lord Jesus, come!

We dare, O Christ, to hope, though we
Can scarcely fathom it, that she

For whom you died, will gratefully
   Assume her privileged seat, and be
      Your banquet's best beloved, while you
      Enclothe your majesty anew,
      And, holding over all full sway,
      Become our servant on that day.
O come, Lord Jesus, come!

Though now, O Christ, as in a glass,
   We dimly see, yet face to face
Is our desire. And yes, alas,
   Our love is weak, but we embrace
      The blessed hope that we will shine
      With borrowed brightness all divine,
      Because we will on that great day
      Be satisfied, and no more say,
O come, Lord Jesus, come.

General Index

heart of the matter, 55
heaven, 95, 168–69
hell, 115
heresy, 136
hip-hitching, 65–69
holiness, 63, 74, 138–39, 267, 268
holistic view, 235n3
holistically near, 196–199, 202, 231, 238
Holy Spirit: indwelling of, 24; inspiration of,
    220; presence of, 162; and the resurrec-
    tion, 91–92; transformation of, 99; work
    of, 12, 22, 23–24
honor, 144–45
hope, 59–60, 64
human glory, 39
human means, 12
humility, 20–21, 158, 173
hypocrisy, 50, 255, 267
hysteria, 273–75

idleness, 122–23, 273–75
illness, 152
illumination, 28
image of God, 40
imagination, 63–64
immeasurable riches, 175
immortality, 98
imperfect love, 79–80
imperfections, 72, 139–40
impurity, 102
incarnation, 13, 173, 241
incentive, to hasten second coming, 241, 283
instantaneous transformation, 101
interpretation, history of, 180
isolation, 166
Israel, towns of, 188–90

Jerusalem, destruction of, 127n3, 130, 186,
    229, 236, 238–40
Jerusalem war, 236
Jesus Christ: becoming a curse, 62; blood of,
    80; body of, 97; as bridegroom, 169–70;
    death of, 108; as divinely near, 199–1;
    enjoyment of, 162; glory of, 26, 36–37,
    39–40, 87; as judge, 110–11, 114–16; as
    Messiah, 28–29; as our dwelling place,
    168; as potentially near, 194–96; predic-
    tions of, 42–45, 126–28; presence of, 22;
    resurrection of, 15, 91–92; revelation of,
    41n1, 60; righteousness of, 115; suffering

of, 41; teachings of, 66–68; temptation
    of, 48–51; wrath of, 109–10
John the Baptist, 28–29
joy, 57; after death, 163–64; entering into,
    164; and patience, 264–66; reward of,
    154–59; of wedding feast, 169–70
judgment: according to works, 135; pardon of,
    80; and rescue, 208n2
justice, 61, 115, 265, 270–72
justification, 19n2, 73–74, 76, 79, 88

kingdom, 282–83
knowledge, 25–26, 27

Ladd, George Eldon, 106n1, 127n3, 186–87,
    189–90, 196, 283–84
last days, 185, 196, 201
lawlessness, 126, 128, 221, 262, 266
Lewis, C. S., 98
light, 27, 139–40
Lord's Supper, 279–80
loss: experiencing sinlessly, 153–54; sanctifica-
    tion of, 159
love: as defective, 137; failure of, 221–22; and
    faith, 75; fruit of, 77–79; as imperfect,
    79–80; of second coming, 259; as super-
    natural, 30; of truth, 132–33
lovelessness, 127

man of lawlessness, 123–24, 128–30, 210,
    233, 234, 241n9, 243–44, 275, 277
marriage supper of the Lamb, 169–70,
    207
martyrdom, 127, 212
marveling, 51–54, 102–3, 120–22
maturity, 82
meeting, 224–25
mercy, vs. wrath, 113–14
Messiah, 37, 39, 113, 249
metaphor, 67
mind of the flesh, 24
miracles, 129
moral transformation, 100
motivation, 140
mysteries, 159, 169
mystery of lawlessness, 131

natural knowledge, 25, 30
natural person, 23–24
new birth, 83, 139

Scripture Index

❅ desiringGod

Everyone wants to be happy. Our website was born and built for happiness. We want people everywhere to understand, embrace, and apply the truth that *God is most glorified in us when we are most satisfied in him*. We provide a daily stream of new written, audio, and video resources to help you find truth, purpose, and satisfaction that never end. We've also collected more than forty years of John Piper's speaking and writing, including translations into almost fifty languages. And it's all available free of charge, thanks to the generosity of those who've been blessed by the ministry.

If you want more resources for true happiness, or if you want to learn more about our work at Desiring God, we invite you to visit us at desiringGod.org.

desiringGod.org